From the Marco Polo Bridge to Pearl Harbor

JAPAN'S ENTRY INTO WORLD WAR II

By David J. Lu

Director, Institute For Asian Studies, Bucknell University

FOREWORD BY HERBERT FEIS

PUBLIC AFFAIRS PRESS, WASHINGTON, D. C.

PUBLISHED IN COOPERATION
WITH BUCKNELL UNIVERSITY PRESS

FOREWORD

It has become essential to make an intense effort to understand how wars come about. Surveys of the route which nations have travelled into past conflicts provide the needed instruction. And, as tales, they command interest and attention, for they record and explain the most momentous human decisions, the acts of rulers and peoples under stress, of personal and national aspirations, envies, hatreds, fears, mistrusts, and delusions.

Such historical studies are also apt to be disheartening. For the course they trace, whether it be of the coming of the wars that cram the pages of the Bible, or of those between the Greek city-states, or of the Crusades, or those of the Napoleonic period, or of the prolonged and devastating struggles between Slavs, Poles, Teutons and Swedes in Central Europe, or of the Balkan Wars, or of the two great World Wars are similar in so many ways, if not identical. The interaction of the hostilities and fears of the opponents, the behavior of the rulers, civilian and military, of the orators and expositors and columnists seem so often to have the same basic and repeated rythym.

In this volume, Professor David Lu, with trained skill and excellent perspective, inspects the path followed by the Japanese government from 1937, when it began its major assault against China, to December 1941, when it plunged into war against the United States. His account of this "path to calamity" is thorough and considered, while preserving a lively sense of the meaning and excitement of the main steps along the path. He has made productive use of the great collection of the archives of the Japanese government, especially those of the Japanese Foreign Office. These revealing records have enabled him to write an esteemable diplomatic history. But not only that. He conveys a greater understanding of the experience by his competent exposition of the way in which it was affected by the form and operative methods of the Japanese government, by the divisions and rivalries which deflected Japanese policy, and by his insight about the nature and purposes of the main Japanese personalities.

In the concluding chapter, Professor Lu displays his grasp of the determining elements of the events related. In his judgment there were two main immediate causes of the war: Japan's refusal to retreat from China and the refusal of the United States and its

iii

associates to continue to supply oil and other essential materials to Japan.

The stubborn will of the Japanese government to retain the control in China which it had achieved by force of arms he attributes primarily to the will of the Japanese Army. That military organization was able to dictate the fate of the nation because of the mode of arriving at official decisions, its appeal to the Japanese people, its close alliance with Japanese industry and the Japanese press, and its readiness to resort to threat and assassination. Correcting the prevailing view, his account reveals that the Japanese Navy was not steadfast in its opposition to the measures which resulted in the war; after the imposition of the oil embargo it also became inclined to favor resort to war rather than a compromising retreat.

The author's assessment of the importance of the economic sanctions to which Japan was subjected by the American government and its associates is justified. However, I have the impression that he does not take into due account the ways and degree to which the successive Japanese military advances and threats endangered the prospects of victory or defeat of the countries fighting the Axis, nor of the fact that the imported oil and other materials were being used by the Japanese government either for training for war, the enlargement and equipment of Japanese military forces, or as reserve stocks for use in war. The American government, aware of the scope of Japanese expansionary aims, could hardly continue to provide the means by which, if the clash of purposes came to war, the Japanese would kill our people and perhaps defeat us.

Professor Lu, after close scrutiny and consideration, concludes that the Tripartite Pact "played an insignificant role in Japan's decision for war, since the Pact had the Soviet Union, rather than the United States, as its primary target." To this conclusion I must dissent. When in September 1940, the time of utmost anxiety about British survival and the outcome of the war, Japan entered in this alliance with Germany and Italy, it enlisted in the group of aggressors in order to share in the expected spoils of their assault. By doing so, it lost the right to helpful treatment of its economic needs and its reasons for complaint against China. Moreover, the American official impressions of the inclinations and intentions of the Japanese government were sustained by the refusal of the Japanese government to disassociate itself from the Pact, to do more than give ambiguous hints that it might or might not be faithful to its obligations at a time of crisis depending on whether it would gain or lose by doing so. This ambiguity was taken to mean duplicity; and that it was so, Professor Lu's narrative seems to me to confirm.

Of one other feature of Professor Lu's version of the diplomatic tale I find myself unconvinced. To the ideas and acts of Matsuoka, Foreign Minister under Prince Konoye and negotiator of the Tripartite Pact and the Neutrality Pact with the Soviet Union, he attributes not only consistent but restrained purpose. "Despite," he avers, "his bellicose utterances, Matsuoka in many respects is more moderate than his Cabinet colleagues, including Prince Konoye". In my reading of the record, Matsuoka was neither consistent nor moderate. He appears to me to have been confused, the victim of his own volubility and determined to expand Japanese rule by any and all means. Quite correctly Professor Lu surmises that he was activated by a burning wish to become Prime Minister of Japan.

Each reader can test for himself such divergent points of judgment and emphasis that arise in the narrative. But one main conclusion seems at this time of writing definitely established. It is that their engagement in this war was, in ultimate outcome, futile. The Japanese provoked a war they could not win, and refused to admit defeat in time to shorten their suffering and destruction and perhaps retain some of their Empire and the chance to be the leading tutor and economic developer of the vast Pacific area. The American government similarly clung to extreme objectives—the complete military defeat of Japan and the intention to reduce that country to weakness and confine it to the four home islands. Because of our acquiescence in in Russian expansion in the Pacific and our failure to guard against Communist conquest of China, our whole situation in the Pacific is now unstable and in hazard.

The student of international affairs must have faith that in the present ominous crisis both the Soviet authorities and those of the Western World will remain aware, even during the most antagonistic phases of their dispute, that a war between them would be vastly more destructive and futile than that into which Japan plunged as it stumbled along the path from the Marco Polo Bridge to Pearl Harbor. This knowledge should and must control their diplomacy and decision.

HERBERT FEIS

York, Maine

PREFACE

It is not generally realized that Japan entered World War II with almost no hope of victory. Its objectives were limited, namely, to occupy the South Sea regions, to establish an impregnable defense perimeter, and to force the United States into acquiescence. However, there was a growing awareness in the minds of Japanese leaders that once the conflict was prolonged, Japan could not pit its resources against those of the United States in a war of attrition. Odds were heavily against them, yet they chose war. Was it a national *hara-kiri?* Why did Japan enter into war?

Perhaps part of the answer lies in Japan's peculiar political structure which barred it from adopting a flexible policy both internally and externally. There was a dual government with the civilian and military branches each vying for supremacy. Within the civilian branch, there were power struggles among the court circles, *Zaibatsu,* and political parties. The military itself was not free from inter-service rivalry and factional strife.

With the house divided against itself, Japan embarked on the conquest of China and Southeast Asia. First it met only a mild resistance which was followed by severe economic sanctions that cut Japan's vital supply of oil. To counteract western resistance, Japan concluded pacts with Germany, Italy, and the Soviet Union.

The present work is an attempt to provide new light on the events just mentioned. It originally started as a study in Japan's decision-making process, but gradually broadened its character to one more akin to a diplomatic history, in corporating socio-economic factors as well as those enigmatic human elements—jealousy, ambition and intrigue.

The main source of information for the present work is the Archives of the Japanese Ministry of Foreign Affairs. The first group of these documents consists of the day to day correspondence and communications between the Ministry and its officials abroad; and the second group, special studies for desk use, policy guidance papers, and reference works. The third group consists of the proceedings of the Cabinet conferences, inner Cabinet decisions, inter-ministry correspondence (between the Foreign Office and the War, Navy and Finance Ministries), and the proceedings of the Privy Council. These documents are most valuable sources in determining those who were chiefly responsible for basic policy decisions, the process of such policy-making, and the factors that influenced their decisions. The degree of coordination attained between the diverse elements of the Government can be judged from these documents. Research was further supplemented by official documents of the U. S. Government and of Germany, as well as Tokyo War Trials documents. The work also draws on numerous memoirs which appeared in Japan and in this country after the war. As much as possible, memoirs and Tokyo Trials documents are checked against the Archive materials to ascertain their accuracy and credibility.

The author is, of course, indebted to many excellent scholarly works on the same period or subject. Professor Robert Butow's *Tojo and the Coming of the War* was published while this book was already on proofs. The two works are essentially complementary in nature. Unlike the Butow volume, this study is not primarily concerned with assessing Tojo's responsibility in the decision for war.

This study is probably alone in its interpretation of the anti-Soviet nature of the Tripartite Pact, in casting Matsuoka's diplomacy in a more favorable light, in defining the role played by the Navy in the decision for war and in other matters uncovered from documentary sources which were once believed to be burned in the Tokyo air raid.

The author wishes to thank his many colleagues at Bucknell, Professor Nathaniel Peffer of Columbia University, President Hugh Borton of Haverford, and Mr. M. B. Schnapper of the Public Affairs Press for encouragement; Messrs. William T. Fox, Leland M. Goodrich, Franklin L. Ho, James W. Morley, Herschel Webb, C. Martin Wilbur, and Dr. Allen Whiting for reading the manuscript at its various stages and offering helpful suggestions; and Messrs. John Hunt and Andrew Kuroda of the Library of Congress and Mrs. Zagayko and Mr. Howard Linton of Columbia libraries for their patience. Last but not least, the author is grateful to his wife, Annabelle, for tirelessly typing most of the manuscript, providing useful editorial comments and proof-reading. To her and to the three little ones who would otherwise have received more attention, this book is dedicated.

In a sense Pearl Harbor was an inevitable sequel to the breakdown of the balance of power established by the Washington Conference in 1922. Thus the narrative of this book begins at an incident that took place shortly after 1922.

DAVID J. LU

Bucknell University
Lewisburg, Pennsylvania

CONTENTS

NOTE ON JAPANESE AND CHINESE NAMES

Japanese names are given in this book in the conventional manner, that is, the personal name precedes the surname. Macrons are not employed to distinguish long vowels from short vowels, since those who are acquainted with the Japanese language do not require such aid. To those who are not familiar with the language such distinctions are quite often unnecessary.

Chinese names are given in the Chinese order, that is, the surname precedes the personal name.

CHAPTER I

THE PATH TO CALAMITY

The Rise of Military Fascism. It was a rainy summer afternoon on July 8, 1924. From the Miura Peninsula spectators could see seaplanes nosediving one by one to bomb the warship *Ishimi.* Flames were visible from a distance. At five thirty the battered warship offered no more resistance, sank gradually and left a white whirlpool behind her. On the same day at Sagami Bay, *Nagato* and *Mutsu,* ships which were the pride of the Japanese Navy, loaded their forty centimeter guns with live shells and fired upon their sister ships, *Satsuma* and *Aki;* both sank instantly. Thus the Japanese Navy fulfilled its obligation to reduce its tonnage under the naval treaty concluded at the Washington Conference of 1922.

This treaty placed the Japanese Navy in an inferior position quantitatively. Great Britain and the United States were each allowed to maintain 525,000 tons in capital ships during a ten-year naval holiday while Japan was restricted to 315,000 tons, the ratio being 5:5:3. However, there was a compensating factor. The United States pledged that it would not fortify the Philippine Islands. This made Japan the undisputed master of the Southwestern Pacific. Nevertheless the Navy's pride was hurt. It was similar to the inferior feeling Japan experienced at Versailles when the western powers rejected its demand for racial equality. "From this day on, we are at war with the United States," muttered Commander Kanji Kato, who had been a naval aide at the Washington Conference, as he saw *Satsuma* and *Aki* sink. "We shall avenge."

At the Washington Conference, Japan also renounced its shaky claim to the Shantung Peninsula and pledged that henceforth it would adhere to the principle of the "Open Door," disclaiming any exclusive rights for the potentially vast Chinese market. It agreed to terminate the Anglo-Japanese Alliance, the union which had been referred to by a noted journalist, Soho Tokutomi, as "the marriage of a peasant girl (Japan) to a noble prince (Great Britian)." However, Japanese politicians saw the Washington Conference in an entirely different light. The reduction in naval armament would save the national treasury some 117 milion yen annually. Through amicable settlement of dif-

1

ferences at the conference table Japan could possibly regain enough goodwill of other powers to enlarge its foreign trade. No one would have dreamed of this happening to a nation which had opened its door to the West only two generations earlier. Baron Tomosaburo Kato was bestowed the honor of premiership a few months after he returned from Washington as the country's chief naval delegate to the Conference.

In 1925 party politicians also succeeded in reducing the size of the Army. Finance Minister Yuko Hamaguchi refused an increase in the budget for the Army to finance the modernization plan advocated by War Minister Kazushige Ugaki. The nation had not recovered from the shock of the great Tokyo earthquake of 1923, reasoned Hamaguchi, and the Army should learn to live within its budget. General Ugaki accordingly slashed the Army's combat strength by four divisions in order to make room for modernization. Disbanding ceremonies were held throughout the country. "It was an ignominious event," General Ugaki later related. "I wept for my comrades-in-arms."

Hamaguchi became Prime Minister in 1929 and adopted a policy of retrenchment and return to the gold standard, thus severely curtailing the export of goods. He also staked his political life on the success of the London Naval Conference. The Navy was unwilling to sign a treaty unless its minimum demand of a ratio of 10:10:7 in heavy cruisers and auxiliary ships were met, but the Cabinet was willing to compromise. The treaty finally approved granted Japan a 10:10:6 ratio in heavy cruisers and a 10:10:7 ratio in light cruisers and all other auxiliary craft. This compromise met violent opposition from the naval staff which was then headed by Admiral Kanji Kato. When Lieutenant Commander Kusanagi, one of the naval aides at the Conference, committed suicide to "apologize for the sins of the Conference," sympathetic young naval officers rallied behind the slogan, "Kusanagi is dead. Blood for blood!" A few months later Premier Hamaguchi was shot at the Tokyo station, and died the following year.

Hamaguchi's death coincided with the period when the forces of totalitarianism became strong enough to challenge effectively the civil authority. On September 18, 1931, the Army independently embarked upon the seizure of Manchuria. The Minseito government, headed by the irresolute Wakatsuki, had neither the will nor the power to resist the Army's new adventure. The failure of the party government to assert its authority largely lay in its inability to cope with the socio-economic problems that the country faced and in its incapacity to gain popular support.

During the early thirties Japan was beset by the world depression. Its population had been increasing at nearly a million annually, over-taxing the country's food supply. National economy, while steadily expanding, was unable to absorb the 400,000 persons who were annually thrown into the labor market. Although peasants constituted one-half of the total population they shared only one-fifth of the total national income. An average farm family cultivated two and one half acres and received less than eight hundred yen a year. Income status of urban workers was similar. To make matters worse, since the beginning of the modernization period the government had consistently aided industry by shifting the tax burden to peasants and urban workers. It exercised disproportionately high land taxes, consumer taxes, and customs duties to finance industrial expansion. The rapid accumulation of wealth due to industrialization did not raise living standards of the mass of peasants and urban workers from the pre-industrial level which prevailed before the Meiji Restoration of 1868. What the Meiji Restoration accomplished was, in effect, a substitution of a new plutocracy for the old feudal system. To the mass of people, particularly to young officers who came from poverty-stricken farm areas, the situation demanded some radical remedies.

"The masses in this country", stated a Tokyo paper, *Yorozu*, in its editorial of June 19, 1930, "are suffering because of the exploitation of a small capitalist class . . . The people are given the honorable title of 'nation' but they are placed under unspeakable miseries. Our people now clearly understand the deception to which they have been placed in these years. Politics has become the chief instrument of the ruling class to exploit the masses."[1]

It was under these circumstances that the views of revolutionary agitators like Ikki Kita gained acceptance among young officers. "Let us unite, and ask the Emperor to exercise his prerogatives," Kita wrote in his *General Outline of Measures for the Reconstruction of Japan,* a bible of these officers. He urged that the Emperor assume full control of the country, suspend the constitution for a period of three years, dissolve the two Houses, and place the country under martial law. These measures, explained Kita, were intended to give the Emperor complete freedom to suppress the reactionary movement of the wealthy and the peers. The ideal society was one in which private wealth was restricted. No family would be allowed to own more than one million yen in property, and no corporation over ten million. Any excess amount currently owned by them would be "restored" to the Emperor who was, after all, "the rightful owner of such property." Administration of the reconstructed state would be entrusted to an elite group drawn from commoners, ex-servicemen and young officers. Those persons who had been associated with the military caste, bureaucracy, *zaibatsu*, and political parties of the past would be purged from public office. Destruction of the *status quo* would be accompanied by establishment of a socialist state which would control the national economy in the interest of the entire nation. In this way "social justice" would be achieved.

However, social justice should not be confined to the borders of Japan. Any nation had an inherent right to possess what was needed for its own existence. There should be an equal distribution of wealth among nations, and since Japan was a proletariat in the international community, it should open war against "have powers" in the name of justice. Its mission would be to acquire larger colonies for its increasing population and to liberate oppressed nations in Asia from their foreign masters. The conquest of Australia and Siberia and the independence of India were immediate goals. Japan would also help China preserve its territorial integrity. Thereafter Japan would become the protector of Asian nations and, eventually, the hegemonic head of the world. "Peace without war is not the way of heaven," Kita bluntly averred. He urged that Japan undertake a program of naval expansion to meet expected opposition from the United States and Great Britain, and establish a great army against Russia. Thus, what was originally an outcry for social justice within Japan became a blueprint for world domination.

Shumei Okawa, a former intelligence officer of the South Manchurian Railway Company, represented a generation of Japanese who were educated under western influence but retained a passionate love for their traditional ideas. Clothing patriotic philosophy with the garb of mysticism, he maintained that Japan was the first state to be created and that it was its divine mission to unify the world under the benevolent rule of the Emperor (*Hakko Ichiu*). In a war between East and West Japan would become champion of the East, Okawa predicted. He advocated Japanese occupation of Manchuria in order to create a land founded upon the principle of Kodo, or the "kingly way." Thereafter, Japan would assume leadership of the peoples of Asia, eliminate the domination of the white race and emancipate colored people. To accomplish these aims the nation would have to give up its worship of the West, and political parties would have to be swept away. This was the gist of Okawa's "Showa Restoration."

Okawa's followers in the Army General Staff organized the Cherry

Society, a group responsible for two abortive *coup d'etat* attempts in 1931 to install a military government under Generals Ugaki and Sadao Araki respectively. Nissho Inoue, another extremist leader, organized a group called the Convenant of Blood League. It was established with the express purpose of having each member assassinate one of the nation's leading political figures. Former Finance Minister Junnosuke Inoue, and Baron Takuma Dan, Director General of the Mitsui concern, fell victims to the Blood League. In May 1932, several young naval officers invaded the official residence of the Prime Minister and murdered Premier Tsuyoshi Inukai. Those who were responsible for his death escaped with only minor sentences, and were even lauded for their patriotism in trying to remove party politicians. The government's unwillingness to impose stronger sentences encouraged further violence. Murder became an accepted political weapon, and terrorism gained in respectability once it was done in the name of the Emperor. One Japanese diplomat aptly called this "the government of assassination, by assassination, and for assassination."[2]

Inukai's death sealed the fate of party government. The cabinet of Admiral Makoto Saito, Inukai's successor, was termed the "National Unity Cabinet." The premiership was no longer held by the head of the majority party in the lower house, but by whoever was acceptable to the armed forces. Political parties, however, still retained five important portfolios in the Saito Cabinet. Finance Minister Korekyo Takahashi continued his policy of limiting the budget of the armed forces and employing a mild inflation to cope with the acute economic situation.

The moderate cabinet of Admiral Keisuke Okada who succeeded Saito also bore the name of the National Unity Cabinet. The Army was hostile and political murder was again revived. General Tetsuzan Nagata, Director of the Military Affairs Bureau, was slain in his office by Lieutenant-Colonel Saburo Aizawa, a disgruntled member of the young officers group. In the February election of 1936, despite Army opposition, the Minseito party which supported Okada won a majority in the lower house. Less than one week after the election, the extremist group revolted against the government in one of the most serious and agonizing uprisings in modern Japanese history, known as the February 26 incident.

The incident involved junior officers and a regiment of troops of some 1,400 men who had been ordered transferred to Manchuria. They successfully staged a series of assassinations and seized several key points in Tokyo. Finance Minister Takahashi; Lord Keeper of the

Privy Seal Admiral Saito, the former Prime Minister; and Inspector
General of Military Education General Jotaro Watanabe were killed
at their homes. Admiral Kantaro Suzuki, the Grand Chamberlain, was
wounded but later recovered. The mutineers also attempted to assassinate Premier Okada but killed his brother-in-law by mistake. The
incident aimed at overthrowing the Okada Cabinet and setting up a
government friendly to the Army. In these respects the incident was
similar in intent to the abortive March and October incidents. But
this time it was conducted on a grand scale and was a temporary success. Ironically, the success was due partly to the fact that the Army
had been disunited. For some time, the Army had been divided into
two factions: One was the Kodoha, or the Imperial Way Faction led
by Generals Sadao Araki and Jinsaburo Mazaki. The other was the
Toseiha, or the Control Faction, led by Generals Juichi Terauchi and
Kanji Ishihara and the late Tetsuzan Nagata. Both factions originally
started as an anti-Choshu group but split into two during the thirties
along the ideological lines advocated by Kita and Okawa. The Imperial Way Faction feared Russia and communism and was willing to adopt
a policy of restraint toward the western powers and China. The Control Faction wanted an outright expansionist policy and was increasingly pro-Germany in its foreign policy orientation. In economic policies both detested capitalism and advocated a state planning system.

Young officers belonging to the Imperial Way Faction were the moving spirits behind the mutiny. But until its political complexion was
made clear the Army High Command hesitated to take steps against
it. At first the assassins were lauded for their pureness of heart and
for their desire to restore the "national spirit." But the Emperor insisted on its suppression, and the Control Faction took full advantage of
it. In its final phase the revolt was considered as mutiny and troops
were repressed.

During the revolt the insurgents were told by Army authorities:
"We share the same opinion with you in respect to the enhancement of
the true aspect of the national character. So we will make efforts to satisfy your wish in this respect. We will demand that the Cabinet put
it into force. Your objectives shall thus be attained. Therefore, you
ought to lay down your arms, now that you have succeeded in carrying things so far."[3] These words were almost prophetic.

When the Hirota Cabinet was formed on March 9, 1936, the Army
was clearly in the driver's seat. General Count Terauchi, who was identified with the Control Faction, became the Minister of War. The
price of his joining the Cabinet was that the selection of each of the

ministers had to be first approved by him. Terauchi promised to "restore discipline" in the Army, and secured Hirota's pledge that the government would accept certain army-sponsored policies.

To show his determination to enforce discipline, General Terauchi ordered the execution of seventeen young officers belonging to the Imperial Way Faction who took part in the revolt. To act "in accordance with his Imperial Majesty's wishes," he placed on the reserve list four full generals and expelled them from membership in the Supreme War Council. Among them were Generals Mazaki and Araki, heretofore his arch rivals. Overnight, the Control Faction emerged victorious and the Imperial Way Faction was vanquished.

To ensure against Mazaki or Araki returning to power as War Minister, Terauchi recommended that the Imperial Ordinance of 1900 be restored, requiring the War and Navy Ministers and Vice-Ministers to be officers on active duty. The Privy Council acted on the suggestion without dissent.

Whatever the motivation behind it, the restoration of the Imperial Ordinance of 1900 placed in the hands of the Army a stronger weapon to deal with the civilian government than the one it had possessed before. The Prime Minister was stripped of his power to select his own War Minister both in fact and in law. Customarily the new War Minister was selected by agreement among the Big Three of the Army — the outgoing War Minister, the Chief of General Staff, and the Inspector General of Military Education. But so long as the Prime Minister could draw his War Minister from the reservists, the Army Big Three were more accomodating. The change in the law obviated the need for such accomodation. The War Minister on active duty was placed under the authority of the Chief of General Staff for operational purposes. Through the War Minister, the Army Chief was able to dictate the formation of national policy. Should the Cabinet disagree with the Army, the Chief of General Staff could always withdraw the War Minister and precipitate a cabinet crisis. If a new premier-designate was unacceptable to the Army, it could refuse to nominate a War Minister, thus preventing the formation of a cabinet.

The months immediately following the February 26 incident thus saw the Army in a new position of strength. The Control Faction took advantage of the incident to blot out its rivals and to impose its will on the civilian government. Thereafter the Army was dominated by a group which was "committed to continental expansion abroad and a controlled economy at home."[4]

The Structure of Japanese Government. The failure of the parliamentary regime to withstand these repeated political crisis was partly due to the weakness within the political parties themselves, and partly due to the system inherent in the Japanese Government. The two major parties were closely associated with the Mitsui and Mitsubishi concerns, the two greatest *zaibatsu* of Japan. Consequently they lacked a basis of popular support. Manhood suffrage was adopted in 1925, but it did not help advance representative government.

The House of Representatives (*Shugi-in*), which was an elective body, had to share equal power with the House of Peers (*Kizoku-in*), which was not an elective body. Furthermore, the Diet (*Gikai*, the composite of the House of Representatives and the House of Peers) held only limited control over the nation's finances. The Meiji Constitution provided that if a proposed budget failed to pass in the Diet, the current budget would be automatically continued. The Diet exercised its control over the executive branch of the Government chiefly through its power of interpellation and censure. Altogether the Constitution carefully circumvented the power of the Diet to the advantage of the executive branch of the Government.

The executive branch of the Government was the composite of the Cabinet, the Privy Seal, the Ministry of the Imperial Household, and the extra-constitutional *Genro*, or elder statesmen. At the helm stood the Emperor.

The Meiji Constitution endowed the Emperor with limitless power. While the Japanese political system recognized a separation of powers, all the organs exercising these powers were subordinated to the Emperor. "The Divine Right of the Emperor," said one Japanese authority, "is the fundamental principle on which the Japanese polity was first established and on which it still rests."[5] The Emperor was the immutable symbol of national unity, and his person sacred and inviolable. He exercised legislative powers, gave sanction to laws and issued imperial ordinances when the Diet was not in session. The Emperor was the Chief of State as well as Commander in Chief of the armed forces. He determined the organization of different branches of Government and had Supreme Command of the Army and Navy. His executive functions also included making appointments, ratifying treaties, receiving foreign envoys, issuing rescripts, declaring war, attending Privy Council meetings, and conferring with ministers.

No specific mention of the Cabinet was made in the Constitution. The latter had only one article dealing with the Ministers of State. They were to "give their advice to the Emperor, and be responsible for it.

All laws, imperial ordinances and imperial rescripts of whatever kind, that relate to the affairs of the state, require the counter signature of a Minister of State."[6]

However, through the years the Cabinet had become a strong central executive organ. It exercised legislative power by issuing imperial ordinances while the Diet was not in session. This included the power to issue emergency financial ordinances. Theoretically the ordinances were subject to review by the Diet when it reconvened, but in practice the legislative body did not make any attempt to override them. Thus the Cabinet was able to rule by decrees and provide appropriation for its own needs — either military or civilian. The militarists used this device to support their war efforts during the Sino-Japanese conflict.

The limitation to the Cabinet's power came from the separation of civil and military affairs. The Emperor had the Supreme Command (*Tosui taiken*) of the Army and Navy which was exercised not through the Cabinet but through the Chiefs of Staff, Board of Marshals and Fleet Admirals, and the Ministers of War and Navy. Civilian members of the Cabinet were not permitted to advise the Emperor on the "command" of the Army and Navy. The term "command" was interpreted to include matters pertaining not only to strategy and tactics, but also to the formulation of overall policies for national defense.

The separation of civil and military affairs had the effect of weakening the position of the Foreign Office. Although the conduct of foreign affairs in any modern nation requires close coordination with military and fiscal policies, this baffling situation existed in pre-war Japan: while the War and Navy Offices were allowed to interfere in foreign policy decisions, the Foreign Office was not permitted to share the least of military secrets. Thus losing its independence of action, the Foreign Office became the maidservant of the War Office. Dual diplomacy was inevitable under these circumstances.

It was still possible, however, to eliminate the dual diplomacy, if a certain central organ could coordinate policies of the military and civilian branches of the government. On the surface, the office of the Prime Minister was uniquely fitted to perform this task. "The Minister President of State stands at the head of the Ministers of State," said the Imperial Ordinance Regarding the Organization of the Cabinet. He also "reports affairs of state to the Sovereign and, in compliance with imperial instructions, has general control over the various branches of administration."

However, the Prime Minister's chain of control was broken with respect to the War and Navy Offices. His two service ministers and the two Chiefs of Staff enjoyed the privilege of *Iakujoso*, a free access to the Emperor. Even after the Cabinet Council had decided on a certain policy, the War or Navy Minister could reverse himself and bring his differences directly to the Emperor. These two Ministers also had an upper hand over the Prime Minister, since they were not appointed by him. The power to select the War Minister rested in the hands of three men — the Chief of Staff, Inspector General of Military Education, and the outgoing minister — who made their choice from Generals and Lieutenant Generals on the active list. The Navy had the Chief of Naval Operations and the outgoing minister select its new minister from Admirals and Vice-Admirals on the active list. Resignation by one of the service ministers would result in the fall of a Cabinet if the Army or Navy failed to name a successor. Refusal by the Army or Navy to name its minister would mean that a new cabinet could not be formed. In effect, the Prime Minister served at the pleasure of the Army and Navy. Thus he was hardly in a position to coordinate policies decided by various branches of the government.

Neither could the Privy Council, the "highest body of the Emperor's constitutional advisers," fill the gap left open by the system of dual government. Established in 1889 to become "the palladium of the Constitution and of the law," the Privy Council was set up for the purposes of "planning far-sighted schemes of statecraft and of effectuating new enactments, after a careful deliberation and calm reflection, by instituting thorough investigations into ancient and modern history, and by consulting scientific principles."[7] It was composed of statesmen chosen for their distinctive careers. Cabinet Ministers by virtue of their offices were entitled to sit in the Council as Councillors with the right to vote. All statutes, imperial ordinances and treaties needed its approval. Despite its broad reviewing power, however, the Council lacked jurisdiction over administrative matters. Its deliberations were confined to matters submitted to it by the Cabinet. It could neither review actions taken by the Supreme Command nor resolve a conflict between the Cabinet and the Supreme Command.[8]

All of these considerations point to the fact that the Emperor alone could exercise the central authority to coordinate diverse policies adopted by the Cabinet and the Supreme Command. However, during the Showa period, exercise of this authority became increasingly difficult, due largely to declining influence of the *Genro* and also to Emperor Hirohito's personal inclination.

The *Genro* was an extra-constitutional institution. The term could be translated collectively as Council of Elder Statesmen, or singularly as an elder-statesman. These elder-statesmen were the Emperor's most trusted advisers. No major decision was taken unless they were first consulted. They derived their prestige from the outstanding services to the country during and after the Meiji Restoration. With the exception of Prince Saionji—who was a court-noble (*Kuge*)—the *Genro* were chosen from members of the Choshu and Satsuma clans. When the clan government was in power, the *Genro* represented the final authority. If a conflict arose between the Cabinet and the Supreme Command, it was referred to the *Genro* for a final decision. Japan was indebted to them for maintaining the unity and solidarity of the nation during the Meiji and the Taisho eras, which saw Japan being transformed from a medieval to a modern state.

Prince Saionji was the sole surviving member of the *Genro* in the thirties. A believer in constitutionalism and parliamentary government, he desired the *Genro* as an institution to die with him. Consistent with this belief, he often declined to advise the throne on the affairs of state leaving the task to constitutionally appointed advisers. In his later years, he carefully confined his activities to recommending candidates for premiership to the Emperor. Even this he declined when it became evident that the militarists were virtually in control of the government.

An attempt was made to establish another extra-constitutional institution to perform some functions of the *Genro* during the Showa period. It was the Council of *Jushin,* to which elder-statesmen who once served as Prime Ministers were invited to join. They had neither the power nor the prestige enjoyed by the *Genro*. From time to time they were consulted on the selection of the next Prime Minister but otherwise performed no signficant roles in political scenes.

The actual task of recommending candidates for premiership to the throne fell to the Lord Keeper of the Privy Seal. He could do so either on his own or upon consultation with the *Jushin*. He also served as liaison man between the throne and the government. Anyone who desired an audience with the Emperor had to clear first through his office. Thus he exercised considerable influence on national policies. But his stature did not become great enough to wear the mantle of the *Genro*.

Had there been determination and willingness on his part, the Emperor still could have exercised his prerogatives without his powerful advisers. However, Emperor Hirohito had been taught to be a constitutional monarch and believed that his task was not to interfere in the policies decided by his ministers, He was a biologist and probably would have preferred his laboratory to the throne. What Japan needed was a German *Kaiser*, not a British king. By not exercising his prerogatives, the Emperor created a power vacuum which no individual could fill.

The Army Vies for Supremacy. Emperor Meiji once termed each soldier his *fidus Achates,* a trusted retainer. Naively but sincerely, many soldiers felt that they were to save the Imperial Household from peril in time of need. It was their duty to refute false doctrine and bring out the truth. Party government had done the country no good and impaired the dignity of the nation. So when the central authority waned and no one was capable of filling the power vacuum, men in uniform — especially those in the Army — were ready to step in "for the sake of the Empire."

The February revolt of 1936 brought the Army closer to fulfilling its allegedly sacred mission. For the first time in two decades the factional strife was ended. Furthermore, the restoration of the Imperial Ordinance of 1900 gave the armed services power to dictate the policy decision. On top of all these, Eiichi Baba, the Army's choice, was placed in the key position of Finance Minister.

Baba was an advocate of semi-war economy in peace time and was ready to grant the Army greatly expanded expenditures. The Army took in the Navy as its partner. In an effort to divide evenly the expanded budget among themselves the two service ministries decided the "Basis of National Policy" on June 30, 1936. It supplemented the Army's traditional northward expansion policy with the Navy's new southward expansion policy. On August 11, the entire Cabinet adopted the "Basis" as its own. The principles stated therein were:

"(1) Japan must strive to correct the aggressive policies of the great powers and to realize the spirit of the "Imperial Way" by a consistent policy of overseas expansion;

"(2) Japan must complete her national defense and armament to secure the position of the Empire as the stabilizing power in East Asia;

"(3) Japan hopes to stabilize Japan-Manchukuo national defense; in order to promote economic development, Japan intends to get rid of the menace of the U.S.S.R.; to prepare against Britain and the United States and to bring about close collaboration between Japan, Manchukuo and China; in the execution of this continental policy Japan must pay due attention to friendly relations with other powers;

"(4) Japan plans to promote her racial and economical development in the South Seas, and without rousing other powers will attempt to extend her strength by moderate and peaceful measures. Thus with the establishment of Manchukuo, Japan may expect full development of her natural resources and develop her national defense."⁹

As a means to achieving these ends, the Army was to expand its Kwantung and Chosen forces to the extent that they could deliver the first decisive blow against the Soviet Far Eastern Army at the outbreak of war. The Navy was to build up an impregnable fleet to ward against possible encroachment by the U. S. Navy in the Western Pacific.

On the same day the Cabinet also decided upon the "Basic Administrative Policy toward North China," which was originally drafted by the Army. The purposes of this policy were: to assist people in North China in achieving perfect independence in administration; to set up an anti-Communist, pro-Japanese area; to secure necessary materials for Japan's national defense; and to improve transportation facilities to guard against possible invasion by Soviet Russia. This would make North China a base of cooperation between Japan, Manchukuo and China. All told, Japan intended to subjugate North China à la Manchuria.

The policy thus ended the *immobilisme* that had long plagued successive cabinets. For once the Government adopted a positive continental policy. But somehow in embracing the Army-originated plan, the Cabinet showed its capitulation to the militarists. Henceforth it would be the Army, not the Foreign Office or the Cabinet, who would be guiding the formulation of Japan's continental policies.

In effect, the new policy also placed an official seal of approval on what the Army had been pursuing singlehandedly in North China since the conquest of Manchuria. In 1933 the Kwantung Army advanced south of the Great Wall and forced the Tangku Truce, requiring Chinese troops to evacuate the Tientsin area. Then in 1935, there were the Ho-Umezu and Chin-Doihara Agreements providing for withdrawal of Chinese troops from Hopei and Chahar. With these areas forming a *cordon sanitaire*, the Army hoped Manchukuo could be protected against Comintern activities and renewed Chinese nationalism.

In order to placate Japanese demands, the Chinese Nationalist Government agreed to the establishment of a Hopei-Chahar Political Council in the winter of 1935, with a pro-Japanese General, Sung Che-yuan, as its chairman. But this Council remained loyal to the Central Government in Nanking and did not develop into an autonomous government as the Japanese Army had first hoped. Meanwhile, the Army's China policy was driving a wedge in Japan's relations wtih the western powers. In 1935 Great Britain sent its chief economic adviser, Sir Frederick Leith-Ross to China to aid in a currency reform program which greatly strengthened the fiscal foundation of the Nanking Government. This was a reversal of Britain's policy from 1931 to 1933 which was on the whole favorable to Japan rather than to China. The cleavage between Japan and the western powers widened on November 25, 1936, when Japan and Germany signed an Anti-Comintern Pact providing for co-operation in "defense against the disintegrating influence of communism." This Pact contained secret provisions which were in the nature of a military alliance against Soviet Russia, but could also be employed against the western powers. In 1936 Japan's cooperation on naval matters with the western powers ended. It withdrew from the London Naval Conference when both the Washington and London Naval Treaties expired.

Internally, the Nationalist Government of China was recovering from civil strife. In 1934 the Communists were forced into the long march from Kiangsi through western China to northwestern Shensi, and it appeared that the Communist remnants might eventually be driven to Outer Mongolia and thus be eliminated as a factor in Chinese civil politics. However, in defeat, the Communist Party shifted from a policy of civil war against the Nationalist Government to one of a united front against the Japanese invaders. This policy appealed to the new national patriotism, and enabled the Chinese Communist Party to pose as a unifying national force rather than a party dedicated to class struggle. The policy of the United Front was adopted by the Nationalist Party in January 1937 after Chiang Kai-shek was kidnapped in Sian by Young Marshal Chang Hsueh-liang. Chiang Kai-shek's acceptance of a policy of "forebearance in domestic issues in order to achieve internal solidarity to fight against foreign enemies" was viewed with disdain by the Japanese Army whose success in China depended on a divided and weak China. The choice before the Army was whether it should immediately crush the Chinese while they were still weak, or seek cooperation with the Nationalist Government and bring it under Japan's influence.

General Senjuro Hayashi, who succeeded Koki Hirota as Prime Minister in January 1937, adopted a conciliatory policy toward China. The four ministers—Foreign, War, Navy, and Finance Ministers—decided that Japan should aid China's unification movement by economic offensive in order to eliminate British and American influences in China. The Kodama Economic Mission was sent to Nanking with attractive terms of economic cooperation. But before the Mission could achieve its objectives, the Hayashi Cabinet fell.

Prince Fumimaro Konoye was chosen by Prince Saionji to head the new Cabinet. Konoye was close to the Emperor and had served as the President of the House of Peers. He was popular and, being a lineal descendent of the most respected house of court nobles, enjoyed immense prestige unmatched by others. In Saionji's opinion, Konoye was the only person who could stem the tide of military fascism. The Army, though frustrated in its desire to install General Gen Sugiyama as the next premier, decided to cooperate hoping that Konoye's prestige could be used to further its control over other departments of government. Hopes and fears were mixed, and the future was still uncertain. It was under these circumstances that Tokyo received news of the Marco Polo Bridge Incident.[10]

CHAPTER II

OUTBREAK OF THE SINO-JAPANESE CONFLICT

The Marco Polo Bridge Incident. Near the Marco Polo Bridge, on the night of July 7, 1937, a Japanese regiment was holding an unscheduled maneuver. At 11:40 p.m. several shots were heard. A quick rollcall revealed one private missing. The Japanese commander demanded a search of the city of Wanping for the missing soldier. When this was rejected, a skirmish ensued and on the next day, the Japanese commander issued an ultimatum calling for the surrender of the city. On July 9 the parties agreed to a truce which was broken only two hours later.

The Konoye Cabinet was thirty-three days old when the incident occurred. At first the news was treated lightly. War Minister Sugiyama expressed complete surprise at the outbreak of the incident, and promised that it would be localized. However, on July 11, he proposed preliminary measures for mobilization, contending that in order to secure the apology and future guarantee by the Chinese, it would be necessary to reinforce the North China Army which had only 5,000 men. For this pupose he suggested that reservists at home be called to active duty and contingents in Manchuria and Chosen be put on an emergency basis. The Cabinet conference approved his proposal with the reservation that troops be sent only to protect Japanese lives and to secure the safety of the North China forces.

Konoye agreed to Sugiyama's demand for two reasons. He feared that the War Minister might resign and thus cause the fall of his Cabiet. On the other hand, he also hoped that by adopting a strong China policy, he might be in a better position to control the government independently of the War Minister. He even agreed to issue a proclamation which would justify the despatch of troops and state that North China was within Japan's defense perimeter.[1]

There were talks of sending Foreign Minister Koki Hirota to Nanking to settle the matter amicably. Not knowing the ultimate intent of the Army, he was reluctant to assume the task. Furthermore, the Army itself lacked central authority to decide which policy to follow. Those in the General Staff Office were against an involvement in China, while those in the War Office generally favored it. Had the General Staff been allowed to have its way the conflict might have been localized. General Kanji Ishihara, the most influential strategist in the General Staff, once remarked that no soldier would be sent to China as long as he lived. Yet the break in the chain of command was working in the War Office's favor. It permitted the despatch of troops to continue, despite the reports that all was calm on the front.

Reinforcement of the Peking area, completed by July 27, set in motion a new wave of conflict. General Kazuki, the newly appointed Japanese commander of the expanded North China forces, demanded that General Sung Che-yuan evacuate his troops to the south of Peking and Tientsin. General Sung, who owed to the Japanese his position as Chairman of the Hopei-Chahar Political Council and was the most pro-Japanese of all Chinese generals, refused. Heavy fighting ensued in which the Chinese lost 5,000 men in a single day. General Sung then firmly aligned with Nanking taking orders from Chiang Kai-shek. On July 28, the Chinese Peace Preservation Corps, attached to another Japanese-sponsored East Hopei regime, killed their Japanese officers and then massacred some two hundred and thirty Japanese civilians. Even if some in the Japanese Army had desired conciliation with China, this incident made it impossible. The North China forces proceeded to occupy Peking and Tientsin which fell on July 29. In the meantime, the Army mobilized three divisions and requested the special session of the Diet for an emergency appropriation of 97,000,000 yen. The Diet approved it without debate and passed a resolution of thanks to troops in North China. The Cabinet's indecision and the Army's lack of control had pushed the unwanted war into full gear.[2]

It was at this point the Emperor stepped in ordering Prince Konoye to start negotiations with Nanking. The Army agreed provided there was a way of saving face by making China ask for peace. Shinichiro Funazu, president of the association of Japanese textile industries in China, was in Tokyo at that time. He was the Cabinet's choice as secret emissary to negotiate with Kao Tsung-wu, Chief of the East Asian Section of the Chinese Foreign Office. No diplomatic officials, not even Ambassador Kawagoe, were to interfere in Funazu's mission. But somehow, the arrival of Funazu in Shanghai and the return of Kawagoe from North China coincided. Kawagoe decided to try his hand and met with Kao on August 9. Kawagoe's proposals included the following: (1) that a designated area in Hopei Province as well as six provinces of Chipei become a demilitarized zone; (2) that the Tangku Truce be abrogated; (3) that Japan agree to the liquidation of the Hopei-Chahar and the East Hopei Councils, and to direct administration of the area by Nanking;   (4) that Japanese forces in China be reduced to *status quo* prior to July 7; and (5) that the principle of economic cooperation between Japan and China in North China be observed.   Kao was left with the impression that there was some hope for a rapprochement with Japan.   Tokyo, however, felt that it was frustrated in its attempt to have China take the initial step in truce negotiations.

At any rate the hope for negotiated peace was short lived. Lieutenant Oyama, an officer of the Japanese Marine Corps, and his driver, first class seaman Saito were killed by Chinese sentries when they sought to enter the Shanghai municipal airport at night.   The Japanese Consul General in Shanghai demanded that the Chinese Peace Preservation Corps which was responsible for the incident be evacuated to the outskirts of the city.   The mayor refused contending that Japanese reinforcement of the Marine Corps and the despatch of additional warships to otherwise peaceful Shanghai were the causes of tension which made the incident inevitable.   Nanking also charged Japan with aggressive intent in Central China.

At first the Army was reluctant to become involved in Shanghai. But the Commander-in-Chief of the Third Fleet, whose headquarters was in Shanghai, requested the despatch of ground troops.   This request was supported by Navy Minister Mitzumasa Yonai who departed from his usual moderate views.   The upshot of this was mobilization of reservists followed by a Cabinet statement placing all the blame squarely on the Chinese.

On August 25 the Japanese Third Fleet ordered a closure of the coast line of Central and South China which applied to all Chinese merchant ships.   On September 5 the closure was extended to cover the coast line of North China as well, with the exception of Tsingtao and other port cities where third powers' concessions were located. Ostensibly the closure was not intended to infringe on foreign rights or commerce.   But in effect Japan was claiming belligerent's rights without accepting corresponding duties.   The closure cut deep into China's customs revenue.   In allowing the conflict to spread to Shanghai, Japan also placed itself in a position to challenge directly the economic supremacy of western powers in China.

Reactions of the West. The initial reaction of the western powers was one of cautious restraint.   Both the U.S. and Great Britain hoped the hostilities might be localized. "We avoid entering into alliance or entangling commitments," said Secretary of State Cordell Hull on July

16, "but we believe in co-operative effort by peaceful and practicable means in support of the principles" of the Good Neighbor Policy, which also applied to the Far East. He also implied that he would agree to the modification of existing treaties "by orderly processes carried out in a spirit of mutual helpfulness and accommodation," leaving the door open for peaceful negotiations to settle the China question.[3]

The Japanese took Mr. Hull's stand to mean that the United States had adopted the policy of noninvolvement. They were especially gratified that President Roosevelt had not proclaimed neutrality according to the Act of April 30, 1937, and had thus allowed Japan to continue importing gasoline, oil and scrap iron from the United States to support their war efforts in China.

London, while making continuous representations to Tokyo for a peaceful settlement, broadly hinted that it was ready to help in any useful form of mediation. Great Britain had huge financial and commercial stakes in China, and it was to its interest that peace be preserved. It was willing to cooperate with Japan, if conditions were clarified, peace restored and its commercial activities allowed to continue. When hostilities spread to Shanghai, Great Britain was the first to offer its good offices for mediation through its local representatives.

However, an anti-British incident occured which marred Prime Minister Chamberlain's policy of appeasement. Sir Hughe Knatchbull-Hugessen, the British Ambassador to China, was wounded by a shot fired from a Japanese airplane while traveling from Nanking to Shanghai in his car on August 26. In expressing the Japanese Government's official regret eleven days after the incident, Hirota told Sir Robert Craigie, the British Ambassador to Japan, that the Ambassador of a friendly power should notify Japan of his impending travel whenever passing through a danger zone. Here Hirota was clearly pressing for British recognition of Japan's belligerent rights in China. Japanese closure of Chinese coastal waters and their interference in the Chinese Customs Administration had jeopardized Great Britain's legitimate economic interests, but no serious diplomatic steps were taken to correct the situation.

The Soviet Union became the first power to offer its assistance to China's cause. A treaty of non-aggression was signed on August 27 between Russia and China. Though sudden, this was not completely unforeseen, since the treaty was a logical sequel to the United Front which was formed early in 1937. It provided a means through which communist influence could further penetrate into China. Though in retrospect, it was this communist infiltration which brought about the

ultimate destruction of Nationalist China, in 1937 the non-aggression
pact was good news for a country which had to fight for its very existence. On the practical side, the treaty permitted China to acquire
certain military equipment from Russia. The treaty gave the Japanese
a good propaganda weapon. After all, they maintained, the pact confirmed Japan's suspicion that further Bolshevisation of East Asia was
in progress.

The western powers' desire to stem the tide of aggression found its
first expression in President Roosevelt's "quarantine" speech delivered
at Chicago on October 5, 1937. "When an epidemic of physical disease
starts to spread," said the President, "the community approves and
joins in a quarantine of the patients in order to protect the health of
the community" against the spread of the disease: "War is a contagion,
whether it be declared or undeclared . . . We are determined to keep
out of war, yet we cannot insure ourselves against the disastrous effects of war and the dangers of involvement. We are adopting such
measures as will minimize our risk of involvement, but we cannot have
complete protection in a world of disorder in which confidence and
security have broken down."

Just what Mr. Roosevelt meant by "quarantine" was not made clear
at the time. But according to one account, he had in mind an extreme
form of sanction against aggressors like Japan who had sent its troops
to the territory of another nation.[4]

The Japanese Government took a rather dim view of Mr. Roosevelt's
speech. Japan could ill afford to lose the United States' economic
friendship or its neutrality. The ruling circles were also worried with
the gloomy prospect of entering into hostilities against the United
States. The Lord Keeper of the Privy Seal, Yuasa, thought the Japanese Government should take steps to make public the reactions of the
western powers to the conflict in China. The report, no matter how dis-
tasteful it might seem, would arouse the nation to the necessity of peace
rather than war.

The Foreign Office also recommended that Japan adopt a policy of
cooperation with the United States and Great Britain. As a first step
toward that direction, Foreign Minister Hirota prevailed on War Minister Sugiyama to hold a news conference with A. P. and U. P. cor-
respondents. Sugiyama obligingly told the American newsmen that
Japan entertained no territorial ambitions and would welcome foreign
capital for the development of China. The Army in China was then
firmly instructed not to bring trouble on foreign residents and to keep
in close contact with them to avoid misunderstanding.[5]

However, the period of cooperation with the western powers was short-lived. The League of Nations looked to the United States for leadership in dealing with Japan but Washington gave no encouragement. The League then took a lukewarm stand of condemning Japan on one hand without promising aid to China on the other. The Brussels Conference of signatories to the Nine-Power Pact on China dwelt on generalities, such as the sanctity of treaties, without producing any concrete proposals. To the League, Japan stated that the former's intervention would only complicate matters in China. As for the Brussels Conference, it refused to attend and allowed Italy to serve as its spokesman. Meanwhile reports from various foreign capitals indicated that Mr. Roosevelt's "quarantine" speech was poorly received. Tokyo also learned that Mr. Hull was shocked by the President's improvision in delivering the speech, and that the isolationist sentiment was still running high. It was safe for the Foreign Office to assume that the economic sanctions Japan feared were not forthcoming. The aggression in China, the Foreign Office concluded, could continue without any foreign intervention.[6]

The Fall of Nanking. At first the Shanghai affair was the Navy's concern. But the Chinese fought gallantly, endangering the lives of Japanese marines. This caused Navy Minister Yonai to request the despatch of Army troops to Shanghai. Early in November an Army division landed on the Hangchow Bay and established itself in a position to strike at Shanghai and Nanking. On November 19 Soochow fell in Japanese hands. That was the signal for the fall of Greater Shanghai. The next day, the Chinese Government announced that the capital would be moved to Chungking, the commercial center of western China. The executive branch, however, remained temporarily in the Central China city of Hankow. In North China, Chinese resistance suffered a similar fate. Taiyuan, the provincial capital of Shansi, changed hands on November 8.

Japan's march toward Nanking was marked with two instances of flagrant violations of foreign rights. The American gunboat *Panay* was sunk by a Japanese naval air squadron. The Navy claimed that is was unintentional, even though the weather was good with clear visibility and the American flag was recognizable from a distance. *U.S.S. Panay* also communicated its position to the Japanese at regular intervals. This information could have been withheld from the naval air squadron by the Army. The latter in requesting the former's aid simply stated that Chinese soldiers were fleeing from Nanking in ships which

ought to be bombed.   It was also possible that the local army was not
happy with the Navy's insistance on respecting foreign rights.   On the
same day, an artillery regiment under the command of Colonel Kingoro
Hashimoto shelled the British gunboat *Ladybird* and took it into cus-
tody.

The two incidents left perplexing problems for the Foreign Office,
which had to make apologies and payment of reparations.   It was clear
that the Foreign Office could not restrain the Army from committing
further violations of international rights.   The actions of the Army
would prevail and the Foreign Office had to bear the consequences.
The Navy, however, was gravely concerned about the incidents.   The
commander of the squadron who was responsible for the sinking of
U.S.S. Panay was promptly removed from his post.   "We have done
this," explained Vice Navy Minister Isoroku Yamamoto, "to suggest the
Army do likewise, removing Hashimoto from his command."   But
Hashimoto was allowed to stay.   The day after the incident, he marched with other soldiers into Nanking which fell to the Japanese.

Chapter III

WAR EFFORTS AND PEACE OVERTURES

The Trautmann Mediation. As summer gave way to fall, the Japanese Army was still deeply involved in the China theater. "Crush the Chinese in three months, and they will sue for peace," War Minister Sugiyama declared when the conflict first started. But Chinese resistance had been unexpectedly strong. General Sugiyama's "crushing blow — generous peace" formula was a complete failure. On September 2, 1937, the North China Incident was officially renamed the China Incident recognizing the fact that the conflict had spread to other parts of China.

By October the Army General Staff became greatly alarmed. It feared that Soviet Russia might take advantage of Japan's involvement in China and suddenly attack Manchuria. Japan could maintain its balance of power in Manchuria until June or July of 1938. After that, the Kwantung Army would not be able to keep pace with the Soviet Far Eastern Army's rapid expansion and in a power contest a defeat would become almost certain. The conflict in China had been draining Japan's available manpower and other resources.

The idea of asking German mediation originated with the General Staff. The court circles and the Konoye Cabinet would have preferred England as mediator but would settle for Germany if the latter could relieve them from their "unwanted war." [1] The Cabinet's acceptance of the General Staff's position was reflected in its adoption of peace terms which included an autonomous Inner Mongolia, greatly expanded demilitarized zones in North China and Shanghai, cessation of anti-Japanese activities, China's possible adherence to the Anti-Comintern Pact, reduced customs duties, and respect for foreign rights in China. These terms were communicated to the Chinese Premier, Kung Hsiang-hsi, on October 28 through German Ambassador Trautmann. Thus began the Trautmann mediation.

Germany enjoyed the confidence of both parties at that time. With Japan, it was a partner in the anti-Comintern pact. With regard to China, it was gaining foothold as a friend of that country. After the defeat in the First World War, the Reich relinquished its special rights and the Shantung concessions. Hitler gave Chiang Kai-shek arms, sent a military advisory group, and fortified the Shanghai area. Its repute as an "honest broker" was not challenged by either one of the belligerents. Germany also had its own reasons to undertake the mediation. It was not ready to abandon its newly won commercial interests in China which were endangered by the conflict. Nor could it afford to see its ally weakened by prolonged warfare in China jeopardizing their chance of checking the Soviet Union.

The mere fact that mediation was initiated suggested that General Ishihara, head of the Division of strategy in the General Staff, had won a battle in the faction-ridden Army. He had consistently favored immediate cessation of hostilities in China in order to guard against Russia. In contrast Sugiyama had seen in the extension of the conflict an opportunity to reestablish control within the Army. Sugiyama had the support of General Terauchi and of the main current of the Toseiha, or the Control Faction. Ishihara's views appealed to Prince Konoye who was seeking a means to counter-balance the predominant influence of the Toseiha. The acceptance of the German mediation would have weakened the War Minister's political position and thus indirectly would have curtailed the Toseiha's influence, since Sugiyama was one of the leaders of that faction.

The Chinese Government received the mediation offer with cordiality. After a meeting with Premier Kung and Foreign Minister Wang Chung-hui, Trautmann requested to see the Generalissimo. Chiang Kai-shek readily agreed to a meeting. At that time the executive branch was located in Hankow but Chiang still remained in Nanking.

When Trautmann saw Chiang in Nanking on December 2, the latter was ready to accept the mediation. He expressed the hope that Germany would remain as a mediator throughout the negotiations, and that the administrative and territorial integrity of North China be preserved. Chiang's move was supported by his top military aides, Generals Ku Chu-tung, Pai Chung-hsi, Tang Sheng-chih, and Hsu Yung-chang, who had previously met together that day. The Generals were concerned that Japan might impose additional conditions other than those presented by the German Ambassador. Vice Foreign Minister Hsu Mo assured them that there was none. With this General Pai summed up the Generals' sentiment: "If this is all they are asking, what are we fighting for?"

The essence of the Chiang-Trautmann talk was communicated to Japanese Foreign Minister Hirota on December 7 through Ambassador Dirksen. But the fall of Nanking was regarded as imminent, and the Japanese Government decided to defer its answer.

Nanking changed hands on December 13 and the War Minister stiffened his attitude. Sugiyama would agree to peace only if China would extend *de facto* recognition to Manchukuo, establish special administrative areas both in North and Central China, and pay necessary reparations. These conditions were much severer than those originally presented by Trautmann and were apparently unacceptable to the Chinese Government.

A day later the North China Army established a puppet regime in Peking, disregarding the wish of the Cabinet and the General Staff. Sugiyama and his friend General Terauchi, who commanded the North China Army, had in effect successfully torpedoed the General Staff-originated peace moves. Meanwhile the entire Cabinet found itself being forced into accepting Sugiyama's conditions as the basis for future negotiations.

To implement its new policy, on December 21 the Cabinet drafted an "Outline of the Policies to Be Taken With Regard to the China Incident," the first major policy paper of its kind since the outbreak of the conflict. It stated that in case the negotiations with Nanking proved futile, Japan would take special measures in the occupied areas of North and Central China immediately. For North China, the program consisted of (1) strengthening the puppet North China regime, whose territory was expected to encompass the three provinces of Hopei, Shantung and Shansi, and a part of Chahar, and (2) establishing a development company which would be required to coordinate its activities with those of Japanese and Manchurian heavy industries. No puppet government was contemplated in Central China in the near future, but if it were established, Shanghai would become an open port.

The revised conditions without the details were transmitted to Premier Kung on December 26. Kung was adamant, declaring that it was a clear breach of faith on Japan's part, but still left the door open for the continuation of negotiations.

Meanwhile the Military Affairs Bureau of the War Ministry drafted a formula which called for non-recognition of the Chiang regime, and peace negotiations with a puppet regime. On the other hand, the General Staff Headquarters still clamored for direct negotiations with Chiang Kai-shek in order to bring about an early end to the conflict. Foreign Minister Hirota became increasingly impatient. On January 4, 1938, he confided to Dirksen that new military operations were planned and a quick reply from China was necessary. He was particularly perturbed that the Chinese Ambassador in Washington had held conversations with President Roosevelt. This seemed to indicate that

China had informed England and America of the conditions. Japan could not tolerate any third power other than Germany discussing its terms.

By January 10 Dirksen could sense that the break of negotiations was in the offing. "The pressure from the nationalistic wing has increased, so the moderate wing will give in if a positive answer is not soon received from China," reported the Ambassador.[2] Dirksen's observation was correct. On Sunday, January 9, and Monday, January 10, two liaison conferences between the Cabinet and Supreme Command were held. They agreed that an Imperial Conference should be called to confirm the China policy decided by the Cabinet. The *Genro*, Prince Saionji, was horrified at the prospect of the Emperor placing his seal of approval on a policy with which he had no sympathy. But the mere fact that the conference was to be called represented a victory for the War Office over the General Staff Headquarters. Once the policy was approved by the Imperial Conference, it would become binding, and no one could challenge it. In maneuvering toward this end General Sugiyama — whose authority as War Minister was once seriously questioned — again placed himself as master of the hour.

As expected, the Emperor said nothing at the Imperial Conference on January 11 which simply ratified the terms previously agreed upon by the liaison conferences. The terms were similar to those decided by the Cabinet Conference of December 21, except Japan would now require China to extend *de jure* recognition to Manchukuo, and to allow Japan to station troops in unspecified parts of China to supervise the carrying out of the provisions of the truce agreement once it was signed. Simultaneously, additional troops were despatched to occupy Hankow.

The Chinese Foreign Minister's reply came on January 13, after being warned by Trautmann of the danger of procrastination. It restated that the Japanese terms were too broad and that China wanted to be apprised of the nature and content of the newly submitted conditions. To Hirota, the Chinese reply represented an evasion. "China had all the necessary facts for an answer," he angrily told Dirksen when the latter related the Chinese position. In discussing the matter, the Cabinet Conference decided to stop the negotiations entirely.

The General Staff balked. At the January 15 liaison conference, Vice Chief of Staff Tada insisted that the decision reached at the Imperial Conference of January 11 be reversed. In this instance, Tada was acting on the advice of his subordinate, General Ishihara, who still wanted peace at any cost so Japan could be prepared against Russia.

Hirota explained that there was little hope of arriving at a peace settlement. The Chinese Government had known the conditions offered but claimed they had no knowledge of their scope. This being the case, the only alternative was to shift the emphasis to war. To this Navy Minister Yonai agreed, since the Navy was in no particular haste to conclude peace with Chiang Kai-shek. Finally the Supreme Command yielded and gave the Cabinet full authority to break off the negotiations.

It was a crucial decision. Hirota apparently knew that Chiang Kai-shek had failed in his effort to secure American aid, and felt Japan would gain more in the end by adopting a strong policy. Another factor which influenced Hirota in taking that position was the intense rivalry existing within the government. The Foreign Office was jealous of its own prerogatives and resented any peace moves started by the General Staff.

On January 15 Premier Kung made an oral statement to Trautmann, declaring that China really desired peace with Japan. He explained that China was not evasive in asking for further details of the basic conditions. When this message was communicated to Hirota through Dirksen, the former simply indicated that Japan wished to abandon peace negotiations and calmly thanked Dirksen for Germany's efforts in the past. According to Dirksen, Kung's message was deciphered by the Japanese intelligence and Hirota had knowledge of its substance before it was given him. At any rate, Hirota adopted a very inflexible attitude. Dirksen warned Hirota that the continuation of war would incur world condemnation, and would have a bad effect on German-Japanese relations. Germany did not desire Anglo-Japanese relations to be strained any further. Nor did it wish Japan to be weakened in a protracted war in view of the renewed Russian threat. Germany also feared that China might be Bolshevised. To this Hirota replied that Chiang Kai-shek had been falling under communistic influence and the war would not aggravate it. He declined to comment on the possibility of a prolonged war and evaded the issues of a declaration of war and military actions against Canton and the Hainan Island.

On the afternoon of January 16 Premier Konoye publicly declared that henceforth, "the Imperial Government shall cease to deal with the National Government of China, and shall rely upon the establishment and growth of a new Chinese regime for cooperation." Prince Konoye later explained that the declaration was made at the request of Wang Keh-min, head of the puppet regime in North China, who wanted to gain status for his infant regime. This declaration sealed the fate of

the mediation. Ambassador Kawagoe was recalled. The Chinese Ambassador in Tokyo, Hsu Shih-ying, also left his post. The semblance
of friendly relations which had existed between the two countries up
to that moment was completely broken.

The failure of the Trautmann mediation thus revealed the weakness
of the Konoye Cabinet. Prince Konoye favored the mediation but was
forced to yield to the demands of War Minister Sugiyama. Foreign
Minister Hirota was not sympathetically inclined to Konoye's initial
move and secretly favored Sugiyama's position. Navy Minister Yonai
was not interested in the mediation that would ultimately place the
emphasis on defense against Soviet Russia. It would have meant that a
greater portion of defense appropriations would go to the Army, and
the Navy would not be able to continue its expansion program. Faced
with these oppositions to the mediation, Prince Konoye was powerless and the support of the Army High Command could not change the
existing power alignment in the Cabinet.

When he first took office, Konoye sought to rule by "conferences and
compromises" in order to "diminish the existing frictions and oppositions
within different segments of the country." The events from the Marco
Polo Bridge incident to the Trautmann mediation proved this method
unworkable. The next few months found Prince Konoye doggedly pursuing a new course, attempting to remake his Cabinet and to strengthen
his own political position.

Attempts Toward a Unified War Policy. In order to understand the
position in which Prince Konoye was placed, one must examine prior
attempts he had made toward establishing a unified war policy.

After the Marco Polo Bridge incident, for some time Konoye entertained the idea of amending the Constitution to enable the Cabinet to
control defense policies. Fearing that the Emperor might veto the
scheme he then turned to the idea of forming a war-time Cabinet, with
only a few members becoming the nuclei, to which all policy-making
functions would be delegated. Other members were to be demoted
to the ranks of administrators, each heading a governmental agency.
The Cabinet would thus include only the Premier, War and Navy
Ministers, and two or three other civilian members. Konoye would go
so far as to include the Chiefs of General Staff and Naval Staff as constituent members of the Cabinet. In turn the Cabinet might thus sur-
pass the General Staff Headquarters in authority and prestige.

The idea was a complete failure. It did not pass the stage of being
drafted on paper. As a substitute, a Cabinet Advisers' Council was

formed.   Generally the move was interpreted as reflecting Konoye's desire to establish a quasi-war Cabinet.   Among the members chosen for the Council were: General Kazushige Ugaki, the dark horse of Japanese politics who was unable to form a cabinet in 1936 because of the Army's opposition;   and Seihin Ikeda, a pro-western financier who was general manager of the Mitsui concern.   Later the Council also served as a reservoir from which Prince Konoye could fill vacancies arising in his Cabinet.

At first Konoye intended to make the Council his policy planning board, but the idea was discarded. The Council could not reach definite recommendations at any of its meetings. Home Minister Eiichi Baba sarcastically remarked that the Council had no other function than to keep the councillors' mouths shut.   These people were far more valuable as friends within the Cabinet than enemies outside of it.

Early in October 1937 Marquis Koichi Kido was drafted to become Minister of Education. Kido had been the President of the Board of Peerage in the Imperial Household Ministry and was close to the Emperor.   Count Yoriyasu Arima thought the combination of Konoye and Kido exceptionally good, their merits and faults balancing one another.   Kido himself was more reserved, viewing his own appointment "only as a means of assisting Konoye."

After this Cabinet reorganization, Konoye launched on another venture advocating the establishment of the Imperial Headquarters, with the Prime Minister himself serving as one of the constituent members. In this Konoye met with stubborn resistance from the military.   On November 17, 1937, the Imperial Headquarters Ordinance of 1904 was repealed and replaced by a new miltiary ordinance.   It provided for the establishment of the Headquarters without a civilian as its constituent member, thus breaking the precedent set during the Meiji period when Premiers Ito and Yamagata sat at the Headquarters conference table.   Henceforth, "matters relating to the Supreme Comand" were to be issued in the form of *gunrei* (military ordinances) without reference to the Cabinet.

A week later, the Imperial Headquarters was officially set up in the Imperial Palace.   However, the Army and Navy agreed to hold liaison conferences between the Cabinet and the Headquarters as often as possible.   To the Prince who was eager to establish a central organ to formulate unified policies, this was merely a face-saving device. Prince Saionji was surprised that the Prime Minister and Foreign Minister were not included as members of the Headquarters.

National Mobilization Law and War Economy. As events soon demonstrated, Konoye's success in bringing about the establishment of channels through which policies could be coordinated was thus more apparent than real. The Army, on the other hand, was able to draw more political power to itself through a series of Cabinet reorganizations and the passage of several Army-sponsored bills.

As early as July 10, 1937, only three days after the Marco Polo Bridge incident, the Army started talks for establishing a comprehensive productive power expansion plan for Japan, Manchukuo, and China. The plan chiefly aimed to perfect the foundation of national defense, and was restricted to essential industries requiring expansion under a unified plan. This would include the control of foreign exchange, curtailment of nonessential imports, stockpiling of iron and oil, subsidizing of munitions and other industries, and development of greater transportation facilities.

The problem the militarists had to face was twofold: First, the economy had to be transformed to a war-time basis; Second, the inborn weakness that plagued Japanese industry since the Meiji period — namely, the lack of natural resources within its own territorial limits — had to be reckoned with. Japan had little gold reserves or foreign currencies, and western powers were not likely to invest in its market to finance its war of aggression.

On August 11, 1937, the gold production law was enacted. It was to encourage gold production and provide government supervision of the disposition of gold. Steel industries were also brought under control during the same month.

On August 14 temporary regulations under the exchange control law — which had been in existence since May, 1933 — were issued. Effective September 27 of the same year, the government was empowered to prohibit or restrict the import or export of certain goods and to regulate the manufacturing, distribution and use of goods produced from imported raw materials. The limited supply of foreign exchange was, henceforth, to be used for the import of munitions or materials to make them. Certain types of raw materials, including cotton, wool, leather, wood, hide, pulp, and rubber were placed under a strict licensing system. The export of goods needed for war were forbidden. Various types of government-sponsored industrial associations were established to handle distribution of materials among themselves.

The temporary capital adjustment law was also passed during the same month. This was intended to force the country's savings into heavy industries. Under the law, no corporation could be newly established or could undertake an expansion program without first obtaining the Government's permission. On the other hand, heavy industry—mainly the munitions industry—was accorded preferential treatment in securing loans from the semi-official Industrial Bank of Japan and Hypothec Bank of Japan.

Foreign Minister Hirota, in his additional capacity as the President of the Government Planning Board, guided the passage of these important bills in the Diet. But once the measures were adopted his usefulness was terminated. On October 25, 1937 he was quietly dropped from the presidency of the Planning Board in order to give him "more time to devote to his main duty of directing the formulation of foreign policies." His replacement by a lesser figure, however, enabled the Army to make further inroads into the decisions involving the nation's economic policies.

The new laws had a far reaching effect even beyond carrying out war efforts in China. The Army made use of these laws to prepare for a greater strife which might come in the near future. "What worried us most," commented Lieutenant Colonel Kenryo Sato, who was from June 1937 to July 1938 an investigator and Secretary of the Government Planning Board, "was the fear that this incident might cause the breakdown of our Armament Expansion Plan and the Five-Year Production Expansion Plan. So we decided to see that the China Incident would not end in a war of attrition on our side."

"Accordingly, generally speaking, we spent 40% of our budget on the China Incident and 60% on armament expansion. In respect to iron and other important materials allotted to the Army, we spent 20% on the China Incident and 80% on the expansion of armament. As a result, the Air Force and mechanized units were greatly expanded and the fighting power of the whole Japanese Army was increased to more than three times what it had been before the China Incident. I believe that our Navy, which had suffered very little attrition in the China Affair, had perfected and expanded its fighting power. Of course, productive power of the munitions industry had been expanded seven or eight fold as a rough estimate."[3]

A bill to circumvent the power of the Diet, to bring the country under direct economic control of the Government, and to assist generally in the establishment of national defense as advocated by the Army was under consideration since 1936 under Hirota's premiership. After the Marco Polo Bridge, the general mobilization law embodying these features became a political necessity. The Government Planning Board which was greatly expanded under Konoye's

Cabinet undertook a study of steps to be taken in this direction. In order for the Army's war production program to succeed, the help of industrialists was urgently needed. Yet there was no inducement for them to take such an expansion program as the Army desired. Most industrialists felt that the conflict would be of short duration and were naturally reluctant to pour all their resources into the war industry which would be suicidal to their own well-being. The mobilization law, among other things, would provide security from ultimate loss and thus encourage the industrialists to undertake the tasks the Army desired.

The year 1938 marked the fiftieth year Japan had been under the Meiji Constitution. The 73rd Diet was convened on January 22 to celebrate this occasion. But the Diet was faced with the passage of an act which was most contrary to the spirit and letter of the Constitution.

On February 19, the Konoye Cabinet approved the final version of the National Mobilization bill which called for the control and use of all manpower and resources for national defense. During wartime, it would provide for government control of labor, materials, land, equipment, business agreements, investment, prices, and publications. In time of peace, it would provide for labor conscription, technical training, storage and conservation of materials, compulsory wartime planning, and research. The Government could grant subsidies, guarantee fixed profits, or compensate for losses.

Article 18 of the bill would give the Government the right to order formation of control associations and to set the pace for the new economic structure. In some quarters, passage of the mobilization law would thus be regarded as the beginning of military control of all private industries.

The Army was confident of its passage without any difficulties. Lieutenant Colonel Sato was able to forget his parliamentary etiquette. To a bothersome query he answered: "Shut up!"

In a way Sato's utterance was symbolic of the declining influence of the Diet. Political parties were disunited. Already there were talks of dissolving them, and it was reported that ninety members of the once powerful Seiyukai Party favored such a move. There were intimidations by outside rightist groups. Isoo Abe, the venerated president of the Social Mass Party was attacked by a mob. On February 17 headquarters of the Seiyukai and Minseito were occupied by a rightist group for ten hours, during which the Metropolitan Police did nothing to stop the violence.

All the Diet could do in this situation was to gain a few points and concede the essentials. The Diet was able to attach two riders; one prescribing that the Government should not use its unprecedented ordinance power but instead should resort to legislation whenever possible; the other stating clearly that the new law should not apply to the current conflict. The most objectionable features of the bill—bans on free assembly, dissemination of news and publication of newspapers—were dropped. On March 16 the bill passed the Diet.

Political parties emerged from the 73rd Diet badly split, with many of their members accepting the Army's views in order to gain political advantages. Yonezo Maeda and Chikuhei Nakajima organized a pro-Army group within the Seiyukai. Saburo Hisahara of the same party began advocating a one-party system for Japan. The Minseito was also shaken. One faction desired compromise with the Army while the other wished to merge with the Seiyukai to form a united front. Against this setting was a tragi-comedy enacted by Suehiro Nishio, member of the Social Mass Party. He made a concurring speech for the passage of the mobilization bill and exalted the Prime Minister: "Please assume the command of our country and lead us like Mussolini, like Hitler, and like Stalin." The reference to Stalin was offensive to the Diet, even though it did applaud the names of the other two. Nishio was promptly expelled from the Diet.

What did the National Mobilization Law mean to Japan's future? Here the following opinion of the Tokyo Military Tribunal is pertinent: "Every aspect of the national life was to be so ordered and controlled as to produce the maximum pitch of warlike efficiency. The entire strength of the Japanese nation was to be harnessed and developed with this single end in view. The National General Mobilization Law provided the instrument through which that goal might be achieved."[4]

Remaking of the Cabinet. When the 73rd Diet ended, Konoye began to question his ability as a statesman. By normal standards, his efforts were successful. He had guided the reluctant Diet to give the Army the power it desired. All the major bills passed with little or no substantive modification. But what was ahead? The Army which benefited most from his leadership showed no sign of ready cooperation. General Sugiyama still occupied the position of War Minister. He was not communicative and always evasive. Would there be any coordination of basic policies while Sugiyama was in his Cabinet? How could Konoye assert himself as Prime Minister and exercise all his prerog-

atives? How could the war in China be ended? Was it not better for
Konoye to step aside and yield the leadership to someone who was
not identified by his prior position? Word was spread by the Prince's
close associates that he wanted to resign and was intending to recommend Education Minister Kido, President Chuji Machida of the Minseito, or General Ugaki as his successor.

The Army was sufficiently alarmed. It still needed Konoye's ser-
vices and was willing to let Sugiyama go if that would induce Prince
Konoye to remain in office. It swiftly took the initiative by having
Prince Kanin, a royal prince who was serving as Chief of Staff, force
Sugiyama's resignation.

Lieutenant General Seishiro Itagaki, who was commanding the Hsu-
chou campaign, was regarded by many as a proponent of a non-expan-
sion policy in China. "While we were tied up in China, Soviet Russia
was expanding its power through its five-year plan. Its military establishment became superior and constituted a threat to us. My policy
as Minister of War was to rebuild national defense by eliminating the
cause of conflict in China," he later told the Tokyo Military Tribunal.[5]
Itagaki did not belong to the Kodo faction—which was discredited
after the February 26 revolt — but appeared to be sympathetic toward
their views. His presence in the Cabinet could well counterbalance
the predominating influence of the Tosei (or Control) faction. This
was the man Konoye wanted and the Army Big Three consented. The
prospective change of the War Minister made it possible for several
influential people who were reluctant before to enter the Cabinet.

Seihin Ikeda, general manager of the Mitsui concern, was the first
one to agree to enter the Cabinet and assumed the Finance and Commerce portfolios. Once before, Ikeda had been offered the post of
Welfare Minister with the understanding that he was to serve as
Konoye's chief of staff in the latter's intricate policy decisions. At that
time Ikeda declined, but with the exit of Sugiyama in sight and with the
offer of two ministries which were dear to his heart, the picture was
different. His only condition was that his old friend, General Ugaki,
should also serve in the Cabinet. Although Ugaki had never dreamed
of becoming Foreign Minister, when Foreign Minister Hirota offered
to resign, Konoye persuaded Ugaki to take the post. Hirota was an architect of strong policy toward China. Ugaki, on the other hand, was
considered a moderate. He had many personal friends in the higher
echelon of the Nationalist Government and his views were generally
well received in Chungking. He would become the Foreign Minister,
he told Konoye, provided the latter agreed to discard his January 16

statement saying that Japan would not deal with Chiang Kai-shek. To this Konoye tacitly agreed. Ugaki's appointment was hailed by Chung-king with Chang Chun, one of Chiang's close associates, sending him a telegram of congratulations. Only Prince Saionji looked at the development with dismay. The post of Foreign Minister was often subjected to severe criticism, and to place Ugaki in that position would mortgage his future reputation. This would endanger Ugaki's chance of becoming the next Prime Minister which Saionji still desired.

In another move to strengthen the Cabinet, Kido relinquished his additional duty as Minister of Education to concentrate on being Minister of Welfare. The post he gave up was given to General Araki, a former Minister of War, and one of the leaders of the Kodo faction. In so doing, Konoye hoped to curtail the influence of the powerful Tosei faction.

On May 26, 1938, Ugaki, Ikeda and Araki officially took over their respective ministries. The Tokyo stock exchange reacted favorably. The prestige of the Cabinet also climbed to a new height. A week later Itagaki also assumed his new post.

The May 1938 Cabinet change had various implications. Basically the Konoye Cabinet remained as a coalition of the court, military, and financial circles. However, it became a strong coalition and the combination of Konoye, Ugaki, Ikeda, Yonai and Itagaki was the best Japan could expect. The Five Ministers' Conference consisting of these five men became a workable instrument, effectively coordinating war, foreign and domestic policies.

Outwardly all five ministers were dedicated to the cause of ending war in China. However, less and less effort was made toward this end. With the National Mobilization Law to safeguard their interests, the *Zaibatsu* found cooperation with the military worthwhile. As to the military, the conflict provided a means to further their expansion program. Prince Konoye and the court circles were also reaping dividends from this new era of good feeling between the military and the *Zaibatsu*. Their cooperation was a basis on which political stability could be attained. Thus in the China conflict, all interested groups found certain advantages.

The only group to suffer from the Cabinet reshuffle was the Tosei faction. With the exit of Sugiyama it lost an effective voice in the higher echelon of the civilian government. However, this confirmed the trend that had been in existence for some time. After the decline of the rival Kodo faction, the Tosei faction had lost much of its *raison d'être*. Without a rival to contend with, the faction had been splitting into several smaller groups. Thereafter, power struggle in the Army would be resumed not along the ideological lines advocated by the Tosei and Kodo factions, but along the geographical power bases with which individuals were identified. Generally speaking there were two main groups: one identified with Manchuria; and the other with North China. The interplay of these two groups would bring about certain foreign policy complications as one group would advocate stronger policy against Russia, while the other would insist on complete subjugation of the Chiang Government.

Ugaki's Diplomacy. According to Itagaki, Ugaki's entry into the Cabinet was an important key to the Cabinet's reorganization. It precipitated a new emphasis in foreign policy. Ugaki's entry coincided with Anthony Eden's exist in England. Lord Halifax, his successor as His Majesty's Secretary for Foreign Affairs, was in favor of a reconciliation with Japan. In his first press conference, General Ugaki declared: "We have had special relations with Great Britain in our traditional friendship. I will do my best to restore them and make them even closer than in the past." Ugaki's overture was endorsed by the Japanese press and was also well received in Britain. Mr. Butler, Under Secretary for Foreign Affairs, responded to Ugaki by indicating to the House of Commons on June 27, 1938 that the British Government would gladly take any steps in its power, alone or in conjunction with other powers, to bring about the cessation of hostilities in China.[6]

These conciliatory remarks prompted both sides to review their policies toward each other. General Ugaki told Sir Robert Craigie, the British Ambassador to Japan, that Japan's policy was one of friendly cooperation with Britain, and that British rights in China would be respected. Sir Robert was reported to have said to Ugaki that it was only a matter of time before Japan would become master of the Far East. Great Britain was too far away and could not match Japan's might in this region. Therefore, Japan should be a little more patient in its dealings with China. Ugaki figured that Great Britain had a far greater stake in the Far East than the United States, and the latter would generally follow the former in its Far Eastern policy decisions. It was thus imperative to reach an understanding with Great Britain.

However, the scope of the talks was eventually confined to British rights in the occupied part of China. Although there was a flow of goodwill at certain moments, Ugaki was too powerless to commit the Japanese Government and Craigie was unwilling to part with all the existing British rights in China. The two parties were still poles

apart. The only visible result came from the British offer of mediation in the Sino-Japanese conflict through Ambassador Archibald John
Clark Kerr in Chungking. The Five Ministers' Conference — newly
formed after the Cabinet reorganization and consisting of the Premier,
Foreign, War, Navy and Finance Ministers—decided to decline the
offer graciously without shutting the door entirely. It was an attitude
of wait and see, which was sharply criticized by Prince Saionji.[7]

In his negotiations with China, Ugaki had no better luck. Chang
Chun's congratulatory telegram set off a chain of events which at one
time looked rather promising, but simply stopped there. In receiving
the telegram Ugaki immediately wired back to Chang Chun asking
if the latter would consider coming to Japan to negotiate a settlement.
Chang agreed. But Ugaki had a second sober thought; he became
fearful that Chang's known pro-Japanese attitude might prejudice the
chance of his success. He suggested H. H. Kung instead, to which
Chungking gave its tacit agreement. Ugaki instructed Consul General
Nakamura in Hong Kong to meet with Kung's private secretary Chiao
to work out details of the proposed conference. As Ugaki understood
it, Kung was ready to come to Nagasaki in a Japanese warship.[8]

In preparation for Kung's visit, Ugaki drafted several basic conditions: e.g., that Manchuria should become independent; that Japan
would not seek any further territorial concessions and would respect
China's sovereignty and administrative integrity; that China should
cooperate with Japan until such time as it could independently carry
out anti-Communist campaigns in North China and Mongolia; that
economic and cultural cooperations should be maintained by Japan,
Manchukuo and China; and that China should indemnify losses suffered
by Japanese citizens during the conflict.

These conditions were severe, and foreshadowed the ones offered to
Wang Ching-wei's government two years later. If enforced, these
provisions would make China Japan's protectorate. The need for
peace terms not "so exacting as the ones proposed when Trautmann was
the go-between" was recognized by General Itagaki, but "the government policy had been far from further reducing them." The War
Office would have preferred that China curtail its Army and delegate
to Japan its air and naval defense.

The proposed peace negotiations did not go any further than Ugaki's
drafting these conditions. A border incident broke out at Changkufeng, where the boundaries of Korea, Manchukuo, and Russia met.
This incident commanded Ugaki's full attention and the negotiations
were permanently tabled.

The Changkufeng incident demonstrated the military might of Russia and a lack of discipline and control in the Japanese Army. The Army High Command which had grown weary of the prolonged war in China took the border clash as an opportunity to force the long awaited decision that Japan withdraw from China in order to prepare for war against the Soviet Union. Prince Kanin and General Itagaki vainly sought an imperial sanction to despatch troops to the disputed area. Itagaki, in putting forward his request, stated that both the Navy and Foreign Ministers were in favor of such a move. The Emperor who had advance knowledge of the Cabinet's position at once reprimanded the War Minister's duplicity. Reluctantly Itagaki had to agree to diplomatic negotiations. The matter was referred to Ambassador Mamoru Shigemitsu in Moscow.

Behind the Army's insistance for an open break with the Soviet Union was their intelligence report stating that there was no concentration of forces in that area, and that there was a reasonable assurance that Russia would not choose to fight back at that particular time and location. The intelligence report also added that the relations between the Army and the Secret Police were at a breaking point. It was possible that Ugaki might have given a qualified yes to the Army's request for the despatching of troops. But the Navy was very much against it. They were more concerned with the air power that Soviet Russia held in relation to that of Japan's, and were not willing to fight skirmishes with the Soviet fleet which consisted mainly of submarines.

On June 30 a full scale war broke out at Changkufeng. Japan had one full division with an artillery company, and troops were also moved in from Korea. Russia countered also with tanks and mechanized troops, and later both sides used their airplanes. In this encounter, Japan suffered at least 1,200 dead and wounded. It was a disastrous defeat. To make matters worse, the new German Ambassador to Tokyo visited Ugaki saying that the Reich Government did not consider it feasible to enter into military alliance with Japan at that time. There had never been any formal negotiations on this matter, but the Army High Command and German officials had been carrying on informal conversations. The news intensified Japan's feeling of isolation and insecurity. In the meantime, Ambassador Shigemitsu pleaded from Moscow that military action be stopped at all costs.

On August 3 the Army High Command decided to yield. A week later new instructions were sent to Shigemitsu empowering him to negotiate with the Kremlin. The conditions included were that Japan would retreat to the line of July 30, that the delimitation of the border

line be decided by both sides on the spot later, and that Japan would
retreat at least eleven kilometers from the alleged border line. These
conditions were clearly a concession of defeat. Shigemitsu made the
most of these conditions and at least in principle let the Russians agree
that the delimitation of the disputed area be decided on an equitable
basis. On paper both sides agreed to retreat from the border but the
hill which had been contested by the two powers was immediately re-
occupied by the Russians after the Japanese withdrew. Japan made
no protest and Russia's *de facto* possession of the disputed hill was
never questioned.[9]

With the Changkufeng incident settled, the Army's agitation against
Ugaki was again intensified. Previously it had staged several anti-
British demonstrations not as much against Great Britain as against
Ugaki personally. Unquestionably, Ugaki was of premiership calibre.
In spite of his failure to form a cabinet in 1936, Prince Saionji still considered Ugaki the best qualified to succeed Prince Konoye. Should
the Ugaki-Craigie talk bring forth fruit, it might make Ugaki an un-
beatable candidate to assume the premiership. This was precisely
what the Army wanted to avoid and thus was staged the anti-British
demonstrations. The Army also pushed its campaign toward Hankow
and discussed plans to occupy Canton. The former was in Central
China on the Yangtze River, the latter near the British crown colony
of Hong Kong. Occupation of either of these cities would infringe on
British rights and thus dash the hope of a rapprochement which would
have been most embarrassing to the Foreign Minister.

In September the Five Ministers' Conference agreed to the establishment of a central organ to manage matters concerning China. This
would take away many of the functions traditionally assigned to
the Foreign Office. Ugaki had no strong feeling whatsoever toward
this but it gave him pretext for a grand exit. By the end of the
month, he resigned. "Mr. Konoye was deeply disappointed," related
Cabinet Secretary Kazami of the event. "The position of the Cabinet
began to shake. It was as if a bolt were lost, and the entire structure
was about to collapse. Mr. Konoye secretly prepared for his own
resignation."[10]

Later an experienced diplomat, Hachiro Arita, took over Ugaki's
position, but the political magnetism Ugaki had carried with him
was lost. "I hope you are not resigning," Vice War Minister Hideki
Tojo said to Konoye at the door after the latter received Ugaki's
resignation. "No," the Prince answered. This pleased Tojo. But

the Prince was no longer the same man, which was also true of the Cabinet.

The Konoye Cabinet was still to continue in office. But the departure of Ugaki ended the effective coalition which was established by the May 1938 Cabinet reorganization. The machinery for policy coordination—the Five Ministers' Conference—was still employed, and in domestic matters the Cabinet maintained its unity. However, in the foreign policy questions the Cabinet became badly split, as demonstrated in the negotiations for alliance with Germany.

CHAPTER IV

ALLIANCE NEGOTIATIONS WITH GERMANY

The Anti-Comintern Pact. The motivation behind the negotiations with Germany in 1938-1939 was the desire to conclude an open alliance against Russia to replace the secret alliance as contained in the Anti-Comintern Pact of November 25, 1936.

The Anti-Comintern Pact consisted of three short articles which were published, and a supplementary protocol which amounted to a secret alliance against the Soviet Union. The published part of the pact spoke in ideological terms, recognizing that "the aim of the Communist International . . . is to disintegrate and subdue existing States by all the means at its command," and therefore, the contracting powers had agreed to "inform one another of the activities of the Communist International, to consult with one another on necessary preventive measures, and to carry these through in close collaboration."

The first of the three articles in the secret addendum provided that should either of the signatories become the object of an unprovoked attack or threat of attack by the U. S. S. R., the other would do nothing to aid Russia. The second article pledged that during the duration of the pact both parties would "conclude no political treaties contrary to the spirit of this agreement without mutual consent."

On procedural matters, the pact also established a new precedent. It was negotiated by the Bureau Ribbentrop and the Japanese Army High Command, rather than through the respective foreign ministries. Foreign Ministers of both countries were hardly informed of the development of the actual negotiations. Japanese Military Attaché in Berlin General Hiroshi Oshima pointed out that the content of the pact, especially the supplemental understanding, was in the nature of military consideration, and thus it was he, not the Ambassador, who was responsible for the conclusion of the pact. The Military Attaché reported directly to the Chief of General Staff and was not subordinated to the Ambassador.

By 1938 the secret alliance was no longer adequate. Japan was deeply involved in the China theater, and the prospect of a protracted war magnified the threat from the North. An open alliance with Germany against Russia seemed to the Army High Command to be the logical answer. It would not only alleviate the threat of Russia invading Manchuria but would also allow Japan to shift its Kwantung Army—regarded as the best in the Far East—for better use in China, either in its new strategic move toward Hankow or in conquest of Canton and other South China territories.

General Oshima was again ordered to sound out Germany's views on a closer link between the two countries. Accordingly, Oshima visited von Ribbentrop at his villa at Sonneberg early in January of 1938, but nothing concrete came out of this meeting. At that time, Ribbentrop still lacked official status in the Reich's government and was unwilling to commit himself.

However, a month later signs pointed toward a closer cooperation between the two countries. On February 4 von Ribbentrop replaced von Neurath as Foreign Minister of the Third Reich. At the same time Hitler finally gained supreme control of the German Army. In a show of goodwill to Japan, Hitler recognized Manchukuo on February 20, recalled General Falkenhausen who served as Chief of the German Military Mission in Chungking, and terminated other military aid to Chiang Kai-shek.

Encouraged by the German goodwill gesture, the Army immediately began to study the desirability of concluding a pact with Germany. The Military Affairs Bureau of the War Office was charged with the task and later recommended that separate treaties be concluded with Germany and Italy.

The purposes of these treaties were to isolate Russia from the western powers and to prevent it from intervening in the China Incident either alone or in conjunction with western powers. Should there be an intervention by the powers Japan would fight a full scale war against Russia, while fighting a limited war against Great Britain and France. For these reasons, the proposed alliances should apply to Russia only. In all other cases, benevolent neutrality would be observed. By the end of June, the Army's recommendations became the official position to the Konoye Cabinet.[1]

Just how much of the above cited recommendations were communicated to Oshima is not clear. In any event when Oshima met with Ribbentrop in the early part of July, he merely asked if Germany were willing to come to an agreement with Japan which would bind the two powers to consult one another in the case of an attack by Russia. No definite answer was given on that occasion. A few days later the two conferred again. While stating that he was acting on his own authority, Ribbentrop nevertheless strongly suggested that Germany would not agree to a pact limited to consultation, and hinted that Germany and Japan should conclude a treaty of general application not confined to Russia. At this meeting Oshima agreed to send one of his associates, Major General Kasahara, as a courier to report back to the Army High Command in Tokyo.

While Kasahara was on his way to Tokyo, the Konoye Cabinet reached a basic policy decision. On July 19, at the Five Ministers' Conference, the members agreed that as far as Germany was concerned Japan would endeavor to "extend the basic principles of the Anti-Comintern Pact to become a military alliance against Soviet Russia," and as far as Italy was concerned to "conclude a secret agreement that would be used as a restraint against Great Britain." Both of them were to aid Japan in solving the China Incident. On the basis of this decision, General Ugaki, the Foreign Minister, came up with draft proposals for a Japanese-German mutual security pact and a Japanese-Italian neutrality pact.

Before the Five Ministers' Conference had a chance to act on Ugaki's proposals, Kasahara arrived in Tokyo. It became apparent at once that the positions of Japan and Germany with regard to the proposed alliance were still miles apart. In brief, the German position as communicated through Kasahara was:

"(1) If one of the high contracting powers is being involved in diplomatic difficulty with a third power, the high contracting powers will immediately consult one another for a possible course of action.

"(2) In order to remove any threat from a third party, the high contracting powers will assume responsibility to give political and diplomatic support to the power which is threatened by a third power.

"(3) In case of an attack on one of the high contracting powers from a third power, other contracting powers will assume responsibility to enter into military aid."

As discussed above, the pact was to be concluded between Japan, Germany, and Italy. The language of the Ribbentrop proposals was sufficiently vague and was open to varied interpretations. The Japanese Foreign Office agreed in principle to the proposals which would have meant an alliance of general application concluded against western powers as well as against Russia. The only reservation it wanted was that a preamble be inserted in the text of the pact explaining that the alliance was a logical extension of the existing Anti-Comintern Pact. This would soften the impact of the alliance, so it would appear to be an alliance applied only to Russia. Japan was not quite ready to antagonize western powers on whom it was economically dependent.[2]

When the five ministers met again on August 26 sentiment for accepting the Ribbentrop proposals was so strong that the ministers discussed mostly procedural matters. The fact that the negotiations were initiated by a military attaché with the knowledge of the Army High Command did not disturb the Foreign Office or the civilian ministers of the Cabinet. The five ministers, however, wanted negotiations to be conducted by the Foreign Office, and so instructed the War Minister to transfer the matter to it. The War Office was nevertheless given the right to communicate to Germany its acceptance in principle of the Ribbentrop proposals. The Foreign Office's insistence that a preamble be included in the text explaining that the alliance was the extension of the existing Anti-Comintern Pact was accepted as Japan's official policy. This was to become a major hurdle in its negotiations with Germany.

At that time the Japanese Ambassador to Berlin was Shigenori Togo, a career diplomat who later became Foreign Minister in Tojo's War Cabinet. His tenure in Berlin was a brief one. Though he had a German wife and was generally sympathetic toward Germany, he steadfastly refused to be drawn into the party which favored conclusion of an alliance. Thus, even if the Japanese Foreign Office had wanted him to become its instrumentality in carrying out negotiations, Ribbentrop would not have agreed to it. Back from Tokyo, Kasahara asked Oshima why the Ambassador was not consulted. Oshima's answer was that Ribbentrop wanted the opinion of the Japanese Army and feared that Mr. Togo might take exception to his proposals. At any rate, neither Ribbentrop nor the Japanese Army wanted Togo to come between them.[3]

Oshima Becomes Ambassador. The Munich agreement took place September 29, 1938. Oshima was invited to accompany Ribbentrop but conspicuously absent from the scene was Ambassador Togo. The fact that Togo was not present at such an important international gathering was taken by the Army High Command as an indication that Togo was ill-equipped to serve as Ambassador.

In the meantime, the German Military Attaché in Tokyo, General Eugen Ott became Ambassador. This gave the Japanese Army an opportunity to promote Oshima's candidacy as Ambassador to the Third Reich. The Army's move was successful and on October 15 Togo was named Ambassador to Moscow, opening the way for Oshima to become Japan's official representative in Berlin. Thus one of the obstacles to a successful conclusion of the alliance was removed.

Changes were also taking place in Tokyo. Foreign Minister Ugaki resigned at the end of September, and the Foreign Ministry was placed under the inactive guidance of Prime Minister Konoye for the time being. It was not until October 29 that Japan had another full time foreign minister Hachiro Arita who once served under Hirota in the same capacity.

Alliance negotiations were temporarily suspended during the diplomatic reshuffle, and Ribbentrop waited patiently until the early part of November to resume his conversations with Oshima. By that time Togo had already left for Moscow and Oshima was a full-fledged ambassador.

Oshima's telegram of November 11, reporting his meeting with Ribbentrop, caused the Five Ministers' Conference to meet again to discuss the alliance proposals. Arita was a newcomer to this group, and his views were being closely watched. In principle, Arita agreed to the proposed alliance and even remarked that it was a grand idea "killing three birds with one stone." He thought the alliance would be conducive to the settlement of the China Incident, would strengthen Japan's defensive position vis-à-vis Soviet Russia, and would improve its diplomatic position. However, Arita wanted the pact to be an extension of the Anti-Comintern Pact. His new instructions to Oshima were: (1) that the alliance should apply only to the Soviet Union; (2) that Oshima should get German support in removing the Russian threat which in turn would enable Japan to deploy its Kwantung Army elsewhere; and (3) that Japan should receive technical and economic aid from Germany. On this latter point it must be noted that Japan was in desperate need of natural resources and heavy industrial goods. It wanted Germany to share its technical know-how of making heavy tanks and other modern military equipment, and of developing synthetic oil. Arita's conditions would thus commit Japan to nothing, while exerting important concessions from Germany.

Oshima did not transmit the substance of Arita's telegram to Ribbentrop. Instead he cabled back to the Foreign Office saying that he was perplexed. He understood that the alliance was to apply equally to Great Britain and France, and the latest instructions ran counter to prior ones he received as Military Attaché.

Oshima was referring to a certain telegram he received from War Minister Itagaki when General Ugaki was the Foreign Minister. Itagaki proposed that the pact be extended to include Britain and

France in its application and Ugaki gave a qualified approval, suggesting certain changes in the draft proposals. Itagaki took this to mean the Foreign Minister's acquiescence to a pact of general application, and so instructed Oshima. The latter in turn informed Ribbentrop of the War Minister's position.

Oshima's stand was a mere reflection of opinions expressed by many young officers. Even after the Cabinet had defined the application of the pact to be confined to the Soviet Union, young officers continued to advocate an alliance also applicable to Great Britain and France. Their positions were consistently upheld by the Army High Command and the War Office.

The pressures exerted by the Army and by Oshima were kept in check by the concerted efforts of the Foreign Minister and Navy Minister who together represented the force of moderation. They found their ally in Finance Minister Ikeda who feared that severance of relations with Great Britain and the United States would mean Japan's economic suicide. A Harvard graduate, and an acknowledged Anglophile, Ikeda openly opposed the proposed alliance. However, Prince Konoye took no initiative and made no effort to stem the agitation for an alliance against Great Britain and France.

Oshima telegraphed twice to ask for further clarification, but before he could get a new set of instructions, the Cabinet resigned on January 4, 1939, leaving behind the unsolved question of the alliance.

The Hiranuma Cabinet. When the Emperor summoned Lord Privy Seal Yuasa to consider a possible successor to Konoye, Yuasa on his own responsibility recommended Baron Hiranuma, since *Genro* Saionji did not offer any suggestion. From Prince Konoye's resignation in the morning, things continued at a smooth and rapid pace. Yuasa took the 1 p.m. train to Okizu to see Prince Saionji, met with him between 4:15 and 5:15 p.m., left Okizu on the 6:16 train, and at 9:45 p.m., Hiranuma was called in to form a Cabinet.

By general consent Hiranuma's Cabinet was a mere extension of the Konoye Cabinet. The principals exchanged their respective positions. Konoye took over Hiranuma's old post as President of the Privy Council, and Hiranuma stepped into Konoye's office. Furthermore Konoye also agreed to sit in the Cabinet meetings in order to maintain continuity of his policies. Though there were certain misgivings about the constitutionality of a president of the Privy Council sitting in Cabinet meetings, both Konoye and Hiranuma persisted in their ways. In fact, Konoye concurrently assumed the position of Minister without

Portfolio in Hiranuma's Cabinet. Three key ministers of Konoye's Cabinet retained their respective positions. They were Foreign Minister Arita, War Minister Itagaki, and Navy Minister Yonai. Another one of the Big Five, Finance Minister Ikeda refused to remain in the Hiranuma Cabinet, and was replaced by Sotaro Ishiwata who happened to be Konoye's classmate in college. Kido became Home Minister and General Araki remained as Education Minister.

Prince Saionji was quite upset when he heard of the formation of the new Cabinet. In the past, Hiranuma had been mentioned as possible premier many times and Prince Saionji had consistently refused to recommend him. If he had had his way Saionji would have again kept Hiranuma from assuming his post. But now that he was old and his influence waning, the *Genro* bowed to the inevitable.

The new Prime Minister was president of an extreme rightist group called Kokuhonsha. A person of limited vision, Hiranuma served as Vice President of the Privy Council for many years before he was finally promoted to its presidency, having been nicknamed a "permanent vice president."

When Arita agreed to remain in Hiranuma's Cabinet, he extracted a promise from the Prime Minister that the alliance with Germany would not be broadened to include its application to Britain and France, and that the provisions of the alliance would not alienate the friendship of these two powers. If Arita had seemingly had his way, War Minister Itagaki was equally vehement in insisting on the Army's position. He submitted to Hiranuma a seven-point program as a condition of his joining the Cabinet. One of the conditions was that relations between Japan, Germany, and Italy be strengthened. The language employed was sufficiently vague. But from Itagaki's former position, it left little doubt as to where the Army stood.

It seemed as though the pros and cons of the alliance as advanced in the Konoye Cabinet would be repeated again in the Hiranuma Cabinet, except for the change in the Navy's position. The Navy would give a qualified consent to an alliance against Great Britain and France, discarding its former inflexible stand. However the Navy's reasons for agreeing to such an alliance was exactly the opposite of the Army's.

According to Captain Sokichi Takagi, staff officer in the Naval High Command, the Navy was convinced that an alliance of limited application could be more dangerous than an alliance that had no such limitation. They reasoned that if an alliance were limited in its application against the U. S. S. R., the Army's desire to fight against

Russia would be matched by Germany's desire to conquer Eastern Europe. Secret agreements between the German General Staff and the Japanese Army High Command could easily involve the two countries in a war against Russia. Should Great Britain and France fight on the side of Russia (as they did in the First World War), Japan would have to face them unprepared. If the United States would also enter the war Japan would become utterly helpless.

On the other hand, the Navy found in the proposed alliance an opportunity to enhance its basic desires, namely the expansion of naval forces. The Navy feared that if the alliance were concluded against the U. S. S. R. alone, the Army might receive a greater portion of military appropriations than the Navy. If the alliance were concluded on the basis of general application, the Navy could always claim that they also had to be prepared against the combined naval strength of Great Britain and the United States. Thus the Navy saw in the proposed alliance a key to its future expansion.[4]

With the addition of a generally sympathetic Prime Minister, and the change of opinion on the part of the Navy, the Five Ministers' Conference of January 19, 1939 had smooth sailing for the first time. War Minister Itagaki proposed that an alliance could be worked out in such a way that the United States would be specifically excluded from its application and the Soviet Union would become its primary target. Meanwhile, if Germany or Italy were involved in war against Great Britain and France, Japan would consider giving military aid to its allies. Itagaki's proposals were accepted with only slight modifications.

The five ministers, however, immediately realized that what they considered to be a good alliance was still far apart from what the Germans wanted. They decided to send a special mission to Berlin, which would not only instruct the Japanese diplomatic corps on the general foreign policy outline of Japan but also assist in the actual negotiations of the pact. Part of their task was to explain to the German authorities the difficulties that confronted Japan and why it was necessary to have certain reservations in the proposed alliance.

By this time Ribbentrop was growing impatient with Japan's procrastination, and his feeling was shared by Mussolini and Ciano. Actually Japan was not eager to have Italy join as the third partner in an alliance which was primarily intended against the Soviet Union. But it raised no serious objections when Ribbentrop asked for the inclusion of Italy since Italy would be useful to Japan as a power to check Great Britain. On December 29, Toshio Shiratori arrived in Rome as Japan's Ambassador. He had been mentioned as a possible

Vice Minister of Foreign Affairs but his candidacy had been vetoed by the more conservative wing of the government. Shiratori now decided to use his new position as a stepping stone to the Foreign Ministership. Without official instructions, he began advocating the cause which was most popular with young officers, that of closer relations with Germany and Italy. His enthusiasm for that cause was at once detected by Mussolini and Ciano. By January of 1939 Italy was ready for the alliance but Japan was not.

Revolt of the Ambassadors. So far Oshima and Shiratori had moved independently of the Foreign Office, and there were several discrepancies between their positions and that of the Government. The special mission, headed by former Minister to Poland, Nobutada Ito, had the delicate task of restraining the two Ambassadors.

The Ito mission arrived in Berlin the latter part of February, via Rome where it was joined by Shiratori. The contents of the directives sent through the special mission were no surprise to the two Ambassadors. Ciano in his diary of February 6, 1939 noted his meeting with Shiratori who confided that the Japanese proposals would be a compromise measure, and that he did not favor Italy's acceptance of the Japanese proposals. When Ito gave the precise terms of the new proposals, the two Ambassadors were nevertheless disappointed. The Ito directives contained provisions which would confine the object of the alliance to Soviet Russia:

"1. Japan would not render military assistance if Germany and Italy were attacked by countries other than the Soviet Union unless these countries turned communistic.

"2. Japan would explain to third parties that the alliance was intended to strengthen the existing Anti-Comintern Pact and was a mere extension of it."

Ito told the two Ambassadors that unless these two secret reservations were met, Japan could not sign a treaty which would otherwise be regarded as an all-out alliance. Oshima felt the first reservation was especially objectionable, declaring it "a slur on Japan's good faith," and asked Arita for reconsideration. In the meantime, Oshima and Shiratori disobeyed orders and refused to transmit Japanese proposals to the German or Italian Government.

On March 13 the five ministers met again to consider the matter. Arita persisted that the decision reached on January 19 was irrevocable, and there was simply no room for further discussion. He asked Hiranuma to confirm his position. But the Prime Minister ordered him to search for further compromises and concessions. Finally they came up with a new proposal which was to be presented to the German and Italian Governments, if the two would not accept Japan's original proposals. There was no substantial change in the overall objectives of the Japanese, but the language was altered so the text of the alliance could possibly mean that Japan would intervene on the side of Germany and Italy, even if they were involved in war with a third power other than the Soviet Union. On the other hand, Japan wanted to make it clear that this part of the alliance would not become applicable until some future date independently determined by Japan. Also Japan still reserved the right to explain to other powers that the alliance was a mere extension of the Anti-Comintern Pact.

The Army, unhappy about the decision of the Five Ministers' Conference, was again contemplating a change in the Cabinet. Chief of the Military Affairs Bureau, General Machijiri, went to see Lord Privy Seal Yuasa, asking if there was a possibility of concluding an alliance along the lines suggested by Germany without causing a cabinet change. Yuasa reprimanded the General and the latter dropped the matter for the time and changed the subject of his conversation. Oshima and Shiratori threatened to resign if the Cabinet did not conclude an alliance on German terms. They hoped their resignation might be followed by that of the War Minister, thus bringing about a cabinet crisis. Arita complained that the Prime Minister was not sympathetic to his views, and that Oshima sent back telegrams which sounded more like a German ambassador than a Japanese ambassador. Arita took the matter to the Emperor and suggested he would even remove the two Ambassadors if they continued to disobey his instructions.

Early in April, Oshima finally went to Ribbentrop. He felt that the new instructions were more acceptable to Germany and hoped that he and Ribbentrop could work out a *modus vivendi*. When Ribbentrop asked whether Japan would give military assistance to Germany if the latter were attacked by a power other than the Soviet Union, Oshima replied that the pact would permit such an action in principle. On the matter of a separate explanation of the pact to third powers, Ribbentrop told Oshima that the Führer had to be consulted. Oshima failed to explain to Ribbentrop that there would be no pact at all if Japan could not explain the pact in its own way. A similar meeting took place in Rome between Ciano and Shiratori. The latter, after reading the instructions given him, told Ciano that in case war broke out in Europe, Japan would render military aid to Germany and Italy.[5]

When this was referred to Berlin, the Führer thought the Japanese proposals were acceptable, reasoning that the Japanese intention of rendering military assistance was in itself sufficient. However, he insisted that the three powers have the same explanation. Oshima told Ribbentrop that he was satisfied with Hitler's answer. Ribbentrop then called Ciano in Rome telling him that the alliance could be concluded.

Arita was quite perturbed when word reached Tokyo that the two Ambassadors had on their own responsibilities accepted the German proposal. Without the reservations, Japan would no longer have the leeway it desired and the pact could involve the Japanese nation in a war against western powers. Arita's views were not shared by other members of the Five Ministers' Conference. Hiranuma had often favored a closer alliance with Germany along the lines suggested by the Army. Finance Minister Ishiwata was not a man of stature and was easily swayed by the opinion of the War Minister. It seemed as though the revolt carried by the two Ambassadors was a success.

The April 8 Five Ministers' Conference, however, was to turn the scale against accepting the German position. Navy Minister Yonai insisted that the two reservations be kept, since the Navy was not ready to fight against Great Britain and France "Of course, we could perform a friendly demonstration on behalf of Italy, if it were involved in a war against Britain and France," declared Yonai. "We could provide water, food, and other necessary supplies. But beyond this we could not render any effective assistance." He wanted the Prime Minister to be aware of these facts and communicate them to the Ambassadors.

To the chagrin of the War Minister, the Emperor also stepped into the picture. On April 11, the Emperor reprimanded Itagaki for supporting the two Ambassadors, and indicated that he would not permit the deletion of the two reservations. Hiranuma felt that since both the Army and the Navy desired peace and noninvolvement in European wars, with or without the reservations the alliance should be concluded. Unable to see the practical import of the two reservations, he favored their deletion. Home Minister Marquis Kido was sent by Hiranuma as an intermediary to gain the Emperor's acceptance of the Army's view. However, the Emperor's stand was so firm that even Kido himself, a former official of the Imperial Household, felt certain resentment against the Emperor. "After all the Emperor is a scientist," he remarked sarcastically: "He is too liberal and is inclined to be a pacifist. Unless His Majesty modifies his views, I am afraid a serious difference of opinion may emerge between His Majesty and the rightists . . . . His Majesty ought to show greater understanding of the Army in order to be able to lead it and guide it." [6]

At the Five Ministers' Conference of April 21 Arita proposed that the Prime Minister write directly to Hitler and Mussolini explaining the position of the Japanese Government, the negotiations which had taken place so far, and stating that Japan was unable to compromise any further. This proposal sounded like a good way out, but the War Minister insisted that the Ambassador in Berlin should be given another try.

While Japan was plagued with a divergence of opinion, Mussolini felt that Japan's hesitation was all for the good. Impatiently he proposed that a bilateral alliance between Berlin and Rome be concluded immediately. Ribbentrop also decided to impose a definite deadline. He said he wanted an answer from Japan by April 28 when the Führer was to speak at the Reichstag.

Starting April 21 the five ministers were in continuous session almost every day. On April 25 the five ministers tentatively agreed that the Ambassadors be recalled, and the negotiations carried out in Tokyo between the Foreign Minister and the German and Italian Ambassadors. Later they came to the conclusion that if Germany and Italy were unwilling to accept Japan's proposals it would be better that they have no alliance at all. Japan had come a long way to reach this momentous decision. The man behind the Japanese decision was Navy Minister Yonai. Realizing that the Navy was ill-equipped to meet the naval forces of western powers, Yonai was determined to avoid an alliance that could involve Japan in a global war.

Hiranuma's personal messages to Hitler and Mussolini were delivered to the German and Italian Ambassadors on May 5, one week after Ribbentrop's deadline. While these were left unanswered a telegram came from Berlin containing proposals drafted by Friedrich Gaus, Chief of the Treaty Division of the German Foreign Office. Gaus claimed that he drafted these proposals without Ribbentrop's knowledge. However Ribbentrop did know what was going on, and Oshima was responsible for sending his Embassy counselor Usami to meet with Gaus to discuss the content of the draft on an informal basis. Arita suspected that the Japanese Army had given the idea to the German Foreign Office through the Army Attaché.

The Gaus draft consisted of four articles. The first article dealt with the text of the pact, notes to be exchanged after the signature, and a secret agreement. The other three included questions of how the Japanese Foreign Office should declare the intent of the alliance and also an oral declaration to be submitted by the Japanese Ambassador prior to the signing of the alliance. Gaus wanted the Japanese Government to state that the alliance would apply if one contracting power were attacked by a third power which was under the influence of the Comintern. In the oral statement the Japanese Ambassador was to assure Germany that Japan would discuss the applicability of the alliance, including its military phase, with Germany and Italy immediately after the conclusion of the alliance.

Tokyo's reaction to the Gaus draft was mixed. The War and Finance Ministers and Premier Hiranuma favored its acceptance. But they were confronted with the promise they made to the Emperor that the alliance was not intended to involve Japan in a general war against western powers. Arita and Yonai were against the draft and the former threatened to resign if the matter did not go the way he wanted. Hiranuma, fearing a Cabinet crisis, showed some sign of moderation. In the meantime, Oshima, without authorization from the Foreign Office, assured Ribbentrop that Japan would enter war on the side of Germany whenever necessary.

The German Ambassador in Tokyo, General Ott, described the Japanese situation as one of great "schism within the Government." The Prime Minister wanted an alliance without any reservations, but he had to yield and accept the two reservations. "Though this phenomenon is hard to understand by the Axis powers which are used to a clear cut decision," continued Ott, "this is inevitable because of the lack of unified leadership. If the negotiations fail, the Cabinet will face a severe crisis."[7] A similar observation was made by Ambassador Grew, who was about to leave for a furlough in Washington: "I know very well that the pressure on the Government will continue, and if Great Britain concludes an alliance with Soviet Russia it is not beyond the bounds of possibility that either the Government will be forced into a totalitarian alliance or will fall . . . . I think that the present political situation in Japan is full of dynamite and that further assassinations are possible, if not likely."[8]

On May 7 Finance Minister Ishiwata joined the side of those who opposed the Gaus draft. Though his stand strengthened and aided Yonai's and Arita's position, it was offset by the Prime Minister's almost stubborn support of the War Minister. Itagaki felt it was his duty to confer in private with Arita and persuade him to accept the Gaus draft. They had a session lasting more than seven and one half hours without reaching an agreement. Itagaki also visited Yonai and Ishiwata and received no further encouragement.

Hiranuma asked the opinion of the Supreme Command on the subject matter. But within the Supreme Command, opinions were equally divided.

The Vice Chief of Naval Operations wanted the Vice Chief of Staff to reconsider the Army's poistion without agreeing to retreat an inch from the Navy's position. Unable to secure the Navy's agreement, the Army persuaded its figurehead, Chief of Staff Prince Kanin, to ask the Emperor to intervene on the Army's behalf. The Emperor refused. With the Emperor's position made doubly clear, Yonai took the offensive, and on May 9 he suggested that the Cabinet suspend discussion of the Gaus draft. After all, the Gaus draft "merely represented a private opinion" without the sanction of the German Foreign Office, said Yonai. It was "quite odd that we are stuck with it." [9]

The Nazi-Soviet Rapprochement. While Tokyo procrastinated, the Reich Government was already preparing for a great offensive against Poland and western powers, and was sounding out a possible rapprochement with the Soviet Union. On April 17, Russian Ambassador to Berlin Merekalow visited Weizsäcker for the first time in almost a year. This was the start of a series of informal conversations between the Foreign Offices of Germany and Russia.

On May 15 Ribbentrop telegraphed Ott suggesting that Germany might conclude a separate alliance with Italy. The German-Italian Axis would become an essential propaganda weapon against western powers. Only Japan would be blamed for the failure to conclude a tripartite pact. Germany did not intend to discriminate against Japan as an Axis partner, but it did realize that Japan was remotely located. In case of war, Germany could receive much greater aid from Italy than from Japan. Ribbentrop hoped Japan would be awakened by its Axis partners' action and join the pact. He urged Ott to influence his close friends in Japan, including War Minister Itagaki, to decide on the issue. At the same time Ribbentrop brushed aside Hiranuma's personal message which he termed ambiguous, and telephoned Oshima that the Führer felt there were several points on which he could not agree.

A military alliance between Germany and Italy came into being on

May 22 without their third partner. Hiranuma was not dismayed and continued to push his plan for an early conclusion of the alliance. He was neither informed nor aware of the fact that while Japan wanted the alliance mainly as a check against Soviet expansion in the Far East, Germany had already shifted its emphasis from its eastern neighbor to its western neighbors.

The international situation was gradually turning from bad to worse for Japan. Hiranuma was confronted with an unfriendly action of the United States. When Mr. Grew had his furlough in May, Hiranuma asked Grew to transmit his personal message to Cordell Hull which did not bring any favorable reaction. Hull tersely commented that Hiranuma's note was another of the series with which "Japan constantly sought agreements or joint action with us which would have the effect of sanctioning all her brazen expansion in the Orient." Instead of taking "a joint action" as suggested by Hiranuma, on July 26 the United States Government gave a formal notice of its desire that the treaty of commerce of 1911 between the two countries be terminated six months from that date. In the alliance negotiations the Japanese Government had been eager not to offend the United States, and the action of the United States seemed to the Japanese Government unwarranted. It cast a dark shadow over the economic future of the Empire. [10]

Trouble with the Soviet Union also worsened with the outbreak of hostilities at the Manchukuo-Outer Mongolian border of Nomonhan. Japan suffered a crushing defeat by armored divisions of the Russian Army. It magnified the need for an alliance with Germany, and it also served notice that the Japanese Army was not ready for an all-out war against the Russians.

The only consolation the Japanese could get during this period was an amicable settlement of the Tientsin question, on which Arita and British Ambassador Craigie held prolonged talks. The incident started when a Chinese in the service of the puppet government was murdered by a pro-Nationalist Chinese. The political fugitive took refuge in the British Concession in Tientsin. Tokyo requested extradition of the fugitive as well as Japan's limited control of the Concession. Britain, anxious about Europe, conceded both of these conditions in an agreement on July 24. It said in part that "the Japanese forces in China have special requirements for the purpose of safeguarding their own security and maintaining public order in the regions under their control and that they have to suppress or remove any such acts or causes as will obstruct them or benefit their enemy."

Thus Great Britain tacitly recognized Japan's belligerent's right in China. It was a clear diplomatic victory for Japan, since there was no actual declaration of war, and the British recognition gave Japan freer hands in its conduct of war.

The negotiations with Germany dragged on without any visible success. The Navy kept insisting on a restricted alliance and gained converts among German naval circles. Commander Endo, Japanese Naval Attache in Berlin, explained to the German Chief of Naval Operations what Japan expected from the alliance and received the latter's support. Admiral Richard Forster who visited Japan in the spring also agreed with the Japanese Navy and tried to influence Admiral Roeder to this view. The naval forces of the two countries had something in common. Unfortunately the German Navy had little influence in the conduct of foreign policies, even much less than its counterpart in Japan.

War Minister Itagaki persisted in his views that the alliance should be concluded without the two reservations. On August 8, he told the Cabinet that they should accept his terms or resign and gave oral statements to the German and Italian Ambassadors to the same effect. On the other hand, Itagaki wanted Germany to reconsider its stand so it could strengthen Itagaki's hands in the Cabinet. By this, Ott told the German Foreign Office that Itagaki never intended to blackmail the German Government. He urged Germany to give whatever aid it could to Itagaki and bring Japan safely into the Axis column thus destroying any possibility of a further rapprochement between Japan and Great Britain.

Ott's telegram could hardly alter the thinking of the German Foreign Office because the conversations which had been carried on between Berlin and Moscow were bearing fruit. On August 16, 1939, the German Ambassador to Moscow, Count von Schulenburg was able to write to Weizsäcker "the proposal of the visit of the Reich Minister was very flattering personally to Herr Molotov and that he considers it an actual proof of our good intentions."

Ribbentrop visited Moscow as scheduled on August 23, and the non-aggression pact was announced to the world on the same day. Among other things, the pact bound the two parties to "obligate themselves to desist from any act of violence, any aggressive action, and any attack on each other, either individually or jointly with other powers." It also enjoined the two powers from participating "in any grouping of powers whatsoever that is directly or indirectly aimed at the other party." An alliance against the Soviet Union was definitely out.

Hitler had scored a major diplomatic victory over the western powers. He had outsmarted the British and French military missions which were negotiating military agreement with Moscow. The path toward aggression was now paved. It looked as though nothing could stop the Führer from realizing his dream of establishing a greater *Lebensraum* for the Third Reich.

Japan occupied a prominent place in the discussions of Germany and Russia when their non-aggression pact was concluded. Herr Hencke, Under State Secretary in the German Foreign Office, who accompanied Ribbentrop to Moscow, made the following record of the discussion between Ribbentrop and Stalin:

"The Reich Foreign Minister stated that the German-Japanese friendship was in no wise directed against the Soviet Union. We were, rather, in a position, owing to our good relations with Japan, to make an effective contribution to an adjustment of the difference between the Soviet Union and Japan. Should Herr Stalin and the Soviet Government desire it, the Reich Foreign Minister was prepared to work in this direction . . . .

"Herr Stalin replied that the Soviet Union indeed desired an improvement in its relations with Japan, but that there were limits to its patience with regard to Japanese provocations. If Japan desired war, it could have it . . . If Japan desired peace—so much the better! Herr Stalin considered the assistance of Germany in bringing about an improvement in Soviet-Japanese relations as useful, but he did not want the Japanese to get the impression that the initiative in this direction had been taken by the Soviet Union." [11]

The news of the pending conclusion of the Nazi-Soviet pact first reached Konoye on the morning of August 22. The next day Konoye had a conference with Marquis Kido, Interior Minister in Hiranuma's Cabinet. The news took Tokyo by surprise, and Kido was excited. "This will bring the question of the responsibility of the Cabinet. We must all resign." The Cabinet Secretary, Mr. Ota, visited Konoye and reported to him how Hiranuma was upset by Germany's "treacherous" action.

Although he had ignored the Emperor's wishes, Hiranuma was bitter about the Army's misleading him feeling that the Army should shoulder the main blame for this mishap. His Cabinet had been formed with "closer cooperation with the Axis powers" as the keynote of its policy. The alliance became a thing of the past, and the Cabinet lost its *raison d'être*.

As his last official act Hiranuma instructed Oshima to protest to the German Foreign Office against its breach of faith. However, when Oshima saw Weizsäcker, he was persuaded not to present his protest until some other opportune moment. He wired Tokyo that he had complied with the instructions. Actually the protest was not officially handed to the German Foreign Office until September 18, after the end of the Polish Campaign and after the original protest had lost much of its meaning.

On August 28 Hiranuma's Cabinet resigned. There were more than seventy meetings of the Five Ministers' Conference. It was a record number in a short period of less than eight months. These events had proved that the Five Ministers' Conference was no longer an adequate organ to coordinate foreign policy decisions. In the past, the Army had been able to impose its will on the rest of the Cabinet on matters relating to China. But in other areas of foreign policy, the Army could not prevail over the opposition of the Navy or of the financial circles. Japan was yet to find a central organ to coordinate its foreign policy. Without such an organ Japan could not cope with the fast changing international situation so "intricate and baffling", as described by Hiranuma. [12]

CHAPTER V

THE CARETAKER CABINETS

The Abe Cabinet. "Several kingmakers were at work. The task of forming a cabinet became a mere private playground of elder statesmen," was the comment of *Tokyo Asahi* when it reported that General Abe was to succeed Baron Hiranuma as Prime Minister. The selection of General Abe was in itself a kind of compromise, and clearly indicated that Japan was neither ready to dispose of the Army's predominant influence in politics nor capable of reshaping its foreign policies.

At first, former Premier Hirota was the choice of both Prince Konoye and Lord Keeper of the Privy Seal Yuasa. But the news leaked out prematurely and the Army High Command and the War Office openly opposed Hirota. Yuasa's second candidate was former Finance Minister Ikeda whose assumption of the premiership would have generally been interpreted as Japan's willingness to shift from an Axis-centered foreign policy to a western-centered one. Indeed such a shift would have been welcomed by the Emperor and the conservative court circles. For Ikeda's candidacy, Yuasa sought Konoye's cooperation and endorsement, but Konoye feared that the selection of Ikeda might evoke strong resentment among the rightist groups and the latter might resort to political assassination. Yuasa likewise approached Prince Saionji who cunningly stated that he would support Ikeda only if Konoye did so. This ended the matter.

General Abe was one of the two names advanced by the Army as acceptable candidates, the other being General Katsuda who clearly indicated his sympathy with the rightists. In contrast, General Abe was evasive in his philosophy, and had neither political appeal nor administrative experience. He was selected, nevertheless, because as Kido succinctly remarked, "it is not in our best interest to refuse the Army's choice."

If the court circles were complacent, the Emperor was more independent. When he called Abe in to form a cabinet, he commanded the General to: (1) respect the constitution, and rule according to its provisions; (2) respect international amity, and avoid unnecessary frictions; (3) avoid radical changes in the financial world; (4) cooperate closely with Great Britain and the United States; (5) select either Umezu or Hata as War Minister; and (6) exercise due care in selecting ministers for home affairs and legal administration.

The first three charges were customarily given to a Premier-designate, and there was nothing unusual about them. But the last three were given only at the Emperor's own initiative which surprised his Lord Privy Seal. The intent of the Emperor was clear. It was a psychological moment for Japan to shift its foreign policy from an Axis-centered one to one of cooperation with the western powers. He wanted a war minister who could be counted on to exercise discipline and control in the Army; he wanted a home minister and a legal administration minister who could uphold law and order, all in preparation for a contemplated shift in foreign policy. With these three ministers doing the Emperor's will, the danger of any reactionary or subversive activities by the rightist groups might be forestalled. [1]

Abe had expected the audience to be a mere formality, and was quite puzzled. He had heard that the Big Three of the Army had already decided on the selection of the War Minister, and it was neither Umezu nor Hata as the Emperor desired. If he obeyed the Emperor's command, he would risk his cabinet to be stillborn. This dilemma was resolved when the Big Three of the Army agreed to accept Hata and named him as their own candidate.

Selecting the rest of the cabinet members posed no problem. Vice-Admiral Zengo Yoshida became Minister of Navy, Kazuo Aoki became Minister of Finance, and Takuo Godo became Minister of Commerce and Industry. Unable to find a suitable person for the post of Foreign Minister, Abe assumed the portfolio temporarily. The Abe Cabinet was formed on August 30, 1939, and contained no carry-over ministers. This was in sharp contrast to the precedent established by the Hayashi Cabinet in 1937 when most of the ministers retained their respective posts while the Prime Minister changed.

Just what foreign policy Abe might adopt was watched with keen interest. But the subsequent events and Abe's reactions to them were to betray the wishes of those who hoped that Abe might effect a rapprochement with the western powers. On September 3, war broke out in Europe. Unprepared to face the new situation, Abe resorted to a safe course, stating that Japan did not want to be involved in the current conflict, and would devote its full energy to solving the China Conflict.

To help him implement his new policy, Abe suggested that all the belligerent nations immediately withdraw their armed forces and ships stationed in China. If this were carried out, the British and French would quit China, leaving the vacuum in the hands of the Japanese. At that time Italy was still neutral, and it would not be affected by Abe's pronouncement. Nor was Germany affected because it had maintained no troops in China since the end of the First World War. America would still keep its troops in China, but Abe calculated that Japan could occupy any of the posts left by the British or French before the Americans could step in, because of its geographical proximity to China. No longer was there any semblance of cooperation with the western powers. There was no outright hostility, but Abe clearly indicated that his country's position was much closer to that of the Axis powers than to that of the western powers.

The war in Europe was, however, overshadowed by the need to conclude a truce with the Russians. On August 30 the Army High Command abruptly ended a conflict at the Manchukuo-Outer Mongolian border of Nomonhan, ordering the Kwantung Army to retreat from the area where the conflict had originally taken place. The conflict started in June between the Japanese Kwantung Army and the Soviet Far Eastern Army on a dubious pretext but became a war to test each other's endurance and strength. The Russians were superior, at each turn their armored division overpowered the Japanese, leaving no doubt in their enemy's mind of their technological and strategic excellence.

A few days later the truce was made public in which the Army with unusual candor admitted that they did not succeed in this encounter. Diplomatic negotiations were entrusted to Shigenori Togo, the Ambassador to Moscow. On September 16 the truce agreement was formally signed, providing for further delimitation of the border and in effect accepting the Russian terms in toto.

Behind the Army High Command's willingness to sign the agreement was its desire to conclude a nonaggression pact with Russia. When Togo started to negotiate the truce, German Ambassador von Schulenburg offered his good offices for closer Japanese-Soviet relations which Togo refused. But from Berlin, Oshima kept advocating a rapprochement with Soviet Russia. The Army High Command which sought an alliance with Germany against Soviet Russia was easily swayed to this view. Since Germany was a friend of Russia, why not iron out Japan's differences with Russia and form an alliance among these three powers? The balance of power would shift in favor of the three, and the alliance would also have the effect of suppressing British and French influence in China.

During the first three weeks as Prime Minister and Foreign Minister, Abe had to rely heavily on the staff work performed by members of the Foreign Office for policy decisions without taking initiative on his part. But the Foreign Office at that time was hardly a unified body conducive for the conduct of foreign affairs. Its internal administration was lax, and Abe's Vice Foreign Minister Masayuki Tani was powerless. Young career officers freely aligned themselves with young officers of the Army and Navy, and insubordination was not uncommon. [2]

Under these circumstances, Abe decided to appoint a full-time Foreign Minister. His choice was restricted by the Army's twofold demand that no one from the Mitsui concern—meaning former Finance Minister Ikeda—should join his cabinet, and no foreign minister should be selected from career diplomats.

Finally, the choice was Admiral Kichisaburo Nomura, who had already retired from active duty, and at that time was serving as President of the Peer's School in Tokyo. Nomura was a Naval Attaché in Washington during the First World War and knew Franklin D. Roosevelt, then Assistant Secretary of Navy in the Wilson Administration. Abe wishfully hoped that Nomura's personal acquaintance with the President of the United States might pave the way for better relations between the two countries.

First Sign of Economic Sanctions. Several harassing problems were awaiting Nomura as Japan's new Foreign Minister. Chief among them was the question of the commercial treaty with the United States, which was due to expire on January 26, 1940, and for which Japan had already received a notice of abrogation.

The U.S. was the best customer and supplier for Japan, in terms of Japan's imports and exports. Japan had sold roughly 30% of its foreign trade goods to, and purchased a slightly larger percentage of goods from the United States in the early thirties. In 1938, Japan imported $240 million worth of commodities from the United States, of which three-fourths were in war materials, such as petroleum products, heavy capital goods, copper, iron and steel scrap, aircraft and parts, automobiles, parts and accessories, semi-manufactured iron and steel, and pig iron. Slightly less than one-sixth of the $240 million was in raw cotton which in turn kept the Japanese mills spinning to produce more exportable goods to gain the much needed foreign exchange. Japan's reliance on the United States was so great that cessation of commercial relations would not only adversely affect its economic wellbeing, but also its war efforts in China.

The outbreak of war in Europe did not help Japan economically. During the First World War, it was able to invade traditional markets of Great Britain and other belligerent nations and profited from such an operation. Now that it was deeply involved in the China War, its main concern was no longer to export goods for profit but to keep the essential strategic goods flowing to its shores.

So far the President of the United States had neither imposed embargo on goods to Japan, nor proclaimed that his country would become the Arsenal of Democracy. But it was reasonably clear that Japan would suffer from the heavy demand made on the United States by the European War. If there were a treaty, it would ensure the minimum supply of goods. In the absence of such a treaty, however, no advance planning could be made and war efforts would be severely crippled.

Aside from economic reasons, Japan had to weigh America's position toward its policy in China. Great Britain's influence in China was weakened after it concluded an agreement on July 24, recognizing Japan's "special" position, and was virtually eliminated after it withdrew most of its troops following the outbreak of the European War. The most formidable power Japan had to cope with was the United States. If the latter would likewise recognize its special position in China, it could possibly mean the end of the conflict. China, after losing the main source of its support, was not likely to continue the hopeless war.

With these two thoughts — continuation of the commercial treaty and America's acquiescence to Japan's new order—Nomura awaited the return of Ambassador Grew from Washington. Nomura's hands were tied. His staff had consistently recommended firmer policies, and his colleagues, while being allured to the policy of understanding with the United States, were unwilling to concede on essential matters.

A staff report prepared shortly after the United States notified Japan of the abrogation of the commercial treaty vividly revealed Japan's official sentiment. Written by the American Bureau of the Foreign Office, it advocated recall of the Japanese Ambassador to Washington as a means of expressing Japan's displeasure of the United States action. The report declared that Japan would not let the United States use economic pressure to dictate Japan's Far Eastern policy, and it was better to have no treaty than to have one with humiliation.

It did recognize that there was not much hope for Japan to conclude a new treaty with the United States unless the conflict in China was terminated. The position of the two countries in the China Conflict was so far apart that there was little likelihood of mutual understanding unless one party should yield to the other.³ Japan should do the following, noted the report:

(1) Japan should review its stand on the Nine Power Treaty, which it had previously declared to be no longer in effect, and allow participating countries in the Treaty to determine the fate of China for the future: and

"(2) Japan should respect American rights in China, e.g., the opening of the Yangtze for foreign trade, fulfilling its debt obligations, returning American properties in the occupied area, making reparation for the U. S. property damaged in the war, and cessation of the bombings, indignities, and other flagrant interferences with American rights."

These were essentially the same conditions which Ambassador Grew felt, if carried through, would ease "the pressure for an embargo against Japan next winter."

If Japan were not willing to take the above steps, then the alternative ought to come from the United States. The latter should (1) recognize the existence of the state of war in the Far East, as Great Britain had previously done; and (2) amend the Stimson doctrine to conform to the new order in the Far East. Of the two alternatives, the staff report termed the first one impractical since it would mean total abandonment of Japan's new order. The only choice left was to force the United States to accept the second alternative. The United States should accept the new order as a *fait accompli*.

Fujiyama, head of the First Department of the American Bureau and the chief author of the staff report, suggested that the Foreign Minister could offer a neutrality pact to the United States, possibly at the time of Ambassador Grew's return to Japan from his furlough. The pact should include a provision that would bar the United States and Japan from involvement in the European war, and another containing U. S. recognition of Japan's preponderant interests in the Far East consistent with the new order.

Since the United States and Japan were the two "major powers" not involved in the current conflict, observed Fujiyama, the two powers properly allied could become balancers in power politics.

The note—separate from the above mentioned staff report—was submitted to Nomura when he became the Foreign Minister.

Nomura was encouraged by the friendly communications sent by President Roosevelt. According to Tani, his Vice Minister, President Roosevelt telegraphed Nomura upon his appointment recalling their mutual acquaintanceship, and concluded the telegram with this phrase: "I pray for your success."

Ambassador Grew returned from furlough to Tokyo in the early part of October. Instead of seeing Nomura first, the Ambassador chose the meeting of the America-Japan Society as his forum to expound the American position. In a speech presented on October 19 he denounced the "new order" in East Asia because it appeared to include, among other things, "depriving Americans of their long established rights in China, and to this the American people are opposed." Moreover, he pointed out, the American people "have good reason to believe that an effort is being made to establish control, in Japan's own interest, of large areas on the continent of Asia and to impose upon those areas a system of closed economy. It is this thought that accounts for the attitude of the American people towards Japan today." [4]

Ambassador Grew's speech amounted to a restatement of the American position of the past; there was little doubt left as to its actual implication. In essence, America would not agree to a new treaty with Japan unless there was a change of policy in China. The immediate reaction in Japan was one of sharp disappointment. "There has been deplorable ignorance," declared the Foreign Office spokesman, "among the American people concerning conditions in the Far East . . . . American Government should pay full attention to actual facts of the situation" and their opinion "be more constructive and practical."

Just what would constitute "constructive and practical" steps were elaborated in policy papers which were prepared in connection with the Nomura-Grew talks. Nomura's advisers suggested that Japan demand a greater voice in the administration of international concessions throughout China, acquiescence by the western powers to the New Order, and cessation of cultural activities which were connected with political activities. Japan would welcome foreign investments in China on a "business basis," provided the United States and other powers conformed to the Chinese (puppet government's) regulations. Japan would especially welcome funds from the United States and England to stabilize currency in China as the first step toward economic rehabilitation. In return Japan would suppress anti-western demonstrations, respect foreign interests in China, find a way to compensate damages inflicted on foreign properties, lift certain trade restrictions, allow export of tung oil, tobacco, furs and mineral products, and open the Yangtze and Red rivers for limited foreign navigation. If the United States and England refused this "offer," a stringent exchange control would be applied in the occupied part of China.

In no event should Japan allow the commercial treaty to expire. If the United States would not agree to the renewal, Japan should still aim for a stop-gap agreement. This should be done even if the questions regarding the China Incident remained unsettled.[5]

The very thought of their supply of essential commodities being cut off abruptly worried the Army and the Navy. In an unusual spirit of cooperation they got together with the China Affairs Board to form a fact-finding mission in China whose main purpose was to inspect the infringement of foreign interests by the Japanese armed forces, and to determine how such infringement could be remedied. They hoped the conciliatory steps taken by them would enable Nomura to complete his talks with Grew before the new session of the United States Congress convened. However while old cases were being investigated new violations of American rights occurred. When Nomura and Grew met on December 4, 1939, Nomura promised that the Yangtze River would be open to general navigation in about two months but the American Ambassador was not impressed. Nor did the former's plea for a *modus vivendi* after the termination of the commercial treaty evoke the latter's sympathy. Mr. Grew remarked that Japan "had to give concrete implementation of its assurances that American rights and legitimate interests in China would be respected on a nondiscriminatory basis." But the issues at stake were not confined to American rights in China. It was the difference in their China policies that had set them apart. Nomura stated that if commerce with the United States were impaired, Japan would obviously have to seek "other commercial channels." The only promise Grew could give was that after January 26, 1940 no discriminatory charges would be levied on Japanese ships or goods "until such time as further instructions shall be issued." By December 22 it became clear to Nomura that the situation was hopeless, and he so advised the Throne.[6]

Ambassador Grew had sensed an implied threat in Nomura's declaration that Japan would have to seek "other commercial channels."

The Ambassador was correct. On December 28 Nomura met with War Minister Hata and Navy Minister Yoshida to discuss general policy matters. They agreed that Japan should devise ways of occupying French Indo-China and the Dutch East Indies and of granting independence to the Philippines. The inclusion of the Dutch East Indies in their discussions was most significant. Its occupation would enable Japan to maintain the flow of oil supplies without interruption even if the United States should decide on an oil embargo. [7]

As a counterweight against the moves taken by the United States, the three ministers agreed that a rappochement with the Union of Soviet Russia, culminating in the signing of a non-aggression treaty was in order. To pave the way they would yield on the border disputes over Nomonhan, but would insist on the renewal of fishery conventions and on broadening commercial relations. The alignment with the Soviet Union would deter the United States from entering the European War on the side of the western powers, and would also enhance Japan's international standing. After accomplishing this, Japan could undertake to mediate in the conflict between Germany and Great Britain. Here was a blueprint of Japan's foreign policy later to be adopted by Matsuoka in the critical years of 1940 and 1941. However, conspicuously absent from the blueprint was the mention of the Tripartite Pact. The European conflict was then only three months old, the Maginot line still stood fast, and Japan had not quite forgiven Germany's breach of faith of the previous summer.

With the Soviet Union, the situation was different. After the truce of the Nomonhan Incident, the Soviet-Japanese relations were improved. Molotov made a speech favoring readjustment of relations with Japan. Mr. Smetanin was appointed Ambassador to Tokyo, the post which had long been vacant. A temporary fishery convention was signed on December 31, 1939, which was followed by the payment of the last installment of the Chinese Eastern Railway by the Japanese Government. These moves—either contemplated or executed —convinced the Japanese leaders that the signing of a non-aggression pact was no longer an impossibility.

However promising the policy decision might have looked to the three ministers, it was never implemented. Shortly afterwards the Cabinet had to resign, due to mounting domestic pressures in which the Army took no part.

During his tenure of office Abe decreed that the Prime Minister could apply any provision of the National Mobilization Law with a directive signed by him. The decree was issued without the consent of the Privy Council, which customarily reviewed changes in governmental structure. Had the decree come from a Cabinet strongly backed by the military, political parties would not have questioned it. But Abe lacked such a backing, and the parties wanted to challenge Abe's new move which would further circumvent their powers. The parties in turn were joined by the Privy Council. Thus each step taken by Abe was doomed to failure. He was defeated in his attempt to revoke the Civil Service Protection Law by strong opposition from the Privy Council. His plan of establishing a ministry of foreign trade was nipped in the bud when career diplomats in the Foreign Office balked, threatening to resign *en masse*. His desire to strengthen his cabinet received no support from political parties. President Machida of the Minseito party steadfastly refused to join his official family. When Abe approached the presidents of the Minsei, Seiyu, National League, and Social Mass parties asking for their terms of support, no answer was received. The mounting crisis was topped by the deterioration in the national economy. The European War had cut much of the supplies which resulted in a sharp increase in the price of consumer goods. On September 18, 1939, Abe invoked the National Mobilization Law, freezing commodity prices, salaries and wages as of that date. But this action did not counter the simple law of supply and demand. Then there was a bad crop in the western part of Japan. Increase in the price of rice threatened the daily living of the average Japanese family. First the Government granted a higher price, then resorted to a compulsory purchasing plan, but to no avail. Supplies of electricity and coal were critically low in one of the coldest winters. With the approach of the opening of the Diet, political parties decided to take matters in their hands.

On December 21 a committee composed of Diet members on an intra-party basis adopted a resolution calling for a nonconfidence vote in the Diet of the Abe Cabinet. On December 26 major parties joined the move. By December 27, more than two hundred and forty members—representing an absolute majority in the Diet—signed the resolution which had been privately circulated. The sponsors of this resolution asked Abe to take "an appropriate action." The Abe Cabinet resigned on January 14, 1940.

It was a peroid marked with indecision and non-accomplishment. The war in Europe, it was evident, created a power vacuum in East Asia and with it new opportunities for Japan. But the Japanese Army was deeply involved in the China theater and was not able to take advantage of the new situation. Had Japan abandoned its policy of conquest in China, and shifted its energy to that of friendly cooperation with its less fortunate neighbor the outcome might have been different. But such a course would have meant radical over-hauling of its policies pursued since 1931, and Abe was hardly the man to undertake the task. Shigemitsu, who variously served as Japan's Ambassador to London and Moscow, and later as a foreign minister, commented about this period in his prison cell at Sugamo: "The boat called Japan was in a roaring sea without a steering wheel. The engine moved violently, and the ship ran away with no destination." [8]

The Yonai Cabinet. The new captain whom Japan chose to guide its destiny was Admiral Yonai, a moderate in political persuasion, who served three times as Navy Minister.

Since Prince Saionji declined to nominate Yonai or his own candidate for the post, the task fell on Yuasa. However, the latter was not prepared to assume the sole responsibility for appointing a new premier, and sought the opinions of former premiers Okada, Hiranuma, Konoye and Kiyohara individually. None of the former premiers opposed the selection, though Konoye preferred former Finance Minister Ikeda. Saionji then gave his assent to the selection of Yonai.

The smoothness in which Yonai was appointed, and the fact that Ikeda's name was advanced by Konoye who five months ago had declined to back Ikeda's candidacy, suggested that the so-called "liberals" had won the fight. But the Army's influence was by no means dead. Before Yonai's appointment was confirmed, a group of officers advocated the candidacy of Sugiyama, the War Minister in Konoye's cabinet, who was responsible for the spread of the conflict in China. When the Emperor asked Yonai to form a cabinet, he also called in War Minister Hata to ask him for the Army's unqualified cooperation. Some young officers mistakenly thought that the premiership had been offered to Hata. When the news was made known they claimed that the Emperor actually intended Hata to be the next premier but was talked out of it by Yuasa and other elder statesmen. The Army resented Yonai partly because of his moderate record, and partly because of inter-service rivalry. In the attack against the elder statesmen they found their outlet.

On the whole, Yonai's cabinet was well-balanced in its political orientation, and from the Japanese standard, a pro-western one. It lacked the active support of the Army which was offset by the Emperor's expression of faith and with his effort to forestall any differences that might arise between the two competing services.

The major trend of Japanese foreign policy was already set by his predecessor cabinets, and Yonai could not readily change it. The basic approach taken by him was essentially the same as the one followed by Abe. It aimed at terminating the conflict in China, readjusting Japan's international relations without involving it in alliances and entanglements, and ensuring the flow of essential commodities to Japan.

As expected, the commercial treaty with the United States expired on January 26, 1940, and Japan entered into an era of no treaty relations with the United States. The inflexible stand taken by the United States did not surprise Japan. The pro-western segment in the Government generally felt that Japan's overall approach to the U. S.-Japanese relations was wrong, and Japan was to blame for the termination of the treaty. On the other hand, January 26, 1940 also marked the turning point for many so-called moderates to begin supporting a stronger policy against the western powers, including closer relations with the Axis. As Arita, who was again foreign minister in Yonai's Cabinet, succinctly remarked: "The Yonai Cabinet is doing its best to avoid an open alliance with Germany and Italy. But due to domestic considerations . . . Japan wishes to maintain closer relations with Germany and Italy short of an alliance." [9]

The "domestic considerations" Arita referred to were manifold. On January 21, only five days after Yonai's cabinet was formed, a British warship stopped the Japanese steamship *Asama-maru* which was returning from the United States, and apprehended twenty-one German passengers aboard. This happened at a place only thirty-five miles off the shores of Japan, and placed Japan in an uproar. The extremists held Yonai's soft policy toward the western powers responsible for the incident, and turned the subsequent anti-British demonstration into an anti-Government movement.

Then the 75th Diet, which convened on February 1, 1940 became a scene of intense political controversy. This evolved around the speech made by a member of the Diet, Takao Saito. On February 2 Saito criticized the conduct of the China Incident, the Konoye statement and the Wang regime. At least one-half of his speech was ordered deleted from the official proceedings of the Diet, and a complete record is no longer available. But according to one account, Saito mentioned in part that once a war started it was no longer a strife between the righteous and the unrighteous, or between the good and the evil. It was a strife between the strong and the weak, and the weak had to be eliminated for the sake of the strong. "Is it a 'holy war' as the Army pretended?" he inquired. He then counseled the government to stop forcing the nation to undertake unnecessary sacrifice "for the cause which is unknown to itself." [10]

The Army, which had seldom heard criticism of this magnitude, immediately issued a statement terming the Saito speech "mutilating the purposes of the holy war." Political parties were faced with the choice of maintaining their own integrity or bowing to the Army's demand that Saito be expelled from the Diet. Saito had gone so far as to resign from the Minseito party, but refused to resign from his Diet membership. Now the move was up to the Diet where pro-Army Diet members demanded his outright expulsion. Orthodox factions of both major parties hesitated, but in the end the pro-Army faction won. Those who opposed Saito's expulsion were in turn expelled from their own parties. After the differences over the Saito incident, the Seiyukai party was split into two factions, never to be reunited again.

In order to placate the Army, Diet members also formed a volunteer group called "The League of Diet Members for the Fulfilment of the Holy War Aims." On March 9 President Machida of the Minseito party urged the league members to introduce in the Diet a resolution supporting the war aims. The Army once again proved itself invulnerable.

A third development did not involve the Army, but in retrospect it played an even greater role in turning the scale in favor of the Army. This was the replacement of Yuasa by Marquis Kido on June 1, 1940 as Lord Keeper of the Privy Seal. It signaled a new era in Japanese politics. Kido brought with him the zeal for reform along the lines suggested by the Army. Gone was the legalistic mind and the person who represented the last stronghold of the pro-western party in the Imperial Court. Newspaper editorials and comments almost universally hailed the new appointment, terming Kido as a man of vision who clearly understood Japan's political future.

Hitching on to Germany's Victory Wagon. Meanwhile, developments in Europe made it necessary for the Yonai Cabinet to shift its foreign policy into one of active cooperation with Germany. In May, 1940, the battle on the western front of the European theatre was intensified. This was the period which Winston Churchill termed "their finest hour." Fresh from the surprise victory in Denmark and Norway, the Germans invaded Belgium, the Netherlands, and Luxemburg on May 10. On the same day Neville Chamberlain resigned as British

Prime Minister and was replaced by Winston Churchill. On May 28 King Leopold III of Belgium capitulated to the Germans. Italy joined the war on June 10 on the side of Germany, and on June 13 Paris fell to the Reich's Army. On June 22, an armistice was signed at Compiègne between the Second Republic and the Third Reich.

The might of the German mechanized divisions, the manner in which the *Blitzkrieg* was fought, and the retreat of the Allied troops from the beaches of Dunkerque, all served to convince the militarists in Japan that their former convictions were right. "Don't miss the bus," were the words they used in describing the situation they were placed in. Don't be late, they reasoned, lest they lose forever the spoils of the European War.

The first definite indication of the shift in the Yonai-Arita foreign policy came on April 15 while the Germans were engaged in their Scandinavian Campaign. On that day Foreign Minister Arita publicly declared that Japan could not remain disinterested in any changes in the status of the Dutch East Indies, implying that it considered the Indies within its sphere of influence. When Rotterdam surrendered to the Germans on May 15, Japan formally requested that Germany express its non-interest in the Dutch East Indies. Simultaneously a move to gain favorable economic concessions from the Indies was actively pursued. Thailand came under Japan's sphere of influence on June 12 with a Neutrality Pact. When France fell the Germans were asked to recognize Japan's special interest in French Indo-China. Ott urged the German Foreign Office to accede to the Japanese demands because "the strengthening of Japan's position in Indo-China would doubtlessly be in Germany's interest. This would increase the chances for an early end of the China War and would intensify the differences between Japan and the Anglo-Saxon powers." [11]

While asking certain favors from Germany, the Yonai-Arita Cabinet also indicated that it was ready to enter into an alliance. The new Ambassador to Berlin, Saburo Kurusu, proposed that Germany and Japan should cooperate more closely in the sphere of economics. "Today, the most important problem confronting Japan is the establishment of heavy industry," declared the Ambassador. "If in this field Japan could secure the close cooperation of Germany, Japan would gain freedom of action against America." The Ambassador also observed that Japan's future lay in the South. But in order for its southward advance to succeed Japan would have to come to an understanding with Russia. Since Germany also needed Russia's friendship, Japan could cooperate on this matter fully.

Although Japan was eager to follow Germany's steps and to share in the latter's spoils, the victorious Reich was not enthusiastic about it. Japan's Ambassador to Moscow, Naotake Saito, seized the opportunity of Ribbentrop's visit to the Soviet capital, and sounded out the latter on the possibility of an alliance. Ribbentrop coldly rejected Saito's proposals, saying that he could not understand what Japan wanted or the political motivation behind the Japanese proposals. On the basis of these, he refused to discuss terms with the Japanese Ambassador. Saito reported to Tokyo that the Reich Minister was drunk with the taste of great victory.

Germany's initial coolness did not deter Japan from further pursuing the alliance. On July 12 and 16 representatives of the War, Navy, and Foreign Ministries met to draft a proposal for closer cooperation between Japan, Germany, and Italy, and to discuss its various implications.

The draft was essentially a restatement of what had already been discussed in the Foreign Ministry. But it was significant in clearly foreshadowing the actual pact which was signed by Matsuoka. In fact, Matsuoka, while critical of the foreign policy of his predecessor, freely consulted this draft in carrying out conversations with German special emissary Stahmer. The draft stated that Japan and Germany would mutually recognize and respect the leadership of the other in the establishment of a new order in the other's sphere of interest. It spoke of economic and political cooperation, of containing the United States in the Western Hemisphere, of maintaining friendly relations with Soviet Russia, and of interfering with British interests in the Far East in order to bring about Great Britain's early surrender.

The purposes of the proposed pact were explained to be (1) to prevent interference by the United States in the China Incident, or the European conflict, (2) to aid Japan in executing the China Incident, and (3) to insure Japan's "political leadership" in the South Sea regions. Fears of Germany's economic penetration to the South Sea regions, and the consequences of its establishing a system of bloc economy in Europe and Africa with the exclusion of Japan were clearly expressed. Italy's participation in the proposed pact was welcomed on two grounds. First Italy had from time to time expressed its support of Japan's Far Eastern policy, and second, Italy's presence in the alliance could counteract Germany's predominant influence in the event that the latter won the war.

While in every other respect the draft was close to what Germany and the Japanese militarists wanted, it contained a proviso which would seriously undermine the usefulness of a military alliance. It stated that if Germany should request Japan's participation in the war, Japan would decline it. Mr. Anto, a division head of the Foreign Office, who participated in drafting the proposals, explained that the British Empire would collapse with or without Japan's help, and Germany would be in the position to establish its hegemony over Europe and Africa. Meanwhile Japan's internal situation—especially the economic situation—would not allow it to participate actively in the war. Japan, of course, would do everything short of war to aid Germany. In other words, Japan wanted to find a formula which would give it the maximum of war spoils while demanding the minimum sacrifice.[12]

Cooperation with Germany was not the only subject in which the Yonai-Arita Cabinet showed its compromise with the Army. As it finally evolved, the Yonai Cabinet was responsible for the establishment of Wang Ching-wei's puppet regime in China, and thus closed the door for direct negotiations with Chiang Kai-shek. The Cabinet also served notice that Japan was interested in the natural resources of the Dutch East Indies, and demanded Japan's predominant position over French Indo-China. It secured Great Britain's consent for closing the Burma route for a period of three months, thus further cutting the flow of strategic goods into the hands of the Chungking regime.

Despite Yonai's overt gestures to accomodate the Army's wishes, the gulf separating Yonai from the Army was wide. The Army felt that the Cabinet was incapable of coming to an understanding with Germany and finally succeeded in forcing Yonai's resignation on July 16, the same day the proposals for closer cooperation with Germany were adopted.

The immediate excuse for the Army to attempt the unseating of Yonai came on June 29 when Foreign Minister Arita made a radio speech entitled "The International Situation and Japan's Position," in which Arita made decidedly pro-Axis statements.

The Army's objection was that Arita made his speech without their consent. According to Arita, he did not attach great significance to his broadcast, and "simply wanted to give a common sense talk on diplomacy to the nation." He did not choose the broadcast as the only means of communicating the ideas elaborated in his speech. He would have been equally satisfied had the occasion been a regular press conference. At first he did not think the matter important enough to warrant the consent of service ministries. But newspapers started to publish reports of a forthcoming major foreign policy announcement, so he decided to let his Vice Minister talk things over with Vice Ministers of War and Navy. They agreed that Arita could go ahead and make his speech. But later the Army insisted that Arita did not have their backing.

What really incensed the Army was not the matter of prior consent, but the fact that the Yonai Cabinet had seized this opportunity to declare itself as pro-German in orientation. It had identified itself with the main stream of pro-Axis policy of which the Army was the chief protagonist. The Army reasoned that the Government had done so only to save its own political life, and the speech itself merely reflected the policy pursued by the Army in the past. This, concluded the Army, "was Yonai's and Arita's scheme to outdo the pro-German party which had heretofore opposed the present Cabinet." According to Harada, the Army also felt that the end of the China conflict was in sight, and it did not want Yonai to receive the credit. Thus the Army vigorously pushed a movement to oust Yonai.[13]

Arita's speech made first-page headlines on the following day. But the newspapers also carried an item saying the Army was not enthusiastic about the new foreign policy approach. This was in reference to certain remarks made by General Muto, head of the Military Affairs Bureau of the War Office, at the Vice Foreign Minister's official residence, but the result was quite embarrassing to the War Office. Part of the content of the Arita speech had leaked out before it was delivered, and the newspapermen were able to detect a struggle within the Cabinet. The Army held Suma, the spokesman for the Foreign Office, responsible for the premature disclosure and the subsequent embarrassment. Suma was summoned to the Tokyo Military Police Headquarters for interrogation. Privately the Military Police spoke of plans to interrogate Arita and Ishiwata as well, in order to harass the Yonai-Arita Cabinet.

To make matters worse, an attempt to assassinate government leaders, including Yonai, Makino, Okada, Matsudaira, and Ikeda, was discovered on the dawn of July 4. It was organized by a group called Shimpeitai (God's Army) who favored an outright alliance with Germany. The attempt was not carried through, but was viewed by the Army as another sign of non-confidence in the Yonai Cabinet. On July 8, the Vice Minister of War, General Anami, visited Lord Privy Seal Kido and declared that the Army wanted Yonai's resignation, adding that the Army would favor Prince Konoye as the next Premier.

Konoye was not yet ready to assume the premiership again. Since January 1939, he served as President of the Privy Council, a non-political constitutional organ. While in that post, he contemplated for months on how to bring about the formation of a new political party. According to Professor Yabe, Konoye's biographer, Konoye wanted to concentrate on this task before again assuming the premiership. His movement for the new order, as it was called, needed more time to mature. In fact Konoye sent one of his associates, Ryunosuke Goto, to see Cabinet Secretary Ishiwata, requesting that Yonai stay on his job for at least half a year longer.[14]

Prince Konoye resigned from the presidency of the Privy Council on June 24, declaring that his sole intention was to devote his full energy to the new order movement. Despite his disclaimer that he had no other political ambitions, the Army interpreted the move to mean that Konoye was joining his forces with theirs. They circulated rumors that Konoye agreed to the Army's move to oust the Yonai Cabinet. In order to avoid misunderstanding, Konoye had to postpone his return to Tokyo from his villa in the summer resort town of Karuizawa.

By that time the Army's formula of suggestion, persuasion, and intimidation was in full operation.

On July 12 General Anami and General Muto visited Cabinet Secretary Ishiwata hinting that the War Minister would resign unless Yonai withdrew in favor of Konoye and his new order.

Apparently the War Minister was innocent of the plot to unseat the Yonai Cabinet.[15] General Hata was under the imperial command to support the Cabinet when it was formed. This he carried out faithfully. At first Hata tried to find out a *modus operandi* between the Cabinet and the Army. But at that critical hour he no longer represented the Army. His orders in the War Ministry were not carried out due to the difference of opinion between himself and his subordinates. On July 15, Hata resigned, and the following day the Army reported that they could not find a successor.

Before Yonai came to see the Emperor on the afternoon of July 16 to tender his resignation, the Emperor was said to have asked Kido to transmit to Yonai his message that His Majesty had full confidence in the Prime Minister. But it was too late. The wheels were already in motion, and the "Son of Heaven" was powerless to arrest them.

The Army was then strong enough to force both the resignation of a Cabinet it did not approve, and the formation of a new one which it strongly supported. Suppose the Yonai Cabinet had remained in office, could Japan have taken a different course? The answer is likely to be in the negative.

Yonai's Cabinet had engendered a good feeling in Washington, and it was hoped that he might bring about a rapprochement between the two countries. However, records of the Cabinet betrayed this expectation. It would be impossible to brand Yonai's Cabinet as liberal or pro-western, and other Cabinets as rightist and pro-Axis.[16] There had been some differences in degree but not in substance in their policy approach. Many of the major policies adopted by the Second Konoye Cabinet—which replaced the Yonai Cabinet—found their direct counterparts in the policies of the Yonai Cabinet. Among them were the decisions to occupy French Indo-China; to negotiate with Germany for an alliance; and to establish Wang Ching-wei's government in Nanking. The establishment of the Wang government did not end but rather intensified the split between the two camps in the Japanese Government. This was one of the most critical periods in Japan's relations with China.

CHAPTER VI

WANG CHING-WEI'S GOVERNMENT

Escape from Chungking. "With one mind and one moral fortitude, we shall together strive to cure the devastation of war," declared Wang Ching-wei on March 30, 1940, the day his "government" returned to Nanking.[1] Thus a government was born whose main function was to correlate its policies to the whims of its imperial master. The establishment of Wang's government was a tactical victory for the War Office. But it suggested a near collapse of the policy of "total peace," or an early ending to the conflict.

There had always been two schools of thought in Japan on the matter of how to end the war. The first one stressed making China into another Manchukuo, which aimed at destroying the government represented by Chiang Kai-shek, and establishing a new central government in China that would take orders from Japan. The other school aimed at direct conversation with Chungking in order to find an amicable settlement.

Neither school had the upper hand in policy decisions, and Japanese policy on China shifted from one extreme to the other. For example, Prince Konoye made a declaration to the effect that Japan would no longer deal with Chiang Kai-shek. That was on January 16, 1938. Ten months later, he issued the Konoye Principles which were the very antithesis of his former statement and were an overt invitation to Chiang Kai-shek to discuss terms of peace. While Ambassador Trautmann mediated between Japan and China, a puppet regime was set up in Peking, and soon afterwards another one was established in Nanking.

The weakness of the puppet governments was apparent from the outset. Both governments were headed by relatively unknown second-rate politicians and lacked popular support. Each functioned separately, and there was no central control or policy coordination. The Provisional Government in North China was created by the Japanese North China Army, and the Restoration Government in Central China by the Japanese Central China Army. Neither of the puppet governments was responsible to the people they governed or to Tokyo, but to the Army which had created it. In Tokyo's view, the dissonance of the two puppet regimes could be dissolved if Japan could secure the cooperation of Wang Ching-wei and other pro-Japanese figures in the Chungking Government.

Wang Ching-wei was a unique person in modern Chinese politics. Born into the family of a scholar in 1883, Wang studied in Tokyo and took a degree in political science. In the early 1900's he joined Sun Yat-sen's revolutionary movement. In 1910 he and his co-revolutionaries staged the assassination of the Prince Regent in Peking but failed. His brilliant defense for the cause of revolution at his trial made him a national hero and he was not executed. A man of pronounced literary ability, Wang wrote the last wishes of Sun Yat-sen at the side of the latter's death bed. The death of Sun brought Wang into prominence as Chairman of the National Government in Canton. But the glory was short lived. Chiang Kai-shek's *coup d'etat* forced him into exile in France. In 1927 he formed a government with Mme. Sun Yat-sen and Michael Borodin at the triple cities of Wuhan. The collapse of the Wuhan government saw Wang attempting to form a coalition government in Nanking with Chiang Kai-shek. Neither Chiang nor Wang achieved a stature that could control the party and the government. But Chiang was the commander of the armed forces and was able to turn his military gains into political assets. In the following years, Wang intermittently collaborated with and opposed Chiang. From 1932 to 1936, Wang served two terms as Premier. Thus it was incumbent upon him to negotiate with the Japanese who after the Manchurian Incident were determined to encroach further on China's sovereignty. Wang lacked the backing of either the financial circles or the Army. But as the chief disciple of Sun Yat-sen he could always command a sizable following within the Kuomintang. His image as a patriot and revolutionary was not marred by his conciliatory policies toward Japan during his terms as Premier. His insistence on Far Eastern unity based on China and Japan's cooperation enabled him to make many friends in Japanese political circles.

In 1938 Wang Ching-wei was named Vice President of the Nationalist Party. Ostensibly the collaboration of Chiang Kai-shek and Wang Ching-wei was to be resumed. However, by then Chiang Kai-shek was the President of the Party, and was in name as well as in fact the President of the Executive Yuan, the position formerly occupied by Wang. In effect, Wang was given an honorary title with little or no political power. The only alternative left for Wang was to associate himself closely with the right wing Kuomintang members who detested collaboration with the Communists.

On October 12, 1938, the Japanese invaded the Canton area where Wang's home and political base were located. This was an occasion for him to make a statement to a Reuter correspondent that China should accept any reasonable terms Japan might offer. The impact of Wang's statement was immediately felt in Tokyo. Colonel Kagesa was ordered to establish channels of communication with Wang if possible, and Japan's Consul General in Hong Kong was appointed a liaison man between Wang and Tokyo if the former should wish to make contact with the Japanese Government.

When the triple cities of Wuhan fell into Japan's hand, the National Political Council met in Chungking and declared that China would continue to fight to the finish. This went counter to Wang's repeated statements that Japan's "reasonable" peace terms should be accepted. Japan's answer to the Chungking declaration was a statement urging China to become its partner in building a new order in East Asia. Japan's price was that China make a change in its government to show its willingness to cooperate. Prince Konoye, who made the pronouncement, added that Chiang's Government had become a local regime for all practical purposes. It was an overt suggestion on Japan's part asking Chiang to step down and let Wang form a new government.

The strained Wang-Chiang relations came to a final breaking point on December 16. At a private luncheon, Wang suggested to Chiang that both of them should step down to redeem their sins committed against the nation. The language Wang employed reminded Chiang of Konoye's statement. Chiang was infuriated, and the two were no longer on speaking terms.

The final break with Chiang convinced Wang of the futility of remaining in Chungking to pursue his "peace program." A few days later while Chiang Kai-shek was making an address to younger members of the Kuomintang Central Committee, Wang flew over to Kunming, ostensively on a propaganda mission. Then with the aid of Yunnan's military governor Lung Yun, Wang and his aide Chou Fuhai boarded a plane to Hanoi. Later Chen Kung-po, Tao Hsi-sheng, Mei Ssu-ping, and Tseng Chung-ming, his secretary, as well as his wife followed suit.

Prince Konoye greeted the news with a statement on December 22 saying Japan required no cession of territories or reparation from China. However, in order for China to be able to participate in the building of a new order in East Asia, it would have to recognize Manchukuo, join the Anti-Comintern Pact, and allow Japanese troops to station in North China and Inner Mongolia. The conditions were not radically different from the prior ones, but represented certain modifications. They were thus apparently acceptable to Wang Ching-wei as reasonable peace terms.

Before the statement was made public, Wang's representatives Mei Ssu-ping and Kao Tsung-wu met with Japanese representatives Colonels Kagesa and Imai several times in Shanghai to discuss conditions under which Wang could escape from Chungking. The Chinese representatives' blueprint for Wang's escape was that as soon as he reached Kunming, Konoye would make a public statement saying that Japan had no territorial ambitions over China. This was to be followed by Wang's announcement that he had broken away from Chiang Kai-shek. Wang would then go to Hong Kong via Hanoi. From Hong Kong, he would declare his assumption of political leadership in China and would cooperate with Japan to effect an early end to the China conflict. Wang would count on the support of the armies of Yunnan, Szechwan, and Kwangtung. He would try to bring them to his side and would seek to have the Japanese Army make strategic moves. Having married the daughter of a wealthy overseas merchant, Wang should also appeal to the overseas Chinese to come to his aid. Apparently satisfied with the arrangement, the four participants—Mei, Kao, and Colonels Kagesa and Imai—signed an informal document on November 20. The importance Tokyo attached to Wang's movement is shown in two Imperial Conferences held on November 25 and 30, both of which used this informal document as the basis for discussion.[2]

Wang's escape was originally planned for December 8, and Prince Konoye was to make the promised speech in Osaka three days later. But while the Prince was getting ready, word came from Kao Tsung-wu that Wang did not succeed in his escape attempt. Konoye hastily canceled his trip to Osaka. On December 18 word came again confirming that Wang was on his way to Hanoi, with a request that Konoye's statement be delivered not later than December 22.

Though Wang's escape was known to be a possibility for some time, after the failure of December 8, no one—with the possible exception of Colonels Kagesa and Imai—took the matter seriously. Konoye doubted if Wang would become a collaborator. Moreover, he was not certain whether Wang was acting in good faith or working on Chiang's behalf. With Wang in Hanoi keeping tight-lipped silence, Konoye talked himself into believing that the statement was intended for Chungking rather than for Wang's consumption.

Intelligence reports from various quarters seemed to confirm Konoye's suspicion. Consul General Tajiri at Hong Kong, after reviewing all the news dispatches and reports available at his disposal, expressed the opinion that Japan should discount Wang's cooperation. He was convinced that Wang was acting more like an agent for Chungking, and prudence called for Japan's not helping Wang. After all, Wang's escape had gone too smoothly, and Chiang Kai-shek had repeatedly declared that Wang's present "trip" had his personal approval. The Yamazaki Economic Research Institute which was engaged in the study of contemporary Chinese political situations also submitted a report to the Army and to the Foreign Office. It termed Wang as a person not trustworthy and unreliable. "He is a man who plays one faction against another for his own personal gains," said the report. "If Japan should accept him as the head of the Central Government of China, Japan would be the loser. One day he would turn against Japan for his own advantages."[3]

At Hanoi, Wang Ching-wei went through some soul searching. Konoye's statement of December 22 was generally acceptable to him, but it omitted two points which Wang regarded as most vital in the success of his peace movement. In the original secret agreement signed by his representatives and Colonels Kagesa and Imai, Japan's right to station troops in China was restricted to Inner Mongolia for the duration of the Anti-Comintern Pact between the two countries. It also required Japanese troops to withdraw from all other areas (except the Pekin-Tientsin area) within two years after peace was restored. The Konoye statement had substituted "certain specified areas" for "anti-comintern defense areas" in the original agreement, and omitted any mention of withdrawal of troops. Konoye's evasiveness and omission had been the result of domestic considerations. From Wang's point of view, an agreement with Japan without clear-cut assurances on the contested points would have made Wang an outright traitor whose lot he could not bear.

Meanwhile, Chungking was doing its utmost to bring Wang back to its fold. Unconfirmed reports stated that Foreign Minister Wang Chung-hui and Chiang's private secretary, Chen Pu-lei, were sent to Hanoi to persuade Wang either to return or to go abroad at the government's expense. When Chiang found it necessary to make a public reply to Konoye's statement he referred to Wang as a great patriot "whose devotion and dedication to the cause of the party, the nation, and the war have been unexceptionable." Wang left Chungking for health reasons and not because of conspiracy, Chiang asserted. He said that Wang asked for and was granted a four month vacation during which he could go abroad to recuperate from illness.

Within Wang's entourage, opinions were divided. It seemed the future was too uncertain, the task too formidable, and the risk too great to assume. But finally Mei Ssu-ping who negotiated with Colonel Kagesa won, and Wang agreed to make public a peace telegram he would send to Chiang accepting Konoye's various conditions.

Wang's "peace telegram" was reported in *The South China Daily News,* a Hong Kong paper on December 31, 1938. In essence, Wang wanted peace along the lines suggested by the Konoye statement, but differed from it in one respect. He would have Japanese troops stationed only in Inner Mongolia which would be henceforth named a special anti-Comintern area for the purpose of joint defense. Otherwise, Wang found no reason why China should not cooperate with Japan to restore "its sovereignty and to build perpetual peace in East Asia." In his telegram Wang also demanded that Japan adopt a new method of education through which the Japanese public would learn to become pro-Chinese.

Wang's telegram clarified one of the pending issues for Chungking. Those who were sympathetic to Wang's attitude felt that he had gone too far. On January 1, 1939, he was expelled from the party membership. On January 8, Wang made another announcement, accompanied by a secret document concerning a meeting of the Supreme Defense Council of China over which Wang presided. He said the position he was taking was consistent with what had been expressed at the council meeting held at the time of the Trautmann mediation, and that he was carrying on his own shoulders the burden of peace. In doing so, Wang committed a tactical error. Heretofore, Chiang Kai-shek was unable to brand him openly as a traitor in deference to Wang's past record. By revealing the top secret of the nation, he lost ground. The public image of Wang was no longer the chief disciple of Sun Yat-sen but a traitor who was willing to sell out his own country. Many who wanted to follow Wang in his effort to bring about peace felt they should stay in Chungking rather than join him in his flight to Hanoi, lest they also be called traitors.

In the meantime, the author of the Konoye statement resigned his post as Prime Minister and was replaced by Baron Hiranuma. Theoretically Hiranuma was not bound by statements made by his predecessor, and this he exploited to the fullest extent with regard to Wang's movement. The position adopted by him was that of "wait and see" without committing himself as to Wang's future status. Wang's performance since his flight from Chungking had been disappointingly poor. Furthermore, Japan and Wang did not necessarily agree on various aspects of their forthcoming negotiations. No matter how future historians might judge him, Wang was at heart a Chinese. Even if he had been motivated by personal reasons, he was almost to the point of stubbornness in refusing many of Japan's ill-conceived demands. But Japan's initial coolness after his flight necessitated a change in his tactics. He realized that unless he could command the following of some of the most influential Chinese politicans and militarists, he would not be able to accomplish his mission. He also knew fully well that his bargaining power with Japan would come to nought if he failed in this first assignment.

At Hanoi, Wang busily engaged himself in trying to persuade Lung Yun of Yunnan and Chang Fa-kwei of Kwangsi to come to his side. Wang's theme was that with the help of these two military governors he should be able to liquidate the two existing puppet regimes and restore integrity to the Chinese Government. He added that Communist penetration represented a real threat, and all patriots ought to join hands in the fight lest the Kuomintang Party be eliminated by the Communists. The two Generals sent cordial telegrams which amounted to polite evasiveness and did not help Wang's position. Having failed in these atempts, Wang sent Kao Tsung-wu to sound out the Japanese position and to present his own case. This action did not bring results until Wang's life was endangered in Hanoi. On March 21 Wang had a sleepless night and chatted with his wife and his secretary Tseng. Soon after Wang retired to his bedroom, shots were heard from the parlor. Tseng was dead instantly with about seventy shots fired into his body by a machine gun. Wang's wife who was still in the parlor was "miraculously" saved. Though it was well recognized at that time that Wang was not the real target of this assassination plot, Japan was forced to take radical steps to save Wang's life and their remaining hope of establishing a strong puppet government.

The fact that Wang was not the real target was easily confirmed by Chungking's action. In the early part of April, Madame Chiang and T. V. Soong sent personal appeals to Wang asking him to reconsider his stand and go abroad. Their messages also contained an implied threat if Wang did not comply he might be assassinated. Chiang also sent a message asking him to return to Chungking with a promise that the past would be completely forgotten.[4]

The Wang-Hiranuma Secret Agreement. On April 5 the Reuter news agency reported the existence of a so-called Wang-Hiranuma Secret Agreement, which was said to have provided that:

"1. In North China, Japan would occupy the city of Sian and cut the communication lines between the Soviet Union and Chungking, thus threatening the safety of Szechwan.

"2. In South China, Japan would occupy the city of Nanning, located between French Indo-China and Kwangsi, in order to aid Wang's effort to win over the army in Kwangsi.

"3. In Central China, Japan would advance to the city of Changsha and occupy two other strategic points in Hunan and Szechwan.

"4. On Wang's part, he would lead an anti-Chiang and anti-Communist front, head an anti-Communist National Army, and agree to conclude a treaty of peace and friendship with Japan."

Neither the Japanese Foreign Office nor the War Office would confirm or deny the existence of such an agreement. But at that time, Kao Tsung-wu was in Hong Kong, and it is conceivable that the so-called Wang-Hiranuma agreement was the outcome of his negotiations with Japanese agents there. The Japanese Foreign Office Archives confirm that such an agreement existed on an informal basis.

The assassination of Wang's private secretary might have played some part in the Hiranuma Cabinet's hasty decision to dispatch Colonel Kagesa to deal directly with Wang in Hanoi. However, without doubt, the promise of cooperation given through Kao in Hong Kong was the decisive factor. Colonel Kagesa arrived in Hanoi on April 17 to confer with Wang and the French authority for Wang's evacuation.

Wang arrived in Shanghai on May 7, but the situation awaiting him was not a happy one. The Chinese community of Shanghai was under the influence of a man named Ting Mo-tsuen, who was the boss of the underworld. Without his cooperation, Wang was hardly able to establish himself firmly in the city. Meanwhile, the faction in the Japanese Army which established and supported the Restoration Government in Central China showed an increasing degree of hostility toward Wang and of distrust for Colonel Kagesa. This faction was represented by Major General Doihara, who headed the Intelligence Division of the Japanese Central Army with headquarters in Shanghai. Kagesa was junior to Doihara in rank and in years of service. Fortunately, the Colonel had the backing of Generals Itagaki and Tojo, respectively the War Minister and Vice Minister at that time.

Otherwise the movement to install Wang as the head of a puppet government might have been nipped in the bud.

By this time Wang was a tired and rejected man. His determination to establish a new government wavered. In desperation, he decided he should visit Tokyo to find out once for all where he stood in the minds of Japanese leaders and about the future status of his government. Major General Doihara was against such a move, but he was overruled by Tokyo, and it was again Colonel Kagesa who was instrumental in bringing about Wang's visit to a reality.

The Foreign Office and War Office were still not prepared to commit themselves to having Wang head the new central government. That would depend on Wang's cooperation and agreement on basic issues. However, realizing that their excessive demands had made Wang's task difficult, Tokyo was ready to drop the requirement that Wang establish a government elsewhere—e. g., in Canton or Fukien—before being allowed to come to Nanking. It would also agree to temporize the demands advanced by the two puppet governments so Wang's central government could have greater authority. Prince Saionji commented that Wang was a great man and Japan should not try to undermine his prestige. But neither Prince Saionji nor others who were sympathetic toward Wang had any real influence in the conduct of foreign affairs. Meanwhile policy papers drafted by the Foreign and War Offices began to minimize Wang's usefulness in Japan's overall scheme of *Realpolitik*.

In the early part of June 1939, Wang's group reached Tokyo. Wang was polite but resolute, determined to get direct answers from Japanese leaders on his future status. Having been assured by Hiranuma that the Japanese Government would allow Wang to form a government he proceeded to present his ideas to Japanese authorities.

He termed the operations of the two puppet governments a gross failure. This was so because they lacked popular support, having been identified with Japanese aggression. In order for Wang's government to have no such stigma attached, several steps would have to be taken. First, Japan and China ought to end their present educational policies which stressed hostilities and contempt for one another. Second, Japan should not assign political advisers but should deal with Wang only through its duly accredited ambassador; should limit the number of technical advisers to be sent to China; and should not allow technical advisers to meddle in political matters. Third, all revenue collecting agencies—chief among them the customs and salt gabel administrations—should be placed under his government's jurisdiction. This would be doubly important to his government, since part of the revenue collected by these agencies had been used to maintain the two puppet governments. Wang also wanted Japan to set up a definite deadline, not exceeding two years, for the withdrawal of Japanese troops in China after peace was restored. If and when Wang should have an army of his own, it should in principle replace Japanese armies stationed in various parts of China. As to public and private industries and mines appropriated during the war they should be returned to original owners or equitable compensation should be given to injured parties. His government would have to be organized as the National Government of China and not as a new government, and his flag should be exactly the same as the one currently used by the Chungking government. These actions would convince the people that his government was the true successor to Sun Yat-sen's government. He also wanted Nanking to be his capital, and at a predetermined date his government would "return" to it.[5]

Wang's demands were comprehensive. Had they been accepted by the Japanese, he would have become a national hero, giving the needed peace to a war-torn country. But many of his demands touched the points regarded by the Japanese as essential. The ministers in Tokyo gave him only qualified answers, neither approving nor disapproving. And on these shaky promises, Wang returned to Shanghai to continue his quest for building up his government.[6]

The only consolation Wang could derive from his Tokyo visit was its psychological impact on other Chinese people, especially on leaders of the existing puppet governments. Since the two puppet governments relied on the Japanese Government (or on the Army, to be more precise) for support, any encouragement Tokyo would give to a particular person had great significance. Wang, after the initial loss of prestige and influence among his former supporters, found a new source of power in whatever support Japan could give. But reliance on Japan meant Wang was no longer a free agent. Gradually he found himself yielding to the Japanese Army's demands inch by inch. The ensuing negotiations between him and the Japanese Government indicated a tragic retreat.

With Wang's visit to Tokyo, Japan's policy toward the establishment of a new government stepped into high gear. General Suzuki, Chief of the Political Bureau of the China Board initiated a move to silence those who were against the establishment of Wang's regime. They were transferred to non-essential assignments from their intelligence or other essential work. General Doihara, nicknamed Lawrence of China, was removed from his post as Chief of the Intelligence Division of the Central China Army, and was replaced by General Kita, a person of lesser calibre and influence. At one time, Doihara had been responsible for a movement to have General Wu Pei-fu head a new central government as a counterpoise to Wang's regime. Thus his exit signaled a victory for supporters of Wang.

Wang's visit also gave the Japanese Foreign Office impetus to assume the role of policy maker which was previously denied to it. Taking a hint from the current situation in Spain, the Japanese Foreign Office came to the conclusion that it was imperative for Japan to establish a *de facto* government in China. It could thus confront the western powers with a *fait accompli*. They could not ignore the right of the *de facto* government, whether they wanted to mediate or to put pressure on Japan. The Foreign Office would also prefer giving Wang's government greater concessions in order to strengthen its position. But on this point the Foreign Office and the Army differed, and the Army had the upper hand.

Wang Throws Hat in the Ring. Back in Shanghai, Wang established a daily newspaper to serve as his mouthpiece. Just about that time, after more than six months of indecision, Chiang Kai-shek issued a warrant for Wang's arrest. To this Wang replied in the first issue of his paper that the Konoye statement had ushered in a new era in Chinese-Japanese relations. "Chiang erred in his judgment. It is incumbent on Wang to work independently for the attainment of peace." Several days later, Wang expressed a view that withdrawal of Japanese troops from Chinese soil was not the *sine qua non* of peace, showing the first sign of capitulation.

While in Tokyo, Wang had become suspicious of Japan's true intent. He feared Japan was simply using him as a trial balloon, and once his mission was accomplished would drop him and negotiate directly with Chiang. To forestall this, he was determined to solidify his own position. The tactics to be employed were: firstly, to get as many followers as possible out of Chungking and areas adjacent to the Japanese occupied zone; and secondly, to cooperate with the two existing puppet governments with a clear understanding that Wang was to be given unchallenged authority over them. But before these projects could be put into practice, there was another hurdle he had to overcome. That was the popularity enjoyed by General Wu Pei-fu, who was the candidate of the North China Army to head the unified puppet government.

Wang decided it was time for him to travel around to strengthen his position. Because of the geographical proximity of Nanking to Shanghai, Wang had less to worry about the outcome of his power contest with the Restoration Government in Nanking. On the other hand, North China and South China offered great difficulties and challenges. Wang's first trip was to the North, ostensibly to see Wang Keh-min, Chairman of the North China puppet regime, but actually to find out for himself whether General Wu was really interested in forming a government. On June 25 and 27 Wang had lengthy conferences with Wang Keh-min in Tientsin and repeatedly issued invitations to General Wu to join them in political talks. Despite the pressure from the Japanese, the old General steadfastly refused.

The conferences with Wang Keh-min brought no concrete results. Soon after Wang's departure, Wang Keh-min held a press conference declaring that the two had not discussed anything about the establishment of a central or coalition government, and that whatever Wang Ching-wei might say about the points discussed in their meetings was neither supported by him nor by his government. He also left the impression that he and Wang had had a basic disagreement.

In the following month Wang met with Liang Hung-chih, Chairman of the Restoration Government. This time the atmosphere was more cordial, but Liang would talk terms strictly on a give-and-take basis. He would cooperate with Wang only if he was to be named Premier in the proposed central government.

Wang's itinerary ended in Canton, the place of his birth, where he had a meeting with the intermediaries of General Chang Fa-kwei. The latter was Wang's life-long friend and at that time was serving as Military Commander of the Southwestern region. Even after Wang's flight from Chungking, the two had corresponded, which seemed to confirm their close friendship. Wang's wife secretly met with Chang in an attempt to enlist his support but to no avail. On August 15, the day after the Wangs left Canton, General Chang issued a statement in no uncertain terms condemning the stand taken by Wang. Their friendship was over. The appeal Wang had once possessed was diminished, if not completely eradicated.

A series of conferences between Wang and Japan followed after the former's return to Shanghai. Wang had relied heavily on the principles elaborated in Konoye's statement, and on his own personal contact with the five ministers. But in the course of negotiations Wang found a deep discrepancy between what he interpreted to be Japan's intent and what the Army in China actually demanded.

On October 10, 1939, the China Army Headquarters was established with General Toshizo Nishio as Commander-in-Chief and former War Minister General Itagaki as Chief of Staff. With Itagaki's appointment to the key position, opposition to a Wang Ching-wei government subsided. This meant that for the first time, Wang would have one central authority to deal with and did not have to worry about being involved in jurisdictional disputes between the North China and Central China Armies. However, Wang's troubles were by no means over. While pledging to support Wang, Itagaki also advocated direct negotiations with Chiang and entertained the thought of going to Changsha to meet with Chiang personally.

On November 1, Colonel Kagesa informally gave Wang what were to be the basic demands of Japan. A Foreign Office representative who met Wang two weeks later found him still in a state of shock, unable to go along with the demands contained in the note given him by Kagesa. The note spoke of a meeting between Wang and the heads of the two existing puppet governments. The implication was that unless Wang was willing to accept Japan's terms, the two puppet governments would be kept and Wang would be quietly laid aside.[7]

To sum it up, the Japanese Government did not depart from its basic policy of allowing Wang to establish a government at a later date. It did, however, want to curtail any demands of Wang which it regarded as excessive. In order to do so, certain aspects of Wang's progress had to be arrested. This policy explained the fact that Wang Keh-min was permitted to issue a statement tantamount to a rebuke of Wang's stand and that Wang Keh-min was again instructed to initiate direct negotiations with Chiang Kai-shek through the good offices of J. Leighton Stuart, the famed American missionary educator who headed the Yenching University.

Wang apparently thought of abruptly ending his peace movement, but was not able to do so, because he was no longer the master of his own fate. To better his rather precarious position, Wang endeavored to reduce Japan's demands. The Kagesa draft called for the signing of an anti-Comintern pact which included a provision that Japanese troops should be stationed in North China and Mongolia. Wang fought vigorously to eliminate this condition, knowing that the Japanese demand amounted to an outright infringement of China's sovereignty. The Japanese also demanded that North China should become a separate political entity. The furtherest Wang would go was to set up a political council for the region which would include Hopei,

Shansi, Shantung, and other provinces directly south of the Great Wall. He insisted, however, that Honan province should not be included in this administrative division and should be placed under the jurisdiction of the central government. The power to supervise troops stationed in North China should be conferred to the central government rather than to the political council, Wang contended. Furthermore if there were conflicts in the application of laws and ordinances, those of the central government should prevail.

Wang also demanded that Japan should in principle agree to his central government supervising financial affairs of the North China political council. The Japanese draft called for forty percent of customs revenue and fifty percent of excise tax to be allocated to the political council, thus giving it virtual financial independence. In another of the items concerning North China, Wang wanted to limit bond issuing power of the political council to domestic bonds only, and before each issue could be marketed, there would have to be clearance from the central government. He maintained that matters concerning local affairs in North China should be reported to the central government, and the Japanese Government should refrain from negotiating directly with local authorities.

Another financial question which confronted Wang was Japan's military currency widely circulated in the occupied part of China. Since this was a strictly military matter, the central government would lack jurisdiction. However, its very existence would threaten the financial integrity of the central government, and Wang was determined to bring about a workable solution. In negotiating, the Japanese not only pressed for the retention of the military currency, but also a favorable exchange rate for it in relation to the proposed central government's currency. The Japanese also insisted that North China should be made a financially autonomous region. While the North China Bank would come under the supervision of the Central Bank, it could have its own currency issuing power.

Japan wanted to make Shanghai a specialized area so the great metropolis could later become a center of Japan's economic penetration into China. Wang would go as far as to allow establishment of a joint Japanese-Chinese economic council which could submit advisory opinions on the economic life of Shanghai, and permit Japanese observers to be stationed there. But he flatly rejected the bid for Japanese nationals to sit in the city council.

Wang also insisted that all railroads should be nationalized by his government, even though he would permit joint operation of the

merchant marines and telecommunication networks hoping possession
of railways would enable him to offset Japan's political predominance
in North China.

As to Japanese advisers, if one should be appointed he should obey
the laws of the central government, claiming no extra territorial
jurisdiction.

The tactics Japan applied were to agree in principle with all that
Wang asked, and then gradually adjust the differences in favor of
Japanese terms. Colonel Kagesa would readily admit that Wang could
decide on his own any "domestic matters." But there was a war going
on, and Wang had to make certain sacrifices for the common cause—
meaning that all the Japanese terms had to be accepted during the
duration of the war. By the middle of November 1939, all signs pointed to the collapse of the negotiations. According to one account Wang
wept and hoped to return to Chungking. Japan was also on the verge
of discontinuing the entire movement.

Wang's reluctance to accept Japanese terms had a much greater
political implication than that which was confined to the occupied
part of China. At that time Japan was still uncertain whether Wang
was Chiang's stooge or Japan's ally. Since the conditions presented to
Wang were regarded as the prototype of conditions Japan would
impose when Chiang would also sue for peace, the failure in the
peace movement conducted by Wang would invariably mean an
eventual failure in the prospective negotiations with Chiang Kai-shek.
The outlook for peace—either partial or total—was dim indeed.

Realizing the grave danger threatening the future of Wang's movement, General Itagaki, the new Chief of Staff of the China Army asked
his superior in Tokyo for modification of certain stringent terms. He
felt that Japanese insistence on North China as a separate political
entity was the main obstacle to the success of the negotiations. While
he himself preferred the original demand, under the circumstances,
a change was necessary. The Vice Chief of Staff of the Army High
Command replied that it was beyond his power to modify the conditions, since they had already been approved by the China Board and
had been sanctioned by the Imperial Conference. It was typical of
the Japanese Army to take refuge under the imperial garb when it
suited their purpose. But in any event Itagaki had to go along with
this inflexible stand. The new instructions from Tokyo were that
the establishment of the puppet government could be delayed, but
Japan could not compromise on the basic conditions.

While Itagaki and his colleagues were striving to gain favorable terms for Wang, the North China Army—which cared for Wang the least—again applied their pressure tactics aimed primarily to curtail Wang's influence. The post of the Supreme Commander of the Chinese Army in North China was offered to General Wu on December 1, 1939. But on December 5 the General died. At the time of his death General Wu's villa was surrounded by Japanese troops. Rumor had it that the General was murdered or poisoned by the Japanese.

Within Wang's entourage, two factions developed. One faction favored establishing a government first and talking detailed terms with the Japanese later. The second faction insisted that a deadline had to be set. If by January 1, 1940, Japan did not yield to Wang's minimum demands, all of them should retire from active politics, and let the proposed government be stillborn. They figured that by forcing a deadlock, the Japanese might reconsider their stand and yield on certain essentials.

Just what made Wang Ching-wei finally capitulate to the Japanese demands is not clear. Perhaps it was a combination of various factors —personal as well as political. The death of General Wu might have suggested to him the danger of going counter to Japanese wishes, and he was no longer a man with freedom of action, having lived under the watchful eyes of the Japanese militarists. Or if Chou Fu-hai's words were to be accepted, Wang and Chiang differed only in their methods, but agreed in their ultimate goals of truce and peace with Japan.[3] Thus while yielding to Japan's superior force, Wang was simply opening another avenue for solving the pressing problems. Or it might be possible that Wang finally came to the realization that he could not establish a government solely on his own, and that he needed backing from the Japanese. A certain general called Huang, who was loyal to Wang, invaded and occupied several off-shore islands along the coast of Fukien province. This was originally intended to provide Wang with a base of operation independent of the Japanese. But the project failed since no supply could come to these barren islands without the aid of the Japanese Navy which viewed the entire scheme as a pure misadventure. Then there was the visit of former Finance Minister Ishiwata to Shanghai. Ishiwata came with one major concession to offer, that Japan would allow Wang to develop his own currency, *Fa-pi*, and would aid in its stabilization. Furthermore Japan would agree to withdraw its military currency and other currencies circulated by it. The values of the two currencies maintained by the two puppet governments would not be artificially boosted to embarrass Wang's financial operation. Ishiwata's visit did not bring any concrete result at that particular moment. But it is conceivable that the visit could have tipped the scales in favor of the faction within Wang's camp which wanted to continue collaborating with Japan.

The Tsingtao Conference. Wang's capitulation came in the form of agreeing to attend a conference between himself and heads of the existing puppet governments. Wang arrived in Tsingtao on January 22, 1940, but the air was filled with uncertainty. A day before Wang arrived, two men who had worked closely together with him in his peace movement deserted him and left for Hong Kong. They were Tao Hsi-sheng, a Nationalist theorist, and Kao Tsung-wu, formerly head of the Japanese Division of the Chinese Foreign Office, who conducted initial negotiations with the Japanese resulting in Wang's escape from Chungking. On January 21, 1940, the Hong Kong *Ta Kung Pao* carried a statement by these two men saying that the conditions imposed by the Japanese were even worse than the twenty-one demands, and were inconsistent with the spirit of the Konoye statement which induced Wang to cooperate. They found a divergence of opinion within the ruling circles and the Army of Japan, discrepancies in their actions, and an arrogant manner used by the Japanese Army in treating the Chinese people. They joined Wang's movement because they wanted to preserve the territorial and administrative integrity of China. But after prolonged negotiations with Japan they found the conditions too severe and their goals unobtainable. They were thus compelled to expose the facts to the nation, concluded the statement. The exposure by the two men could not have come at a worse time than this. The bad publicity undermined the importance of the Tsingtao conference and also served notice where Japan—the self-styled champion of peace, co-prosperity and equal rights—stood in relation to its subject nations.

The Tsingtao conference went according to the schedule set up by the Ume intelligence organization.[9] The two existing puppet governments agreed that Wang's government should be called the National Government, and that Nanking should be his capital. They also decided that a Central Political Council should be organized and be held in Nanking to prepare for the establishment of the government. This was a victory for the supporters of Wang. On the other hand, Wang was forced to agree that a political council be set up in North China giving it an autonomous status. The conference ended on

January 27, and on the same day, Wang, his aides, and his Japanese advisers left Tsingtao for Shanghai.

Wang Ching-wei tentatively set March 30 as the day on which he and his government would "return" to Nanking. In the intervening period, Japan sought Germany's immediate recognition of Wang's government, in order to bolster the latter's position. But the Germans were reluctant. Japan did not send enough war materials needed by Germany from the occupied part of China, while Chungking faithfully complied with German wishes. On the other hand, Japan was disturbed by an overt gesture of Ciano, who suggested to Wang the possibility of Italy's recognition in return for some economic concessions. The Foreign Office feared that Japan's hold on Wang might be weakened, and might eventually result in the collapse of Japan's control over China, if Wang were allowed to have free intercourse with other powers. The logic was inconsistent, but the Foreign Office apparently felt the advantages of recognition by Germany— regarded as a first-rate power—far outweighed the disadvantages, while in the case of Italy—not a first-rate power in Japanese eyes— the situation was exactly the reverse. The question of recognition also posed other intricate problems. If Japan should establish normal relations with Wang's government, then technically at least, the act of war in China should be terminated. On what basis could Japan continue to fight on Chinese soil? The question was purely academic, since the Japanese figured that they could do so either by secret agreement with Wang or with informal understanding. But they felt the question had to be answered. The true reason Japan hesitated was that such a step might permanently endanger the chance of negotiating directly with Chungking. Recognition of Wang would drive a deeper wedge between Chungking and Wang, and the resulting enmity would destroy any hope of Wang, together with his sympathizers in and out of Chungking, working as Japan's intermediary in bringing about total peace.

On March 20, the Central Political Council convened in Nanking. Its composition heavily favored Wang's faction and former members of the Nationalist party. Since all the major issues were already approved by the Japanese military in advance, no interference in the proceedings of the Council was contemplated by the Japanese. Wang with the backing of the absolute majority of the Council exercised almost dictatorial power. To give a flavor of orthodoxy to his government, Wang appointed Lin Sen, who was currently Chairman of the National Government, as Chairman of his government as well. But since Lin was not able to return to Nanking, Wang would assume the position of "Acting Chairman" during "the forced absence of Chairman Lin Sen."

On March 30 Wang officially established his government. Lack of support among the Chinese people was evident. The government also had no firm financial foundation, and one of the very first acts of Finance Minister Chou Fu-hai was to sign an agreement with the Yokohama Specie Bank for a loan of $40,000,000.[10] The only visible success Wang attained from Japan was the use of the Chinese National flag with a slight modification, and the assumption of the name "National Government." Otherwise, as one observer from Hankow who visited Nanking reported, it was shocking to see people's "indifferent attitude" toward Wang.

On April 23 General Abe, a former Prime Minister, arrived in Nanking to serve as Japan's first ambassador to Wang's government. Among other things, Abe's mission was to sign a fundamental treaty between the two powers. The actual signing of the treaty, however, did not take place until the end of November of the same year. The protracted period of negotiations was proof that the two parties could and readily agree on basic issues.

As it finally emerged, the basic treaty and the accompanying secret agreements gave Japan all it desired, covering virtually every phase of governmental operation in China. The treaties also recognized that the state of war existed in China, and during its duration Japan should have free hand in undertaking any necessary military operations. Several special areas were established in which Japan's exclusive rights were recognized. The treaties also specified certain areas in which Japan could establish permanent military bases. One of the secret agreements gave Japan unilateral control of the Hainan island similar to a leased territory. Japanese troops were to be withdrawn from China once peace was restored. But several riders were attached to this provision, cancelling its practical significance. Wang was also compelled to sign a treaty with Manchukuo, recognizing its independence. The three powers later signed another treaty, which permitted Japan's hegemony and economic domination over the remaining two partners.

With Wang's government established and the basic treaty signed, another chapter in Japan's China policy came to a close. But it was hardly the solution to the basic problems. The desire for direct negotiations with Chungking was kept alive, both in Wang's camp and in Tokyo.[11]

CHAPTER VII

THE SECOND KONOYE CABINET

Selection of Konoye. In a brief ceremony at the Imperial Palace on July 17, 1940, Prince Fumimaro Konoye again received the imperial command to form a cabinet. Except for the Emperor's casual reference to "the difficult world situation" in connection with the possible selection of foreign and finance ministers, there was no air of an impending crisis.

But beneath the calm was the realization that for better or for worse, Japan was heading toward the time of decision, and Prince Konoye was to be the nation's chosen instrument. Marshal Henri-Philippe Pétain severed relations with the British government on July 5, got the power to establish an authoritarian government in France by a vote of 395 to 3 in the Chamber of Deputies on July 8, and then appointed collaborationist Pierre Laval to be his Vice-Premier on July 12. A few days later, on July 18, the Democratic National Convention in Chicago was to nominate Franklin Delano Roosevelt for an unprecedented third term. Winston Spencer Churchill's outcry that he had "nothing to offer but blood, toil, tears and sweat" was almost forgotten by the Japanese. After the fall of France, the Germans occupied islands in the English Channel, which seemed to indicate that the German *Luftwaffe* would in the end prove to be stronger than the British sea power. Prince Konoye's task was to carry out a program of national consolidation and defense, and for this he was uniquely fitted. For he alone could "perform the astonishing feat of retaining the confidence alike of the Army and of the elements most strongly opposed to all that the Army stood for."[1]

Prince Konoye had long since been the Army's choice as Yonai's successor. But the Prince himself would have preferred Baron Hiranuma to assume the post, at least temporarily. The Prince's reluctance was explained in the fact that he was busily engaged in his New Order Movement, which would eventually bring into being a one party system in Japan. The delay in assuming the premiership was essential for a variety of reasons. First, he wanted to create a public image of the movement as a spontaneous one originating from the people. Should he assume the premiership that public image would be lost

at once. Second, there was an ever present danger of the new political party being infiltrated by the Army. The Army had indicated
its support for the New Order Movement, but obviously for its own
benefit. In his private capacity, Prince Konoye could form a new
party or an organization with the exclusion of the Army, but if an
organization were formed by the Prince in his official capacity as
premier, this would obviously be impossible. Third, political parties
in Japan were at the point of disintegration. By joining their remaining forces with that of Konoye, they hoped to retain their political influence. To forestall this, it was necessary for Konoye to have the
nucleus of his organization well formed. Only in this way could the
will of Konoye prevail and not that of the old guard politicians.

Yet when the position was offered him, Prince Konoye did not refuse. He was riding on the crest of popularity, and did not hide a
certain feeling that he alone could perform miracles in that difficult
situation. His attitude was at once ridiculed by Prince Saionji. "What,
he wants to govern by popularity?" said this venerated octogenarian.
"It's anachronism!"

The Ogikubo Conference. All elements of theatrical suspense were
present when Prince Konoye decided to confer with the War, Navy, and
Foreign Ministers he had designated before he named the remaining
members of his Cabinet. The Navy Minister-designate was Vice
Admiral Zengo Yoshida, a moderate whom the Navy decided to retain. The War Minister-designate was Lieutenant General Hideki
Tojo of Manchurian fame whose inordinate devotion to frivolous details won him the nickname of Private Tojo. In the selection of these
two Konoye had taken no part, since they had to be recommended
by their respective services. The Foreign Minister-designate was
Yosuke Matsuoka, a former president of the South Manchurian Railway Company and delegate to the League of Nations when Japan
withdrew from that world body. He had previously served in Konoye's
first Cabinet as a member of the Advisory Council.

It is almost impossible to delve into the mind of Prince Konoye to
find the reason for selecting Matsuoka as his foreign minister. In his
memoirs, the Prince termed Matsuoka "a problem minister and a dangerous character," but this was apparently an afterthought. Matsuoka
had the power of persuasion and a forceful way of speech which many
Japanese politicians lacked. He spoke of war with Great Britain and
the United States which was interpreted as a pure publicity stunt. On
more than one occasion, he would suddenly shift his tone of voice and

declare that he was at heart a pro-American. Since it was impossible to have any one who had a strong leaning toward the western powers to assume the post of foreign minister, Matsuoka's selection seemed logical. Prince Konoye consulted Matsuoka's predecessor, Arita, and apparently had Arita's tacit consent for his selection. According to Shigemitsu, Matsuoka possessed a liberal view toward China, and advocated that Japan should require no reparation or annexation from China. He unequivocally declared respect for China's sovereignty; this was to be the cornerstone of his China policy. Shigemitsu even hoped that the alliance of Konoye and Matsuoka would become so powerful that the might of the Army would be curtailed.

As to General Tojo, this was his first time to hold a position of political responsibility. The appointment of this relatively unknown person had multiple implications. It reduced the importance of the office of the War Minister, at least temporarily. Tojo was one of many lieutenant generals, and his rank compared unfavorably to that of Field Marshal Prince Kanin who occupied the post of the Army Chief of Staff, and to that of General Otozo Yamada who was then the Inspector General of Military Education. Thus in conferences with the other two members of the Army Big Three, Tojo was always at a disadvantage. His relative unimportance was matched by the corresponding rise in power of his subordinates, especially Major General Akira Muto who remained as head of the Military Affairs Bureau. General Muto, together with Rear Admiral Keijun Oka and Cabinet Secretary Kenji Tomida, constituted the "secretariat" of the Liaison Conference. It was to replace the Four Ministers' or Five Ministers' Conference as a major policy making organ. The *de facto* power thus wielded by Muto could not be overlooked by Tojo. The replacement of the Ministers Conference with the Liaison Conference—which occured one week after the Konoye Cabinet was formed—did not in itself suggest the eclipse of the civil authority. It was rather an indication that the Army and Navy High Commands no longer trusted the ability of their service ministers to communicate their views to the civil branch of the government. It was not the civil authority, but the authority of the service ministers which suffered.[2]

In spite of the reduced status of the two service ministers-designate, the meeting held between Konoye, Matsuoka, Yoshida and Tojo on July 19 was able to produce an outline of basic policies. Although many of the features embodied in these policy decisions were not necessarily new, the conference—known as the Ogikubo conference— gave an illusion that differences between the two services as well as between the civil and military branches of government were ironed out. Prince Konoye took this as a green light for forming his cabinet.

On the matter of economic policy, the ministers agreed that the government was to be given unlimited power in the control of war economy but was not to rule over matters connected with military supplies. On diplomacy, the Axis ties between Japan, Germany, and Italy were to be strengthened to aid Japan in its pursuit for the new order in East Asia. A non-aggression pact with the Soviet Union was sought but combat readiness against that nation was to be maintained at all times. "Appropriate steps" were to be taken in order to incorporate in the new order the colonies maintained by England, France, Holland, and Portugal in East Asia. Though Japan would avoid unnecesary "friction with the United States, if and when the United States should resort to active intervention in Japan's new order, Japan would resolve to expel such an intervention." On the China policy, the ministers agreed to leave the door open for direct negotiations with Chungking, provided the latter would consent to sign a mutual defense pact, to establish a common Far Eastern economic bloc, to abandon anti-Japanese activities, to pledge no further act of war, and to accept the minimum conditions on anti-Comintern activities. As to the possible merger of the Nanking and Chungking regimes, Japan would treat it as a purely domestic question for China. The ministers also approved a plan for establishing a one-political-party system in Japan. This last item, incidentally, was the only question not taken up by the Yonai Cabinet.[3]

Conspicuously a finance-minister designate was absent from the Ogikubo conference. This suggested that Japan's financial policy was no longer independent of military exigencies. It was obvious that the Finance Ministry under the Second Konoye Cabinet was not going to be the stronghold of civilian power it had once been. Nor would there be a finance minister whose stature would be comparable to that of Ikeda who served in the First Konoye Cabinet.

Nominations of other ministers followed after the four ministers reached their basic agreement. The post of Finance Minister was given to Isao Kawada, a bureaucrat who once served as Cabinet Secretary. Akira Kazami, who was Konoye's political lieutenant in the one-party movement and who was the Cabinet Secretary during the First Konoye Cabinet, became Minister of Legal Administration. A newspaperman by profession, Kazami had hardly any legal training or judicial experience to speak of, and his appointment was completely unexpected. Ichizo Kobayashi, President of the Tokyo Electricity

Control Board, became Minister of Commerce and Industry. Another important addition to the Cabinet was Naoki Hoshino, Cabinet Secretary of the Manchukuo Government, who actually controlled the government operations of that country. Hoshino became President of the Government Planning Board, ranking as Minister without Portfolio.

One thing that could not escape observers was that the Cabinet contained many members who had spent their mature lives in Manchukuo. War Minister Tojo once served as Chief of Staff in the Kwantung Army. Matsuoka was President of the South Manchurian Railway. Vice Minister of Commerce and Industry, Nobusuke Kishi also rose to fame in the service of the Manchukuo Government. Hoshino was the power behind the Manchukuo Cabinet. More than anyone else he was responsible for the success of a controlled economy in Manchukuo. These men could transplant the philosophy they acquired in Manchuria to Japan proper. That philosophy in practice was tight military control and government regulated economy. Could Hoshino really make Japan's economy in the image of Manchukuo to prepare the country for war readiness? How would Matsuoka's presence affect the future of the Empire? All of these questions were to be answered shortly when these men pushed their way in an unprecedented haste to remake the country.

One "Party" System in Japan. Establishing the Taiseiyokusankai, or the Association to Support the Imperial Rule, was one of the first major steps Prince Konoye undertook as Premier. Back in May 26, 1940, Prince Konoye, Marquis Kido and Count Arima met in private to design the political future of their country. They agreed that it would not be long before the premiership would fall on Prince Konoye and therefore it was imperative for them to be prepared for that occasion. Prince Konoye's prior experience with political parties had been none too favorable. Despite the national emergency that existed, the parties resorted to "obstructionist" tactics during the time Prince Konoye headed his first Cabinet. This he was determined to avoid at all costs in the future. He wanted existing parties to merge under his leadership, and if he should fail in this first objective, he would then proceed to organize a party of his own. The three agreed that the new cabinet would rely heavily on whatever party Konoye could organize for its membership. Ostensibly, the meeting was held in secret, but its contents conveniently leaked out.

Three days after the meeting took place, one of the leading members of the Minseito informed Kido that most of his fellow party mem-

bers would agree to dissolve their party in order to merge with
Konoye's new party. In the meantime, Kido became the Lord Privy
Seal on June 1, and the new political movement lost an able lieutenant
and promoter. On June 24, Prince Konoye resigned his post as President of the Privy Council. This occured while Admiral Yonai's Cabinet
was still in power. In resigning, Prince Konoye did not hide his intent
of establishing a new political party, and stressed that the party should
become a vehicle in his overall movement for the new order. He
would wash his hands of self-serving political mergers which would use
the new party as a stepping stone to capture power for decadent old
political parties. The political parties were already at the verge of
disintegration, and Prince Konoye's statement only served to heap coals
on the fire.[4]

On the eve of the third anniversary of the Marco Polo Bridge
incident, the Social Mass Party dissolved itself to join Konoye's new
party movement. This came as a complete surprise to Prince Konoye.

"Don't miss the bus" became the slogan for many political party
leaders. This was true of the Social Mass Party. It had for some
time considered shifting its emphasis in order to accomodate the
wishes of the military. It was no secret that the military wanted a
one-party system for Japan, and the Social Mass Party drafted its
plank accordingly. In disbanding itself, the party hoped it could
find favor with the military and gain a new foothold in the new
political arena with the support of the militarists.

The only party to offer any measure of resistance was the Minseito. This was, however, forced upon them and was hardly a matter of
choice. Preliminary to the establishment of the new political system,
Prince Konoye drafted its plank and distributed it to ten odd people
who were concerned with the movement. The plank included a
clause stating that the main body of the Minseito should be left out
of Konoye's new party. One of those who was given the plank was
Sakurauchi, a close friend of Sakurai who was secretary to President
Machida of the Minseito. Since Sakurauchi always told Sakurai of
any political secrets, he was "specifically" instructed not to do so in
this instance. But Sakurauchi disobeyed the instructions anyway,
and Machida was promptly informed of what was going to take place.
Furor raged in the party circles, and Machida decided to start his
own reform movement which could outshine that of Prince Konoye.
This was a calculated risk. If all the parties were to merge and form a
new party, Machida's would be left alone and become impotent.
By starting his movement ahead of others, Machida could hope that

his party might be placed in a far more favorable bargaining position. As to his program, he adopted Konoye's plank in toto—which at that time was not yet published.

Kazami, chief lieutenant of Konoye's party movement appeared to welcome Machida's move. "After all, the nation had felt that no one but Mr. Konoye could rescue it from the peril of our times . . . And no one had exceeded Mr. Konoye in popularity," commented Kazami in his memoirs. "I secretly admired the main body of the Minseito for its courage in starting a reform movement to oppose Mr. Konoye's new party."

The leak through Sakurauchi to the Minseito was possibly a premeditated one. In any event, Machida's reform movement was short-lived. Within less than a week after the Second Konoye Cabinet was formed, Ryutaro Nagai, Minister of Communication under Konoye's first Cabinet, together with thirty-five of his followers resigned from the Minseito to join Konoye's movement. On July 26, the National League headed by Kenzo Adachi disbanded, and the main body of the Seiyukai headed by Chikuhei Nakajima followed suit four days later. The Minseito could not hold out much longer. After its offer of cooperation was rejected by Konoye, on August 14, it also went out of existence.

"Thus at that time, confusion in the political scene was very pronounced," recalled Kazami, "All politicians wanted to catch the new bus, and jumped out of the old one. But they could not find the new bus anywhere. Though they were hoping the bus would come some time, there was no assurance that the bus would take them in. On the other hand, they had destroyed with their own hands the bus they had been riding. It was not surprising to see how confused and disorderly the situation became."

Daily Kazami was swamped with requests for "seats" in Konoye's new political "bandwagon" from the old-time politicians. According to Kazami, this caused Konoye to shift his emphasis from establishing a new political party to forming a political non-party association. Many politicians were very much against such an association, but they were not vocal in their opposition for fear of not being included in the bandwagon.

The Taiseiyokusankai—the Association to Support the Imperial Rule —as it was called, came into being on October 12, 1940. It took the name of an association (kai) rather than a political party (to) and covered people of all walks of life, including civil servants, school teachers, university professors, monks, clergymen, women, and veterans, making an incohesive entity. All Cabinet ministers become ex-officio members of the inner group of the Association. Its financial affairs were taken care of by government appropriation. It was no longer possible to distinguish the government hierarchy from the hierarchy superimposed on the Association. As to policy matters, while the majority would have a voice in decision making, the President of the Association would remain the final arbitrator. There was an element of distinctive totalitarianism. Most revealing were two of the five basic principles under which the Association was to be operated:

"1. The Association shall deny democratic or socialistic ideas and shall not engage in political rivalry for the attainment of power. Nor shall it make party interest and self-serving deals the goals of the Association.

"2. The New Order shall repudiate democratic principles—legislative supremacy, rule by the majority, and equality of all people—and shall recognize that the leader is the supreme guide."[5]

Except for further reducing the Diet into a rubber stamp organization, the Taiseiyokusankai accomplished very little in promoting Prince Konoye's political ideals. It never attained the status enjoyed by the Nazi Party in Germany or the Fascist Party in Italy.

One positive aspect of the Taiseiyokusankai was that it gave the government unchallenged control of all possible channels of mass communication. The public was presumably included in the Association, and on the local level, prefectural governors took over the directorship of the Association in their respective prefectures. Each prefecture was divided into local districts consisting of cities and counties, which were broken into village units. They were subdivided into groups of households called neighborhood groups. These groups were to circulate official papers of the Taiseiyokusankai issued to them through the local unit. In addition, the neighborhood groups were required to hold monthly meetings, reading the directives sent from Tokyo and discussing their contents. Thus a directive issued in Tokyo in the name of the Association could reach the remotest village through a prefectural governor's desk in a matter of days. Where newspaper or radio or other means of communication failed to reach, the Association found a way to penetrate. The Taiseiyokusankai thus became a powerful weapon of mass communication. Its directives were not diluted by the interpretation of local politicians.

To the average Japanese, any directive sent was accepted in its entirety without question. They were to understand it, not to question it. And it was in this aspect alone that the Taiseiyokusankai should be remembered for its positive accomplishment. Yet this was not what

Prince Konoye had been striving for, and by not being able to hold control of the organization, unwittingly he played into the hands of the militarists. There was the vast network of mass communication into which the Army could infiltrate. Once the Army got hold of the organization, its control of the country would become complete.

Later Prince Konoye was to regret his misadventure. "I have traveled various paths in my thinking—socialism, nationalism, and fascism. And I made friends in various camps and schools of thought," he confided to Kenji Tomida, his Cabinet Secretary, "I have often compared myself with Prince Saionji. I now know he is greater than I. He was steadfast in his belief in liberalism and parliamentarianism. I wanted to save Japan from becoming a Nazi nation. Instead, I made a complete mess of the Taiseiyokusankai. In retrospect, the old Prince's belief in political parties was much better. Perhaps there is no better political formula than to let rival parties contend."⁶

CHAPTER VIII

THE TRIPARTITE PACT

Decision to Align with Germany. If the Gallup poll had been taken on September 27, 1940, an overwhelming majority of the Japanese public would have, in all likelihood, applauded the Government's latest "diplomatic triumph," the conclusion of the Tripartite Pact. The press had been daily reporting the victories of Germany while giving little or no account of the advantages enjoyed by England in the Battle of Britain. For the public, the war was already won by Hitler's Third Reich, and the British capitulation was only a matter of time. It would have been plain folly for the government not to hitch Japan's wagon onto Germany's rising star.

The Second Konoye Cabinet was publicly committed "to the advancement of the national fortune by taking a farsighted view of the drastic changes in the international situation and by formulating both constructive and flexible measures to meet these changes." The conclusion of the pact with Germany and Italy was indeed one of such constructive steps. Its future success, however, would depend entirely on how it could be flexibly employed to cope with the changing international situations.

The main architect of this Axis-centered policy was Yosuke Matsuoka, the brilliant but enigmatic Foreign Minister. There were some in the Cabinet—including Prince Konoye and Navy Minister Yoshida—who were convinced of the desirability of a pact with Germany but were fearful that a conflict might arise with the United States as a result. To this, Matsuoka forcefully replied that the pact would be designed to keep the United States neutral for its own benefit. He contended that the pact would deter the United States from further involvement in China and in the European War, and would leave Japan free to defeat China. In his view, a firm front towards the United States would be preferable to a policy of appeasement. Such a stand would not only enhance Japan's prestige abroad but also enable Japan to gain further concessions from the western powers. Matsuoka was a graduate of Oregon University law school. And if anyone still entertained any misgivings about the proposed pact, he was willing to defer them to Matsuoka's superior knowledge of the United States.

The Cabinet—after the two meetings on July 26 and 27, 1940—allowed Matsuoka to conduct singlehandedly alliance negotiations with Germany at an opportune moment, declaring that they trusted in the Foreign Minister's "diplomatic skills." The net effect was that at the end of July 1940, Matsuoka had the kind of power that none of his immediate predecessors had possessed—namely the power to conduct foreign policy without interference from the Army High Command. On August 1, Matsuoka invited German Ambassador Ott for tea and sounded out Germany's reaction to a possible alliance.

Japan's post-war contention that the alliance was a defensive one designed to keep the United States out of war finds its support in this initial meeting. Matsuoka told Ott that the center of world civilization would gravitate toward the Pacific Ocean and both Japan and the United States would play predominant parts in it. He could not bear the thought of seeing the two powers fighting against one another hinting that even after the proposed alliance with Germany were concluded, Japan might still come into an understanding with the United States.

Ott was none too responsive to Matsuoka's advances. His reluctance was easy to understand. An offer of an alliance in the hour of German victory was hardly a welcome one. Furthermore, Berlin was annoyed by Tokyo's persistent request that the former support the latter's demands over French Indo-China. The loyalty of French Africa to Vichy was by no means certain, and any unwarranted pressure by Berlin on Vichy might induce French Africa to join de Gaulle's Free French Movement. In fact, Germany rendered no support to Japan's French Indo-China claims during the months of August and September. On Matsuoka's feeler for an alliance, the Wilhelmstrasse was conspicuously silent for several weeks. This the impatient Matsuoka had to endure. Ambassador Kurusu in Berlin was instructed to approach Ribbentrop to convince him of the desirability of an alliance, but it was to be made discreetly and as the Ambassador's private opinion.

Thus on August 23, when news of the despatch of General Heinrich Stahmer as Ribbentrop's personal representative reached Tokyo, Matsuoka was greatly relieved. It was almost certain that Stahmer would ask for an alliance which would involve military commitment. Tokyo was ill prepared because it was still bound by prior decisions that it could not agree to an alliance which would lead to a war against the United States. The Navy had consistently maintained that it was not ready to shoulder the burden of war against the United States and the alliance should be confined to economic assistance.

Stahmer's despatch forced the Konoye Cabinet to take up a more definite position. On September 4 Konoye, Matsuoka, Tojo, and Sumiyama, Vice Minister of Navy who was substituting for Yoshida in the latter's illness, agreed that unless Japan was willing to make a military commitment, it would be impossible to talk with Germany and Italy. Since it was unlikely that Germany would request military operations against Great Britain, the United States would automatically become the object of the new alignment concluded by the Axis powers. It was a policy of containment against the United States. The memorandum of agreement between the four ministers read in part that Japan and Germany would "mutually cooperate in order not to allow the United States to interfere in regions other than the Western Hemisphere and the United States possessions." [1]

The four ministers planned their world strategy in terms of geopolitics. In their views the world of tomorrow would be divided into four power blocs, one headed by Japan in Asia, one by Germany and Italy in Europe and Africa, one by Russia, and one by the United States in the Western Hemisphere.

The primary objective of the alliance was the establishment of "Japan's sphere of living for the construction of a Greater East Asia New Order." The regions were to comprise "the former German Islands under mandate, French Indo-China and Pacific Islands, Thailand, British Malaya, British Borneo, Dutch East Indies, Burma, Australia, New Zealand, India, etc., with Japan, Manchukuo and China as the backbone." To this end, though, German acquiescence was necessary. The Japanese Foreign Office had been receiving disquieting reports. Consul General Yamaji from Vienna advised that Germany was seriously considering colonization of Sumatra and Java, the two most important islands of the Dutch East Indies. Special envoy Sato suggested that German designs might not be confined to the Dutch East Indies alone but were likely to include French Indo-China as well. Germany's refusal to intervene in favor of Japan in the current French Indo-China dispute served to confirm the worst of fears that Germany intended to replace England and other powers as colonial master in the Far East. It was not surprising that the four ministers stressed "mutual recognition" in each other's sphere of interest. This was the recurring theme during the remainder of the negotiations. It would have the effect of pre-empting the entire Far East as Japan's exclusive sphere of interest without Germany.

Another hurdle Japan had to face was the threat from Soviet Russia. But there the proposed alliance seemed to be the logical answer. By aligning with Germany's might, Japan felt that Russia could be checked. Japan would consider entering into a grand alliance encompassing four powers, Japan, Germany, Italy and Russia. For this purpose, Japan was prepared to assign a portion of the Middle East—e. g., the Gulf of Persia—as Russia's sphere of influence. However, the fundamental distrust of Russia was still present. While desiring cooperation with Soviet Russia, the Foreign, War and Navy Ministries agreed in their policy papers that if one of the powers in the Tripartite Pact were involved in a conflict with Soviet Russia, other members would immediately take appropriate action along the lines contained in the secret agreement of the Anti-Comintern Pact.

On September 5, a day after the four ministers conferred, Navy Minister Yoshida resigned, stating poor health as the reason. This was hardly of any persuasive value since there were clear policy differences. Yoshida had never endorsed an alliance which would actually involve the Navy in a war against the United States. The decisions of September 4 were clearly contrary to the position of the Navy which he represented. Yoshida's resignation removed from the Japanese political scene the last remaining opposition against an alliance which would include military assistance. Admiral Koshiro Oikawa who succeeded Yoshida was more favorably disposed toward the alliance and for political reasons did not actively oppose it. The way was paved for negotiations between Matsuoka and Stahmer.

Soviet Russia Matsuoka's Primary Target. Stahmer arrived in Tokyo on September 7 under instructions not to confer with anyone but Matsuoka. He had two trump cards he could offer. The first was Germany's willingness to allow Japan and the United States to reach an understanding. The second was Germany's assurance that it would become a broker for betterment of Japanese-Soviet relations.

At their first meeting, Matsuoka took an exceptional liking for the energetic secret emissary. "He has a keen mind," wrote the Foreign Minister while still talking to him in one of the meetings. With the portly Ambassador Ott listening intently, Stahmer gave a succinct account of his mission:[2]

"Germany does not want the present conflict to develop into a World War, and wishes to bring it to termination as quickly as possible. It wants the United States to stay out.

"What it wishes of Japan is to have Japan play the role of restraining and preventing the U.S. from entering the war at all costs."

These statements were accompanied by assurance that Germany did
not look for Japan's military assistance in connection with its war with
England, and that Germany would "make use of every means in its
power to prevent a clash between the United States and Japan, and
even to improve the relations between the two, if it were humanly
possible."

On the future of the Japanese-Soviet relations, Stahmer saw "no
insurmountable obstacle in the path" toward a rapprochement. He
told Matsuoka that contrary to the British propaganda "German-
Soviet relations are good," and it was better to reach agreement between Germany, Italy, and Japan first before approaching Soviet
Russia. This did not impress Matsuoka. "It is not the intention of
the Imperial Government to enter into a four power pact including
Japan, Germany, Italy, and Soviet Russia," he flatly stated. For the
time being, Japan would stand to gain by maintaining friendly relations with Soviet Russia. "But we must realize that Soviet Russia
could be left as a great power after the conclusion of the European
war. It would thus become a menace to the new order in East Asia.
Japan and Germany should stand together and find a common policy
against Russia." [3]

Matsuoka also suggested that if one of the contracting powers were
involved in a conflict with Soviet Russia, the other party should not
only refrain from aiding Russia, but also immediately come into consultation to discuss appropriate measures to be taken. Matsuoka was
in effect saying that the Tripartite Pact should be a logical extention
of the Anti-Comintern Pact on which the three powers had previously
agreed. Significantly enough, in his discussions with Stahmer, Matsuoka did not follow closely the decisions reached at the Four
Ministers' Conference of September 4. Instead, he relied heavily on
the paper drafted by policy officers of the Ministries of War, Navy
and Foreign Affairs on August 7. This paper was almost a verbatim
reproduction of the decisions reached by a similar body under the
Yonai Cabinet. It did not name the potential enemy as did the Four
Ministers' Conference, and gave the Foreign Minister wide discretionary power to draft the actual text of the alliance. Matsuoka's departure from the decisions of September 4 was not accidental. He trusted
in his own sagacity and skill as a diplomat more than in the collective
wisdom of his cabinet colleagues.

Matsuoka's desire to make Soviet Russia the primary target of the proposed alliance stemmed partly from his belief that the United States would not resort to force to prevent Japan from establishing its new order. Japan would come to the aid of Germany if the latter became involved in a war against the United States. But Matsuoka thought this was unlikely. The primary objective of the alliance was to eliminate the possibility of American intervention in Europe and Asia. Japan alone was too weak to perform this task, and so was Germany. But the powerful combination of the two would effectively counterbalance the threat posed by the United States.[4] So confident was Matsuoka of the efficacy of the proposed alliance that he even predicted that the Western Hemisphere bloc led by the United States would eventually become a good neighbor of the East Asian Co-Prosperity Area.

An agreement which was brief and flexible enough to allow different interpretations was the ideal of Matsuoka. Thus his original proposals to Stahmer consisted of the following:

"Article 1. Japan recognizes and respects the leadership of Germany and Italy in the establishment of a new order in Europe.

"Article 2. Germany and Italy recognize and respect the leadership of Japan in the establishment of a new order in Greater East Asia.

"Article 3. Japan, Germany and Italy agree to cooperate in their efforts on the aforesaid lines. They further undertake to consult one another on an appropriate and valid means to eliminate and conquer any hindrances that might be presented before them.

"Article 4. The Governments of Japan, Germany, and Italy, considering it as the condition precedent of any lasting peace that all nations of the world be given each its own proper place, have decided to stand by and cooperate with one another with regard to their efforts in establishing and maintaining a new order of things calculated to promote the mutual prosperity of the peoples concerned."

Matsuoka did not delve into the question of military cooperation. Nor did he mention economic or political cooperation. Stahmer had precise knowledge of what the Japanese High Command wanted, and Matsuoka's silence on these key issues was somewhat perplexing. But without pursuing the matter any further he decided to withdraw for the day. The end result of the first day's meeting could be described as both parties having "reached substantial agreement," in diplomatic parlance. The only concrete agreement that the two had was the exclusion of Italy from the negotiating table. This was quite satisfactory to Matsuoka since he thought of the objective of the alliance only in terms of cooperation with Germany.

On the next day Stahmer presented his own draft which generally corresponded with Matsuoka's draft, evidencing Stahmer's eagerness to accommodate. However, he offered a different Article 3: "Japan, Germany and Italy agree to cooperate in their efforts on the aforesaid lines. They further undertake to assist one another with all political, economic and military means when one of the three powers concerned is attacked by a power at present not involved in the European war or in the Japanese-Chinese conflict."

This version would have made the United States and Soviet Russia as potential enemies without expressly naming them. Matsuoka's version would have been noncommittal as far as designation of a potential enemy was concerned. The German version was apparently the minimum condition that the Third Reich expected to exact from Japan. Ribbentrop even suggested that the words "either openly or covertly" should be inserted after the word "attacked" in the above quoted article, broadening its application. He explained that this article would come into play if the United States leased Singapore from Great Britain or occupied some of the Mediterranean islands, for such an action would constitute a covert attack. This proposal was immediately rejected by Matsuoka. Stahmer, speaking on behalf of Ribbentrop, did not take this point too seriously. In fact, he might have offered it as a bargaining point, ready to concede if it were pressed, and gaining another concession from Japan. The minutes of their negotiations reveal that after the rejection of Ribbentrop's proposal, Matsuoka readily accepted two additional clauses:

"Article 5. Japan, Germany and Italy agree that the aforesaid terms do not in any way affect the present political status between the three aforementioned powers and Soviet Russia.

"Article 6. Japan, Germany and Italy will without delay conclude a treaty laying down the details of the application of the aforesaid terms."

Later Matsuoka told the Privy Council that he felt compelled to accept Article 5 lest the Soviet Union think that it was one of the countries to which the provisions for military assistance under Article 3 would apply. "During the time we are building up the New Order, we can ill afford to let the Soviet Union suspect that we are their enemies," explained the Foreign Minister. "By placating the Soviet Union, we hope it will not effect a rapprochement with the United States."

According to Dr. Yoshie Saito, Matsuoka's adviser who was the only one consulted during these negotiations, the Foreign Minister wanted to make it certain that the text of the alliance would be worded so it

would permit Japan's withdrawal from the alliance in case it failed
to prevent the United States from entering the war. He also wanted
the alliance to indicate clearly that it was only defensive in nature.[5]
But in the final hour of negotiations, Matsuoka apparently yielded to
the German demand that the alliance was primarily an anti-American
one. After only three days of negotiations, the Reich's special emissary
and Japan's Foreign Minister hastily reached an agreement.

It was a diplomatic *Blitzkrieg*. No staff consultation was ever made.
This was partly due to security reasons and partly due to the lack of
support of Matsuoka by rank-and-file career officers. When Matsuoka
first assumed office, he fired some forty ambassadors and ministers
en masse in a sweep called the "Matsuoka Hurricane." This brought
enmity from his staff members, and Matsuoka was not in a position
to confide in them or receive their unfaltering support. Matsuoka
also feared excessive participation by Shiratori, his other foreign policy
adviser, which might change the course of his negotiations. Shiratori,
the former ambassador to Rome and an avowed champion of Axis
cooperation, was installed as foreign policy adviser at the behest of
the Army. Once the secret was imparted to the Army through Shiratori, pressure would be applied on the Foreign Office to make the alliance an out-and-out anti-western instrument. Furthermore, Matsuoka
was filled with personal ambition, and wanted to use his success as
Foreign Minister as a stepping stone to premiership. To do so he
had to assume full control of foreign policy and disallow the Army's
persistent interference. He was always ahead of the Army in the
conduct of foreign affairs, and for a while it looked as though the
civilians would have the final word in foreign policy decisions. General
Muto who previously declared that the Army would destroy Konoye
and Matsuoka "if the alliance were not signed," quickly came to the
praise of Matsuoka.

The final text of the alliance as agreed by Stahmer and Matsuoka
was not radically different from the six articles previously discussed.
The pact drafted without the benefit of careful staff work left the
mark of its haste. The very ambiguities Matsuoka wanted to employ
to Japan's advantage proved to be otherwise. As time passed, Japan
was to find that it was inextricably woven into the Axis structure, yet
could not reap the fancied advantages.

The theory that Matsuoka had a free rein in negotiating the alliance
is reinforced by the fact that by September 14, only three days after
Matsuoka concluded his talks with Stahmer, Matsuoka's version was
accepted by the Army and Navy without alteration. This was re-

markable since Matsuoka did not follow closely the decisions of September 4 reached by the Four Ministers' Conference, and since Matsuoka concluded the alliance negotiations without consulting representatives of the two service ministries. In fact, the Army and Navy ironed out their differences along the lines suggested by Matsuoka, with War Minister Tojo telling Lord Privy Seal Kido that there was no longer any difference existing on the alliance question and the Throne should be so informed.

Italy was notified of the pending alliance on September 26, but immediately replied that it would accede to the terms already agreed upon by Japan and Germany. On September 27, 1940, the Tripartite Pact was formally signed in Berlin. For this purpose, an English text was employed since English was used in the negotiations and the texts in the three countries' languages were still unavailable. In Tokyo, Matsuoka held a simultaneous celebration of the signing of the pact. Through the trans-continental telephone provided for the occasion, he was kept informed of the actual proceedings in Berlin. The jovial Ribbentrop invited Matsuoka to pay a state visit to Berlin in the near future.

An imperial rescript was issued on that day, prodding the nation with the new responsibility that Japan undertook by signing the pact. Thus was placed the prestige of the Throne behind the pact, effectively silencing any possible opposition to it. Ambassador Grew who had been trying to "consider the event from every angle," came to the conclusion that "the primary aim of the alliance" was against the United States.[6]

Japan's Reasons for Concluding the Alliance. Why did Matsuoka, a self-professed pro-American, agreed to a pact which might be applied against the United States? To view the matter in proper perspective, it must be realized that Japan of 1940 had an unshakable belief in the ultimate victory of Germany. From this belief, it followed that Japan needed to align with a victorious power in order to strengthen its international standing, and to reach an agreement with Germany before advancing southward, lest Germany claim these regions for itself. The relations with the United States showed little or no hope of betterment, and the improved international situations resulting from the alliance might offset it. There was also a remote possibility that the improved situation might help Japan solve its stalemate in China. The Army had found the might of Soviet Russia unchallengable, and a pact against it impractical. The domestic pressure made it impossible for anyone to conclude an alliance of the kind Matsuoka first envisaged.

The fall of France was concrete evidence that Germany would win the war, wrote a policy guidance paper in the Foreign Office. "Disintegration of the British Empire is inevitable," it continued. "Even if Great Britain would resort to a prolonged war with the aid of the United States, it could not possibly hope to eliminate the progress made toward the establishment of the new order in Europe by Germany and Italy."

A similar conviction explained Matsuoka's Herculian effort to conclude the pact. In Matsuoka's own words, never before in the history of modern Japan, had the country become so "weakened and isolated." The country was exhausted by the China Incident, and the economic pressure applied by the United States was beginning to be felt. Under these circumstances, if Japan tried to change its foreign policy, it would only lead to "appeasement without honor." To turn the scales in its favor, Japan had to rely on the power of another country. Matsuoka confided to Saito that Germany was the power on whose coat-tail he intended to ride, though he admitted that alignment with Italy and Soviet Russia might also become necessary.[7]

Closely connected with the question of the shift in its foreign policy was the question of the South Sea regions. From time to time, Japan had declared its keen interest in these regions by stating that the European conflict should not spread to these regions. "The South Sea regions are not only within the economic sphere of the empire, but also an integral part of Japan's life-line essential to the establishment of its self-sufficient defense structure," said the policy guidance paper. The main hindrance to Japan's ambition—the British and French influence—had gone, and as to the United States, it would not fight against Japan as long as there was a war in Europe. On the basis of these observations, the policy planners concluded that the most vital problem facing Japan was acknowledgment by Germany and Italy of Japan's leadership in the South Sea regions. The first two articles of the pact, drafted by Matsuoka, were widely regarded as the Foreign Minister's great victory. They seemed to amount to a *carte blanche* assuring Japan possession of the vast former colonies of England, France, and the Netherlands. For the Germans who lacked a modern navy, possession of overseas colonies was purely academic. They were more practical minded and apparently felt that the promise as contained in the pact did not amount to much in any event. To show further their generosity, Ambassador Ott formally declared that the former mandated islands were deemed lawfully ceded to Japan by Germany. As to the "equitable compensation" for the islands, General Ott suggested that six bags full of coffee would suffice. But behind the show of generosity was the implied threat uttered by General Ott prior to the conclusion of the pact. "If Japan refuses to align with Germany," said Ott, "Germany might quickly conclude a peace treaty with Great Britain and take possession of the South Sea regions." And this was the very reason Japan was compelled to act fast, Matsuoka explained to the Privy Council.

Had the Japanese Navy been more realistic in evaluating its own strength against any potential threat from the Germany Navy, or had the Foreign Office correctly appraised the current situation by finding that the Churchill Government was determined to continue fighting, the outcome might have been different. But the stumbling block was their blind faith in Germany's invincibility.

This blind faith was matched in degree by the contempt Japan felt toward the United States. Both the Foreign Office and its Minister discounted the likelihood of America's participation in the war. The presidential election was only about seven weeks away, and there was a possibility that a change in American foreign policy might occur. Wendell Wilkie's heated campaign was treated with excellent coverage by the Japanese press, and the candidate himself was given a better than even chance of winning. There was a way in which Japan could hope to influence the outcome of the American election, the Foreign Office figured. Americans did not desire to go to war, nor would they vote for a man who was seeking his third term. If Japan's attitude were softened, it would indicate to the American voters that the foreign policy pursued by the Roosevelt Administration was correct. On the other hand, if Japan took a firm stand and negotiated from a position of strength, its attitude might touch a responsive chord in some of the American voters, notably the isolationists. To this Matsuoka hopefully added that there were twenty million Americans of German descent who occupied important positions in American society. By aligning with Germany, Japan could enlist their support in influencing American foreign policy.

The Foreign Office had long since abandoned the hope of better relations with the United States. As long as Japan was engaged in the China conflict, it was clear that the United States would not renew or renegotiate the commercial treaty. Here again a firm resolve seemed to be the logical answer while the policy of appeasement was not. The recently decreed U. S. embargo of scrap iron served to fortify this view. In the past, appeasement seemed to have brought only failure. Had Hitler not done remarkably well in Munich? Did it not show weakness of democracy as such? These questions found resounding echoes in the recent examples of Japan's own Abe and Yonai Cabinets. Their soft policy toward the United States had provided nothing but frustration. During the tenure of the Yonai Cabinet, Japan started preliminary talks with the Dutch East Indies Government which brought forth no results. This was indicative of the futility of the policy of peaceful penetration. Furthermore, the Foreign Office suspected encouragement by the United States responsible for the stubborn resistance of the East Indies Government. If one doubted the wisdom of a bold policy and alignment with Germany, he would still have to concede that it was the only remaining alternative and hope for Japan. The Konoye Cabinet had promised a radical shift in foreign policy. The Cabinet's very existence was dependent on the support and goodwill of the Army. On the face of it, the alliance was a domestically attractive and externally feasible solution to Japan's problems.

The desirability of adjusting relations with Soviet Russia was also explained in terms of its possible effect on Japanese-American relations. The exclusion from the application of the alliance as provided in Article 5 was intended to avoid a possible repprochement between Russia and the United States, Matsuoka told the Privy Council. On Japan's part, its rapprochement with Soviet Russia would be based on a sheer Machiavellian calculation. Japan wanted to adjust its relations with Russia in order to negotiate with the United States from the position of strength. But once the Russians served Japan's purpose, Japan and Germany should join their forces to curtail any further extension of Russian influence. This policy was consistent with the Army's desire. The Army, while eager to talk business with the Russians, had strengthened its tactical position in the Manchurian border facing Russia. A revealing story was told by Dr. Saito, who shortly after the conclusion of the Tripartite Pact, accepted the position of chief consultant of the South Manchurian Railway Company. He was amazed to see a large segment of the company devoted to extensive research work which did not concern the actual operation of the company. Later he was confidentially informed by a General that the research staff who was under the company's payroll was engaged in a strategic survey, preparing for an eventual war against Soviet Russia.

Another factor that had to be considered was Japan's unfamiliarity with the current status of Russo-German relations. The two countries seemed to be on cordial terms, and Japan feared that Germany might use Soviet Russia to check Japan's southward advance by aligning together and letting the latter attack Japan from the rear. The very thought of this possibility made Matsuoka more amenable to the suggestion of concluding a pact directed against the United States rather than against the Soviet Union. Yet in Matsuoka's mind friendly relations with the Soviet Union could not and should not last more than a couple of years. "Even if the relations between Japan and Soviet Russia were adjusted," commented the Foreign Minister to Privy Councillors. "I doubt they would last more than three years, and in any event after two years we should actively reconsider our position with regard to Soviet Russia." The Privy Councillors were further informed that in case Germany entered into a war against the Soviet Union despite the fact that the two countries had a non-aggression pact, Japan should come to Germany's aid notwithstanding the specific exclusion of Russia from the application of the Tripartite Alliance. On the other hand, if Japan became involved in a conflict with Russia, Germany would have to help Japan. Matsuoka was consistent in his belief that Russia could not be trusted. His explanations at the Privy Council served to clarify his later stand that Japan should go into war against Soviet Russia when Hitler opened fire against Stalin the following year.

In retrospect, the Tripartite Pact was an attempt by Japan to strengthen its international position by jumping onto the seemingly victorious German bandwagon. Japan staked its all in German victory and lost. It was also a diplomacy of bluff, a belief in Japan's ability to actuate the United States to come to terms once Japan attained the "exalted status" of an Axis partner. But most of the minus factors were still unknown, and in 1940 the pact gave every indication of success. In 1945, when the fortune of war was turning against Japan, and Germany was defeated, Prince Konoye was still of the opinion that "given the international situation of 1940, the conclusion of the Alliance was an appropriate, in fact, almost the only policy for Japan." After describing the necessity of aligning with Germany to offset the Anglo-American combination, the Prince registered his anger against critics of his policies: "I do not agree . . . with those who are imbued with pro-Anglo-Saxon sentiments that the Alliance with Germany in the autumn of 1940 was necessarily a dangerous policy for Japan. To argue so is an emotional argument, or else, one constructed after the German defeat has become certain."[8]

Nevertheless, the Prince deeply regretted German breach of faith and the inflexible stand taken by the Army which made changes in his policies impossible.

Matsuoka himself was perhaps sincere in saying that the Alliance was of a defensive nature. Yet he was the one who would have favored undoing what he had helped to create. On the day the attack on Pearl Harbor was announced, he was on his sick bed. Dr. Saito came to see him. There Matsuoka recanted: "The Tripartite Alliance was my worst mistake. I hoped to prevent the United States from entering the war. I wanted to adjust our relations with Soviet Russia through this Alliance. I hoped peace would be maintained and Japan would be placed in a secure position. Instead we see face to face the present calamity which indirectly resulted from the Alliance."

In tears, Matsuoka begged the forgiveness of his Emperor.[9]

CHAPTER IX

THE RUSSO-JAPANESE NEUTRALITY PACT

The Thorny Path to Moscow. The period immediately following the signing of the Tripartite Pact was a period of frustration. The scare tactics employed against the United States were calmly answered by its spokesman Cordell Hull in the following terms: "The reported agreement of alliance does not . . . substantially alter a situation which has existed for several years. . . . That such an agreement has been in process of conclusion has been known for some time, and that fact has been fully taken into account by the Government in the determining of this country's policies."[1]

On September 26, a day before signing of the Pact, the Administration in Washington had already imposed an embargo on all shipment of scrap iron and steel to Japan. This was followed by the decisions to grant additional loans to China, and to maintain indefinitely its Pacific Fleet at Pearl Harbor. These measures were calculated to counteract any of the possible advantages Japan might have reaped from the new alignment.

Of the three measures that Washington adopted, the harboring of the Pacific Fleet at Pearl Harbor made a long lasting impression. Realizing that the United States meant business, Admiral Yamamoto, Commander-in-Chief of the Combined Fleet, spoke of the folly of the new alignment. "If we are to fight against the United States, we might as well be prepared to fight the whole world," commented the Admiral. Predicting Japan's defeat, Yamamoto added that Tokyo would be burned to the ground three times, and the people would hang "poor Mr. Konoye." Prince Saionji lamented that "Takauji (the prototype of an arch traitor) had finally won." The new alignment had intensified rather than lessened Japan's lone-wolf position in international politics.

The Army was in a state of unrest and dissention. The one million men stationed in China had not seen action for months, and there was prospect of a long and dreary winter during which men could expect nothing but continuation of their trench life. Severe cases of tuberculosis were reported from various parts of China. The moral was generally low. Those who were eager for action took matters into their own hands. In South China, a small regiment waged a war of its own trying to cross the border to the British crown colony of Hong Kong. Another unit, which was designated to become a military observer group in Indo-China did not wait for the completion of preliminary arrangements, but opened a frontal attack, crossed the border, and established a beachhead in a most war-like manner. The Army High Command's stand was not to punish these unauthorized actions, but to promise that Tokyo was contemplating an even greater step forward. One of such examples was the assembling of landing cutters in Shanghai earmarked for the projected southward advance.

To implement this new policy, the Army named General Sugiyama to become Chief of General Staff, replacing His Royal Highness Prince Kanin. Sugiyama was personally not opposed to a rapprochement with Soviet Russia and was one of the few Generals not tainted by their former views against that country. His appointment thus signaled an era in which the Japanese Army actively sought an understanding with the Soviet Union in order to facilitate Japan's southward advance.

As to actual negotiations with Soviet Russia, Matsuoka preferred to defer them to Ribbentrop's better judgment, at least for the time being. In Matsuoka's views, Ribbentrop was sincere when he said that Germany was willing to become an "honest broker" between Japan and the Soviet Union. This would have also served the Führer's foreign policy aims. In 1940 Vichy was safely in Hitler's camp, and his influence extended over the Pyrénées to Franco's Spain. A stronger tie with the Soviet Union would have comlpeted his grand coalition against Great Britain, and Japan's accession to the Axis pact was an appropriate occasion to broach the subject.

The first step toward that goal was taken by Ribbentrop. On September 26, less than twenty-four hours before the actual signing of the Axis alliance, the German Chargé in Moscow told Molotov of the pending pact, requesting a much closer tie between the four countries. Molotov was unusually well informed of the alliance negotiations in Tokyo and was aware of the potentially dangerous anti-Soviet nature of the Pact. He gained insight into the nature of the Pact through the Sorge-Ozaki spy ring operating in Tokyo which was not uncovered until October 15, nearly three weeks after the signing of the Pact. Richard Sorge was a German newspaperman and a protégé of Ambassador Ott. His true identity as a Communist party member was not revealed since he had disguised it under his dual membership in the Nazi party. Hidemi Ozaki was a young China specialist who served as Konoye's informal adviser on Chinese questions.

With these two constantly supplying vital information, there was no doubt that Molotov knew precisely what Matsuoka wanted of Soviet Russia. Article 5 of the Pact which stated that the alliance would "not in any way affect" the existing relations between Soviet Russia and the three powers must have sounded strange or even comical to the Foreign Commissar. What Japan wanted was to align with Soviet Russia temporarily and after its aims had been served to join hands with Germany in crushing Russia. From Molotov's standpoint, there was certainly no reason for hastily entering into a pact with Japan. If one was actually executed, its benefits would largely go to Japan rather than to Russia. Japan needed Russia's benevolent neutrality to move southward, but Russia required no help from Japan in negotiating with Germany or with the western powers. Yet Molotov was a practical man, and Matsuoka could have gotten a non-aggression pact for a price. The failure to secure such a pact with Russia was not due to Matsuoka's inaction, but due to the worsening of relations between Germany and Russia.

The fall of France had upset the balance of power in Europe. It had come too fast and too swift for Russia's comfort. In the Balkans, tension had been developing. Around the time the Tripartite Pact was signed, Russia complained to Germany about the excessive number of German military staff officers in Romania, heretofore considered to be within Russia's sphere of influence. The Germans did not hesitate to continue shipment of arms to Finland, while neglecting to fulfil their outstanding commercial obligations toward Russia.

Indeed, it was these difficulties that caused Ribbentrop to write to Stalin urging the despatch of Molotov to Berlin. After reviewing the events following the Polish Campaign, and expressing his conviction that the British Empire would inevitably fall, Ribbentrop clearly indicated that he also wanted to discuss the Russo-Japanese relations in the forthcoming visit of Molotov. It was the "historical mission" of the four powers, averred Ribbentrop, "to direct the future development of their peoples into the right channels by delimitation of their interests on a world-wide scale."[2]

Molotov's visit to Berlin materialized on November 12, while Tokyo was busily celebrating the 2,600th anniversary of the founding of the Empire. Among the topics to be discussed by Ribbentrop and Molotov was: "To consider jointly how the countries of the Tripartite Pact could reach an agreement of some kind with the Soviet Union, expressing the Soviet Union's solidarity with the aim of the Tripartite Pact."

In his meeting with Molotov, Ribbentrop emphasized that he had consistently exerted pressure on Tokyo to promote a Russo-Japanese rapprochement. He assured Molotov that with regard to its *Lebensraum* policy, Japan was oriented not toward the East and North, but toward the South; thus little conflict of interest with Russia.

The last meeting of Molotov and Ribbentrop took place in the Reich Foreign Ministry's air raid shelter. There Ribbentrop submitted a draft of the proposed four power pact to his visitor. It included a declaration by Russia to the effect that it concurred in the aims of the Tripartite Pact; a provision that the four powers would undertake to respect each other's natural spheres of influence; and still another provision stating that the four powers would neither support nor join any combination of powers which was directed against one of the four powers. The accompanying two secret protocols assigned Southeast Asia as Japan's sphere of influence while leaving the territory south of the Soviet Union in the direction of the Indian Ocean as Russia's sphere of influence. Russia also would have gotten freedom of passage through the Turkish straits by revoking the Montreaux Convention.

These promises, from Russia's point of view, were unrealistic. Foreign Commissar Molotov's primary concern was pragmatic. He wanted to avoid an outright clash with Germany while strengthening Russia's hold on the Balkans and Finland. Nevertheless, when he left Berlin he gave the impression that he was sympathetic with the German proposals.

A blow to Ribbentrop's grandiose scheme came less than a fortnight after he and Molotov had their last extensive discusison. On November 26, Molotov told the German Ambassador that the Soviet Union would join the four power pact only if Germany would withdraw its troops from Finland; would allow Soviet Russia to establish military bases in the Bulgarian territory within the range of the Bosporus and the Dardanelles; and would recognize the area south of Batum and Baku in the general direction of the Persian Gulf as the center of Soviet aspirations. As to Japan, Russia would demand that Japan renounce its rights to concessions for coal and oil in Northern Sakhalin.

It must be noted that the price to be paid by Japan for the rapprochement was not too large, and Japan was prepared to pay that much in any event. On October 3, the Japanese Foreign Office drafted a policy guidance paper preparing for the forthcoming negotiations with Soviet Russia. It stated that Japan was prepared to renounce its fishery rights, and if necssary its rights in Northern Sakhalin, in return for a guaranted amount of oil import annually, and other financial concessions. Other conditions for the rapprochement included Soviet recognition of Manchukuo, cessation of aid to Chiang Kai-shek and recognition of Inner Mongolia, three Northern Chinese provinces, French Indo-China, and the Dutch East Indies as Japan's spheres of influence. In return Japan would recognize Soviet absorption of the Baltic states, permit the Chinese Communists to operate in the North-western provinces of Shensi, Kansu, and Ninghsia, and recognize Outer Mongolia, Sinkiang, Afganistan, and Persia as Russia's spheres of influence. The non-aggression pact was then to be followed by an extensive commercial agreement. The compact was also to provide for delimitation of the Manchukuo-Outer Mongolian borders, and for amicable settlement of disputes.[3] On the whole, the Japanese condi-tions as set forth in the policy paper were not unreasonable. If Japan and Soviet Russia proceeded independently of Germany, they could have possibly reached some understanding. But at this particular moment Japan wanted to employ "Germany's pressure over Russia."

For some time Soviet Russia watched Germany's growing influence in Eastern and Central Europe and in Scandinavia with apprehension. Molotov's November 26 note represented his realization that German and Soviet interests were mutually incompatible, and if further ac-commodations were to be made, the Soviet Union ought to be repaid for them abundantly. Germany's offer of a four-power pact provided him with an excellent pretext to advance his demands. Hitler took Molo-tov's latest demands with ill grace. His answer was Directive No. 21, better known as Operation Barbarossa, issued on December 18, 1940. This ordered the German armed forces to be "prepared to *crush Soviet Russia* in a quick campaign even before the conclusion of the war against England."[4]

The Japanese Foreign Office, without knowing the worsening of the Nazi-Soviet relations became increasingly impatient. It was some time before the Japanese fully realized that Germany could no longer serve as the "honest broker." But in the meantime, the alternative policy of negotiating directly with Russia gained momentum.

Impasse in China. One of the reasons which prevented Matsuoka from negotiating with Russia was his preoccupation with the Chinese question. Wang Ching-wei's government was established in Nanking in March 1940, and was eagerly awaiting its recognition by the Japanese government. Despite the fact that special envoy General Abe was at his post in Nanking to negotiate with Wang on the two countries' basic treaties, the matter dragged on for some time without producing any conclusive result.

With regard to China, the second Konoye Cabinet assumed dual responsibility. First, it was committed to end the China Incident at all cost, so Japan could employ the resources and manpower tied up in the China theatre for southward advance. To this end, direct negotiations with Chiang Kai-shek were inevitable. Second, it was also committed to the fostering of Wang Ching-wei's government. These two responsibilities were mutually irreconcilable. The matter was further complicated by the fact that a powerful segment of the Army stationed in China would not allow any other course of action but to recognize Wang's government as the only legitimate one in China. Should Japan proceed to negotiate with Chiang Kai-shek and forsake Wang? Or should Japan recognize Wang at the risk of ending the hope for permanent settlement? Thus Japan was immobilized when a quick decision was imperative.

China had long since been the Army's playground, and the China policy had been conducted by the Army rather than through the Foreign Office. But in the summer and fall of 1940 the Army could not present a united front. Matsuoka took advantage of this situation and secured Tojo's assurance that if the Army failed to conclude a peace treaty with Chungking by the middle of August, he should be permitted to conduct his own negotiations. On the other hand, Matsuoka was also given a deadline. If his efforts produced no result by October 1, then a basic treaty would be signed with Wang Ching-wei instead. It was a compromise move, but one highly advantageous to the Foreign Office. To pursue his "Operation Chungking," Matsuoka relied on his friend Chien Yung-ming, a Shanghai banking magnate, to serve as an intermediary. Chien had known Matsuoka while the latter was President of the South Manchurian Railway Company. Chien's connection with Chungking was reported to be excellent, and through him various proposals to Chiang Kai-shek were advanced. Details of Matsuoka's proposals were lost and little is known of what transpired. They included basic terms which provided for a truce by the end of 1940, and for the merger of the Chiang regime with the Wang government. As to the actual position Chiang was to hold in the new coalition government, Japan would let Wang and Chiang decide, since the matter was essentially a domestic problem for China.

Matsuoka added that Japan would not seek any territorial annexation or reparation. He would, however, insist on the stationing of Japanese troops in China on a "temporary" basis. Consul General

Tajiri in Hong Kong was also instructed to maintain informal contact with Chungking. In the meantime, concurrent negotiations were held with Wang Ching-wei. This was calculated to appease the strong sentiment in the Army that Wang should be supported. At the same time it was hoped that by holding concurrent negotiations, at least one of the regimes might become more amenable to accepting Japan's stringent conditions.

Matsuoka seemed to have boundless confidence in his ability to strike a bargain with Chiang Kai-shek. On October 7—after securing from the Army an extension of his deadline—he announced publicly that Japan would welcome China as its Axis partner, instead of having it "playing a role in the front line of European and American capitalism." Militarily Japan was in a more favorable position. In the summer of 1940 the Burma Road was temporarily closed, and Japan successfully occupied North French Indo-China. This meant that the two most vital routes providing supplies for Chiang Kai-shek were closed. The only route that remained open was the one from Soviet Russia, which was the least important of the three, because of its great distance. Time and again long range strategic bombers displayed their effectiveness against Chungking. It was clear that without foreign aid, Chiang Kai-shek could not long sustain Japan's repeated offensives. Intelligence reports indicated that both the Nationalist Fifth Central Committee meeting and the Seventh National Congress were overwhelmingly in favor of capitulation. Chiang Kai-shek was also confronted with the growing influence exerted by his communist allies. The New Eighth Route Army firmly grounded itself in North China both inside and outside the occupied area. The New Fourth Route Army attempted to attack the Nanking-Shanghai delta area so that the communists could establish a foothold in the key cities of Central China. The attempt was suppressed by General Ho Ying-chin, whose collaboration Wang secretly hoped to obtain. But there was a seed of internal discord, and it would seem to be to Chiang's advantage that he quickly sue for peace and prepare himself against the eventual conflict with the communists.

The effect of the Tripartite Pact on Chiang's mind is less clear. With insufficient intelligence forces to operate, Chiang was forever suspicious of the great powers' intentions. At times it looked as though the balance of power was shifting in favor of Japan, and the danger of a rapprochement between Japan and Russia was imminent. Yet in the end, the Tripartite Pact presented only a potential and inconsequential threat to the Generalissimo. To be effective, the Pact had to be translated into some positive terms—such as the result Japan had been desiring—the complete cessation of foreign aid to Chiang Kai-shek. This end could have been served if Russia agreed to the closing of its route. The new alignment, however, presented exactly the opposite effect. On October 17 the British Government announced that it had decided to reopen the Burma Road. While its strategic value was somewhat dubious, it was a psychological shot in the arm for the Generalissimo's war efforts.

Matsuoka had allowed only three weeks for his plan to succeed. When at the end of that period he found that his initial advances did not bring results, he turned to Germany. This probably accounted for Ribbentrop's informal discussions with the Chinese Ambassador during Molotov's visit to Berlin. Ribbentrop also sought Molotov's cooperation in bringing about a rapprochement between Japan and China.

Yet it was doubtful if Germany could have succeeded in its new mediation effort. For Generalissimo Chiang Kai-shek to embrace the offer of Germany, Japan's ally would have been tantamount to accepting the kiss of death. Pro-German feeling in China was negligible, while pro-western as well as pro-Soviet people occupied important positions in his government. Then there were the stringent terms suggested by the Japanese Army for Chiang's "capitulation."

The continuation of China's resistance against Japan was recognized by President Roosevelt as necessary for Great Britain's continued resistance against Germany, which in turn was essential to the United States security. This gave Chiang Kai-shek an opportunity to approach Washington with the idea of an alliance between China, the United States, and Great Britain as one measure which would effectively counteract the Axis-Tripartite Pact. The suggestion was gently turned down by Washington, but China received further promise of loans and other aid.[5] Altogether Chiang Kai-shek lost nothing as the result of Japan's alignment with Germany.

Recognition of Wang Ching-wei's government was, however, a nemesis to the Generalissimo. Aside from requesting the United States to prevent Japan from recognizing the Nanking regime, Chiang also skillfully maneuvered the Japanese into believing that he was prepared to talk terms with them, provided they would withdraw support from Wang Ching-wei. For instance, in Berlin, Chungking's Ambassador Chen Chieh told Ribbentrop that China would agree to a truce if Japan would withdraw its troops from China. When asked by Ribbentrop, he indicated that withdrawal need not be immediate but had to be established as a matter of principle. Furthermore, at Hong

Kong, the Japanese intelligence organ was told that Chiang Kai-shek sincerely desired peace and had already selected Hsu Shih-ying, a former minister to Japan, as the Chinese representative to negotiate truce terms, and that the Chinese Government was awaiting a similar appointment by the Japanese Government.[6] This information was puzzling to the Japanese Foreign Office, and Matsuoka rightly suspected that Chiang's offer might be a trap intended to forestall Japanese recognition of the Nanking regime. Yet, Matsuoka was determined to pursue his "Operation Chungking." This was even more necessary since recognition of the Wang regime would not of itself bring about the basic settlement Japan was seeking.

Matsuoka was supported in his decision by War Minister Tojo, but when word leaked out that Tokyo was going to steer clear of Wang Ching-wei in favor of peace negotiations with Chiang Kai-shek, the Army stationed in China became defiant. On October 23, special envoy General Abe hurriedly returned to Tokyo protesting such government action. Major General Kagesa, who was instrumental in inducing Wang to flee to Hanoi and in establishing a government of his own, also left Shanghai for Tokyo. Both Abe and Kagesa claimed that the offer made by Chungking was insincere, merely a subterfuge to delay Japan's recognition of Wang. Matsuoka, through his Vice Minister Ohashi, begged Abe to delay signing the treaty with Wang. But the old General threatened to resign from his post if the treaty were not signed as scheduled. The matter was brought to final arbitration at the Imperial Conference of November 13 which decided that Japan would sign a basic treaty with Wang without abandoning the hope of a direct settlement with Chungking.

On November 30, 1940, the basic treaty between Wang Ching-wei and Japan was signed in Nanking. The treaty gave Japan a "legal" basis for its "war-like operations" in China, as long as there was "a threat to the peace and well-being of the two nations" by the destructive activities of Communism. The basic treaty was accompanied by two secret agreements, two exchanges of notes, and a joint declaration of Japan, Manchukuo, and China. These documents made Wang's capitulation complete. Wang was forced to recognize Manchukuo as an independent nation; to allow stationing of Japanese troops in China indefinitely; to lease communication and transportation facilities for military use by the Japanese for the duration of the conflict; to establish "high priority anti-Comintern areas" in North China; to set up "special areas" in the Yangtze delta region, the Hainan Island, and Amoy and its vicinity; to pledge that China would conduct no foreign policies con-

trary to the spirit of the basic treaty; to allow *de facto* joint manage-
ment of the maritime customs and other tax collecting agencies; to
grant other economic concessions; and to promise hiring of Japanese
political advisers and technical experts. Wang was also to repay
Japanese citizens who suffered loss resulting from the China Incident.[7]

The signing of the basic treaty was hardly a jovial occasion for
either Tokyo or Nanking. For Wang Ching-wei the treaty meant
China's perpetual subjugation to the will of its imperial master. Matsuoka gave his consent to the signing of the treaty reluctantly, justify-
ing it only by saying that any further delay in the establishment of normal relations with Wang's government might endanger its existence.
Otherwise, informal negotiations with Chungking were carried out
until the very last moment. War Minister Tojo candidly admitted
that the basic treaty did not represent a permanent "settlement" of
the China Incident. "Even after the conclusion of this treaty," he
told the Privy Councillors, "we shall work toward total cessation of
hostilities, and shall continue to negotiate with Chungking with views
to bringing about the merger of the Wang and Chiang regimes." Tojo
hoped that this could be accomplished by the end of the year. Thereafter, Japan would abandon the idea of peace with Chungking and
would resort to a prolonged war. Matsuoka would have favored continuation of his Operation Chungking indefinitely even after the end
of 1940, if Wang would agree to such a diplomatic maneuver.

Without doubt, the basic treaty killed the chance of an overall settlement of the incident with Chungking. Chiang Kai-shek was aggrieved
by the establishment of a rival regime claiming loyalty and support of
the Chinese people. Prior to the basic treaty, informal contact had
been kept between Wang and Chiang. On occasions this contact
served as the main channel of information, allowing Japanese strategists
to map out their policies toward Chiang. Despite the fact that Chiang
expelled Wang from his membership in the Kuomintang Party, there
was no evidence of personal acrimony. As late as April 13, 1940,
a fortnight after Wang Ching-wei's return to Nanking, Chen Li-fu sent
a message urging Wang to abandon the establishment of a government
under the Japanese and rejoin Chiang in Chungking. Chen Li-fu, who
headed the CC clique, was Wang's personal friend and was also close
to Chiang Kai-shek. The tone of the message could be termed as
nothing but cordial.[8] Signing of the basic treaty quickly changed the
picture. It brought about the angriest denunciation yet to come out
of Chungking which was accompanied by a statement that China was
"determined to fight till the victory is won." It might have been a

self-convincing talk by a rejected regime. But at any rate Japan permanently closed the partially opened door. No peace movement in Chungking was possible thereafter, without being branded as a treasonable act.

Although normally sympathetic toward the Army, Marquis Kido was discouraged at the prospect of a prolonged war in China as a result of the Army's insistance on signing the basic treaty. He was compelled to tell the Emperor: "What we must be aware of is the compromise we allow to the extremists. The result has always been barren. We are now neither able to subdue our external enemy, nor in the position to restore our national strength."[9] The basic treaty with Wang was thus devoid of any constructive element. The extremists had gotten their way, only to find that they had won a battle, but not the war.

Journey to Berlin and Moscow. Once the China question was disposed of, even though quite unsatisfactorily, Matsuoka turned to the question of a rapprochement with the Soviet Union.

The failure of Germany to bring about a rapprochement between Japan and Soviet Russia gave Matsuoka a moment of rethinking. From Vienna, Minister Yamaji consistently and accurately reported the worsening of the Nazi-Soviet relations as the result of their discord over the Balkans. But from Berlin and Moscow, Ambassadors Oshima and Tatekawa reported the contrary. The Foreign Office generally discarded the seriousness of the Balkans situation. But Yamaji's reports were enough to cause doubt in the minds of policy-makers. Japan lacked an effective intelligence network, and it seemed desirable for the Foreign Minister to visit Berlin and Moscow in order to find out for himself what course Japan could chart with regard to these two countries.

Matsuoka apparently had two objectives in mind when he embarked on the journey. One was that he desired a rapprochement with the Soviet Union almost at any cost, except that he wanted no all-out alliance. The other was that he desired an escape clause in the Tripartite Pact, so that Japan could either gracefully withdraw from it or not be burdened with its responsibilities.

One of the aims of the Tripartite Pact on Japan's part was to receive information from Germany on the latest technological development. This was necessary for carrying out its plans for southward advance. However, due to the effective blockade imposed on Germany by the British Navy, the only means of direct communication was often through submarines. If the land route through Siberia were opened, Japan could import heavy machinery and other equipment which would be of immense value to Japan's defense build-up. Thus the Soviet Union's goodwill toward the parties of the Tripartite Pact was of paramount interest to Japan. Aside from this factor, it must be borne in mind that the very success of the Tripartite Pact actually depended on the attitude of the Soviet Union. If the three powers should succeed either in checking the influence of Russia in world politics, or in bringing it into the fold of the Tripartite powers, Japan would be in a much stronger position to bargain with the United States. On the other hand, a hostile Russia would mean an end to Japan's ambition of southward advance, as well as an indefinite postponement of a possible understanding with the United States. As far as Japan was concerned, Soviet Russia held the balance of power, and Matsuoka was prepared to sign a pact with Stalin with or without Hitler's consent.

A discretionary power much greater than normally accorded the head of the Foreign Office in the Army-dominated Japan was given to Matsuoka. In preparation for Matsuoka's forthcoming trip, Vice Foreign Minister Ohashi was ordered to draft a set of instructions for Matsuoka. This draft was then shown to the Prime Minister, War Minister and Navy Minister for their approval. Under normal circumstances, instructions of this nature would have been drafted by the three sub-Cabinet officers of the War, Navy, and Foreign Offices. The Liaison Conference met on February 3, 1941, and approved the Ohashi draft. It thus confirmed the views of the Foreign Office that Japan should be prepared to relinquish its oil concessions in Northern Sakhalin, and if necessary its fishery rights, in return for Russia's guarantee for shipment of 1,500,000 tons of crude oil annually for the next ten years.[10]

Yet it is misleading to assume that the journey was taken for the sole purpose of seeking a rapprochement with Soviet Russia, and that the "courtesy call" was merely a subterfuge to cover up the true intention. The political settlement with Russia would have true significance only if the existing ties with Germany were strengthened rather than weakened. If one of the reasons for taking the journey was to reach a political settlement with Russia, another reason was to iron out any possible differences existing between the Axis powers. Ambassador Ott telegraphed from Tokyo that Matsuoka intended to discuss diplomatic ways and means of keeping the United States out of war. This was to be done by strengthening the existing ties with Germany, and if this proved impractical, Matsuoka would consider undertaking a preventive attack on Singapore. On the first point, Ott was essentially correct. The February 3 Liaison Conference was even more specific in stating that Matsuoka should secure Germany's assurance that it would do its utmost in preventing the United States from entering the war. On the second point, Ott was badly mistaken. The February 3 Conference expressly denied the Foreign Minister power to commit his country to enter into the European conflict, and Matsuoka himself privately confided his unwillingness to attack Singapore. The February 3 Conference went even further. It suggested that Matsuoka obtain Germany's unqualified assurance that it would not request Japan's entry into the European War. While professing no desire to fight on Germany's side, the Conference nevertheless instructed Matsuoka to request German attack on Soviet Russia should the latter invade Manchuria. These self-contradictory positions suggest that in February 1941, Japan still regarded Soviet Russia as its primary enemy, and the Tripartite Pact as the chief instrument in containing Soviet advances and in guarding Japan's interests. As far as Japan was concerned, the Pact was not primarily directed against the United States. As to the proposed political settlement with the Soviet Union, it was a temporary self-serving experiment. In Matsuoka's mind, any pact he concluded with Russia could be discarded once it accomplished its purposes.

Personal considerations also played a part in prompting Matsuoka to visit Berlin and Moscow. Matsuoka had been manipulating to become prime minister. But in order to be nominated to that post, he had to prove to the court circles and to the military that he was a statesman of stature, not merely a crafty diplomat. The visit was ideally suited to accomplish this purpose. First, if he could bring about accord with Soviet Russia, and further strengthen the Axis ties, he would firmly establish himself as the greatest Foreign Minister Japan ever had. Second, the mere fact that he had personal contact with Hitler and Mussolini—two of the most idolized heroes in pre-war Japan—would have raised him up to the exalted status of a world re-known "statesman."

With pomp and fanfare, Matsuoka left Tokyo on March 12, 1941. The original plan was to go directly to Berlin, visiting Moscow only on his return trip. But on the morning of departure, the plan was suddenly changed, making Moscow Matsuoka's first stop. On March 24, Matsuoka had a meeting with Stalin and Molotov which lasted two hours. The Kremlin apparently attached great importance to the visit of the Japanese Foreign Minister and this convinced him that it was possible to conclude some kind of agreement with Soviet Russia. He was said to have presented to the Soviet leaders the "fundamental" issues confronting the two countries and the ways of eliminating existing differences. However, when Stalin wished to reply, Matsuoka asked him to withhold comment at that time. He preferred that Stalin give more thought to the subject and continue the conversation when he returned to Moscow. One area in which Japan was not well informed was the present status of German-Soviet relations. Matsuoka could determine this better after visiting Berlin. In the meantime, it was hoped that the procedure Matsuoka suggested might give Japan an upper hand in the next round of negotiations.

From evidence available today, it is clear that the Japanese Government did not discount the possibility of an eventual war between Soviet Russia and Germany when it was seeking an agreement with Russia. What Japan feared most was a rapprochement between the United States and the Soviet Union. British Ambassador Craigie had previously warned Matsuoka not to approach the Soviet Union. Matsuoka took Craigie's words as those representing Washington's views as well, and feared that an agreement between the United States and the Soviet Union might be in the offing. He thus wanted to forestall a move from the United States to the greater advantage of his own country.

Berlin was eagerly awaiting Matsuoka's arrival. On March 3 Hitler issued a directive which amounted to an agenda for Matsuoka's visit. In this, Hitler declared that it was paramount to the interests of the tripartite nations that Japan be drawn into conflict in East Asia at the earliest possible moment, and that Germany should allow economic and technical aid to flow to Japan and let it share Germany's experience in the war without demanding any compensation. This he thought was a sufficient inducement for Japan to enter the war. Hitler was confident that America could be kept out of war if Great Britain were quickly defeated. Japan could contribute to this end by occupying Singapore. However, Hitler was distrustful of the Japanese and ordered that Operation Barbarossa be kept secret from Matsuoka.

Matsuoka arrived in Berlin on March 26. The importance Germany attached to his visit was clearly shown in the reception accorded him by Hitler and Ribbentrop. Despite the unexpected revolt in Yugoslavia, Hitler found time to hold two long conferences with the visiting Foreign Minister. These were in addition to several other meetings Ribbentrop held with Matsuoka.

Well aware of Matsuoka's intention to conclude an agreement with the Soviet Union, Ribbentrop informed Matsuoka to the extent allowed by the Führer on German-Soviet relations. Matsuoka's impression that the relations between Germany and Russia had worsened was further confirmed by the following words of Hitler: "Germany had concluded well-known treaties with Russia, but much weightier than this was the fact that Germany had at her disposal in case of necessity some 160 to 180 divisions for defense against Russia."[11]

However, the discussions did not dwell on these matters. The prime concern for the German Foreign Office and the General Staff was to induce the Japanese to accept a share of responsibility in carrying out the war against England. "A quick attack on Singapore would be a very decisive factor in the speedy overthrow of England," said Ribbentrop to Matsuoka. The capture of Singapore would "perhaps be most likely to keep America out of the war, because the United States could scarcely risk sending its fleet into Japanese waters." After all, the aim of the Axis powers was to frighten "America into abandoning the course it had chosen and of keeping it out of the war."

Matsuoka was not endowed with the power to negotiate on the matters involving the supreme command, and the Reich Foreign Minister was well aware of it. This was evidenced by the fact that in the past the Germans preferred to talk to the Military Attaché or other military officers rather than to civilian representatives on matters pertaining to strategy. On the other hand, the continued insistence by the Germans on Japan's role in rendering the *coup de grâce* to England convinced Matsuoka that the Reich was ill-prepared to take an all-out assault against the British Isles.

Matsuoka talked in generalities without committing himself to specific actions. He assured Ribbentrop that Germany should not be misled by his words and acts which would show a friendly manner toward the English. He was "assuming that manner not only in order to soothe the British, but to mislead the pro-British and pro-American elements in Japan, until he should one day suddenly attack Singapore." Quoting a famous Japanese statesman who addressed the Navy at the outbreak of the Russo-Japanese war: "Open fire, and the nation will then be united," Matsuoka said the whole Japanese nation would be united at one stroke by the sudden attack on Singapore. "The declaration of war against England should follow" immediately, he declared.

Matsuoka played his game well. In return for these vague promises and assurances, Matsuoka was able to get the vital information he was seeking, that the relations between Soviet Russia and Germany had worsened. Ribbentrop, eager to persuade his visitor not to enter into any agreement with Soviet Russia, even gave the assurance that "Germany would immediately strike if Russia should undertake anything against Japan, and thereby keep Japan free in the rear with respect to Russia." This was another of the objectives Matsuoka was after, and he got it with no corresponding giving on Japan's part. If any credence is to be given to the words of Dr. Saito, Matsuoka's adviser and later his apologist, this was the critical moment in Matsuoka's thinking toward reorientation of the Japanese foreign policy. "If the Nazi-Soviet war became inevitable, the Tripartite Pact would be crippled and become dangerous to Japan," Matsuoka was to have said to Saito. "Thus, I decided to reconsider our approach to the Tripartite Pact."

At this point Matsuoka interrupted his conference with the Nazi leaders and paid a brief visit to Rome. He attached little significance to his meeting with Mussolini, and there is nothing worthy of mention. However the visit to the Vatican was a unique personal experience for Matsuoka.

Aside from "praying together" with the Pope for peace, Matsuoka sought to convince the Pontiff that Japan was not fighting against the Chinese or China, but only against Bolshevism, which was threatening to spread over China and the whole Far East. It was regrettable that the United States and England stood on the side of Bolshevism. The meeting with the Pope produced no visible effect on the conduct of foreign policy. However, so impressed was Matsuoka by Pius XII that he willed to be buried by Catholic rites, despite the fact that he maintained nominal membership in a Methodist church.

The last conference between Hitler, Ribbentrop, and Matsuoka which was held after the latter's return from Rome was devoted to the matter of technical and scientific assistance Germany could give to Japan. Matsuoka told his hosts that Japan would particularly welcome information about U-boat warfare tactics. He impressed on Hitler that such assistance was vital to Japan's preparation for a possible war against the United States. On the matter of Singapore, Matsuoka urged his hosts to be discreet about it. He explained that opposition to the plan of attack on Singapore by political and financial circles would be so great that once the plan was known to them they could do it much harm. In a somewhat evasive manner, he told his hosts that he would admit to the Emperor, the Prime Minister and the War and Navy Ministers that he had discussed the matter pertaining to Singapore. But he would have to tell them that it was done so only in a hypothetical way.

Matsuoka, who had previously lauded Hitler as a leader who could be found only "once in a thousand years," concluded his visit by assuring Ribbentrop that the visit had "exceeded his expectations."

The Neutrailty Pact. Back in Moscow on April 7, Matsuoka was immediately received by the Foreign Commissar. This was only one day after German Ambassador Schulenburg had told Molotov of impending German action in Greece and Yugoslavia. The breach between Germany and Soviet Russia had been widened. Yugoslavia had just concluded a treaty of friendship with Russia which was described by Schulenburg as "unfortunate and undesirable." It was against this background that Matsuoka pushed his way to conclude a neutrality pact. Calculating that eventually Stalin himself would ask to see him, Matsuoka purposely did not request an interview with the First Secretary of the Communist Party. Nor did he indulge in a discourse of "moral communism" in Japan as he had done during his first visit. Serious business began immediately with Matsuoka suggesting to Molotov that Japan intended to purchase Northern Sakhalin. This proposal had previously evoked Molotov's comment whether it was "meant for a joke." Molotov countered by saying that for a non-aggression treaty, the outright cession of Southern Sakhalin would be required as the price and for a neutrality pact, the liquidation of Japanese concessions in Northern Sakhalin. There was nothing new in this proposal. The same ground had been conveyed several times since Ambassador Togo opened negotiations for a neutrality pact in 1939. Matsuoka was doubtful if the Kremlin really desired a pact. When he saw his old friend American Ambassador Steinhardt the next day, he said in effect that the Soviet demands involved major territorial concessions, and he could not possibly consent to them.

Two days later, a *modus vivendi* seemed to work out when Matsuoka abandoned his original plan for a non-aggression pact and agreed to discuss a simpler and limited neutrality pact. But this was as far as they could go. Instead of proceeding further on this matter, Matsuoka took a day's cooling off period and left for Leningrad to attend the presentation of a ballet at the Kirov Theater.

Upon his return from Leningrad on April 11 Matsuoka had another lengthy conference with Molotov, but the result was futile. Hope still remained, however, as Molotov told Matsuoka that Stalin would receive him on April 13.

Stalin was well disposed toward Matsuoka when the two met again. He declared that Matsuoka was "choking him" and made the appropriate gesture. This melted the ice. In return for a "non-aggression clause," which Matsuoga sought, Stalin asked that the inviolability of the territorial integrity of both Manchukuo and Outer Mongolia be included in the text of the pact. Matsuoka agreed to the substance of Stalin's request, but insisted that it be made in a separate agreement attached to the main text. At the conclusion of the talk, Stalin also dropped the demand for an outright elimination of Japanese concessions in Northern Sakhalin, for which Matsuoka had to promise that he would persuade the Japanese Government to give up the Northern Sakhalin concessions within the next few months. This was later put in the form of an exchange of notes in which Matsuoka was forced to use the word "liquidation" rather than "adjustment" in describing the disposal of concessions.

The treaty was simply worded and was for a period of five years. It provided for maintenance of friendly relations, respect for the integrity of each other's territory, and maintenance of neutrality in case either party was attacked by one or more third powers. In the accompanying "Frontier Declaration," Japan pledged to respect the territorial integrity of the Mongolian People's Republic, while the Soviet Government made an identical pledge with regard to Manchukuo.

Although the scope of the pact was limited, it was exactly what Matsuoka and his colleagues had been seeking. By that time, Matsuoka had to abandon hope of bringing Soviet Russia into the Axis camp. Under the circumstances, it was deemed unwise to proceed further than necessary. Thus the treaty was not patterned after the Non-Aggression Pact of 1939 between Russia and Germany. The adaptation of that text would have clearly aligned Soviet Russia with the Axis powers by delimiting the respective spheres of influence and gaining Soviet promise for cessation of aid to China.

The Japanese Foreign Office doubted if the pact would affect the existing relations between Soviet Russia and China. Matsuoka simply hoped that Chiang Kai-shek might abandon his stubborn resistance in view of the favorable relations that Japan was maintaining with Soviet Russia and other great powers. Even a seasoned observer like Ambassador Grew in Tokyo thought that Soviet aid to China would eventually end, and that the agreement would "strengthen the hands of and stimulate those elements in Japan which favor a vigorous prosecution of the southward advance."

The effect of Soviet aid to China was negligible. But the Neutrality Pact provided security for Japan in the north, while giving it a free hand to advance southward. This lessened the danger of a possible two-front war with Russia on one hand, and the United States and England on the other.

Even though Japan virtually ignored the desire of its Axis partners in concluding the pact, outwardly the semblance of unity was maintained. Ribbentrop and Ciano congratulated Matsuoka, and the latter reiterated that "the pact did in effect fulfill one of the basic objectives of the Tripartite Pact as originally contemplated, and brought it nearer to the path of true accomplishment." He termed the Neutrality Pact the logical extension of Japan's traditional *Hakko Ichiu*, meaning that the universe should be placed under the benevolent rule of the Japanese Emperor. "It has declared to the world without qualification our peace-loving good-neighbor policy." He boasted that together with the Tripartite Pact, the Basic Treaty with the Wang regime and the mediation of the Thai-French Indo-Chinese dispute—all concluded within the past six months under his leadership—the Neutrality Pact served to notify to the world "the sincere desire of the Empire" for peace. Matsuoka had reason to boast. He had concluded a pact much desired by the Japanese militarists in short order, a feat rarely matched in Japanese politics. A German observer in Tokyo felt that the Japanese Foreign Minister had taken a hint from the Germans and had carried out his task extremely well. "He has mastered our *Blitzkrieg* diplomacy," commented Boltze, the Chargé in the absence of Ambassador Ott.

As to the price, Matsuoka paid exactly what the Japanese militarists were prepared to pay. The "liquidation" of Japanese concessions in Northern Sakhalin was previously agreed upon by the Japanese leaders. In return he got the promise of extending the fishery treaty—the barometer of the Soviet-Japanese friendship in the pre-war years—and of concluding a commercial treaty. The commercial treaty would include a clause specifying that the Soviet Union would deliver to Japan for a period of five years, 1,000,000 tons of crude oil annually. The period could be extended subject to future negotiations. This, incidentally, was the minimum condition set by Navy Minister Oikawa.

Despite the fact the pact was "limited," it did not deter the Japanese militarists from becoming jubilant. The Foreign Minister himself was not thinking in terms of a lasting pact. He felt that the pact should be subject to revision within the next two or three years. At that time, reorientation of Japan's foreign policy would become necessary. What Matsuoka and his military colleagues in the Cabinet sought was a pact which would leave Japan's northern front secure, allow it to advance southward, and place it in a favorable international position which would enable it to negotiate with the United States from the "position of strength." Given a year or two, these tasks would be accomplished. The defect in the pact seemed to be covered by the non-aggression clause, and the pact as a whole would serve Japan's purposes well.[12]

The pact was signed in the Kremlin at 3:00 p.m. (Moscow time), April 13, 1941. A brief ceremony followed with Stalin himself personally serving the champagne while Matsuoka helped to arrange chairs. Later the two appeared arm-in-arm for an official photograph under the portrait of Lenin.

Then the time of departure came. Stalin unexpectedly appeared at the Moscow station to give Matsuoka a big send-off whereupon Matsuoka initiated a bear hug.

"The departure of Matsuoka was delayed for an hour and then took place with extraordinary ceremony," noted German Ambassador Shulenburg witnessing the occasion. "Apparently unexpectedly for both the Japanese and the Russians, both Stalin and Molotov appeared and greeted Matsuoka and the Japanese who were present in a remarkably friendly manner and wished them a pleasant journey. Then Stalin publicly asked for me, and when he found me he came up to me and threw his arm around my shoulders: 'We must remain friends and you must now do everything to that end!' Somewhat later Stalin turned to the German Military Attaché, Colonel Krebs, first made sure that he was a German, and then said to him: 'We will remain friends with you—in any event (*auf jeden Fall*)!'[13]"

Back in the train away from the excitement, Matsuoka quietly contemplated the means of gaining control of the Japanese Government. He began to work on the speech he was to deliver upon arrival in Tokyo at the Hibiya Hall. The speech was to include a sharp criticism of his Cabinet colleagues, including Prime Minister Konoye and Baron Hiranuma. With his job well done, the Foreign Minister was confident that both the public and the militarists would support his bid to become prime minister.[14]

Matsuoka's diplomatic victory was short-lived. The Neutrality Pact had been concluded in order to (1) prevent a possible rapprochement between the United States and Soviet Russia, (2) place Japan in a securer position so that it could negotiate with the United States from a position of strength, (3) discourage the continued resistance by Chiang Kai-shek's Government, and (4) permit Japan to advance southward without fear of being attacked by Russia from the rear. The Pact's success would depend on two unknowns. First, there would have to be no war between Germany and Russia at least for two or three years. Second, the Japanese Army would have to permit the Foreign Office to negotiate with the United States with greater flexibility. Everything was in suspense, and in victory Matsuoka was sowing the seed of his own destructoin.

CHAPTER X

THE SOUTHWARD ADVANCE

Onslaught on French Indo-China. On September 23, 1940, the Japanese Army crossed the Northern French Indo-Chinese border, thus opening a new phase in Japan's southward advance. The fact that this occurred just four days before the signing of the Tripartite Pact was no accident. The Konoye Cabinet's policies which aimed "ultimately at the construction of a new order in Greater East Asia," were not to be taken up separately, but to be pursued concurrently. In a sense, the decisions "to foster a strong political tie with Germany and Italy, and to take active steps in the adjustment of diplomacy towards the Soviet Union," were preludes to the "settlement" of southern problems.

French Indo-China and the Dutch East Indies constituted the nuclei of Japan's southern problems. Of the two, the French Indo-Chinese question had to be solved first and firmly since it was more immediate. Tongking was the terminus from which one of the major supply routes to Chungking originated. Indo-China was of great strategic value in that it was the natural gateway to Southeast Asia. The region was rich in rubber, tin, and rice. The Dutch East Indies presented a different picture. Oil was the product Japan desired from the islands. Once the supply could be secured the actual military occupation of the islands would become unnecessary. Thus, in contrast to French Indo-China, a soft policy or "diplomatic" persuasion was to be adopted towards the Dutch East Indies.

Prior to the outbreak of war in Europe, Japan entertained no territorial designs toward French Indo-China. Its objectives were to gain French recognition of the state of war in China and of Japan's belligerent's rights, just as the British did after the disputes over the Tientsin Incident. Back in 1938, Japan repeatedly asked the French Indo-Chinese authorities to halt shipment of war materials to Chungking and had received no satisfaction. The War, Navy, and Foreign Ministries advanced the idea of bombing the Yunnan railway which was built by French capital, forcing a diplomatic settlement. But no concrete action was taken until the fall of 1939.

When the war broke out in Europe Japan was no longer constrained from bombing the Yunnan railway. Simultaneously, the Army took military action in Kwangsi province, directly to the north of the French colony, where most of the French interests in China were centered. However, it was not until the collapse of resistance in Europe that the French Indo-Chinese authority heeded the Japanese demands to have a military observers group stationed in its territory and to stop shipment of war materials.

The acquiescence came after a considerable show of force on Japan's part. On July 19, 1940, the Yonai Cabinet decided that military action would be employed if the diplomatic means should fail to produce the desired result. An ultimatum was sent to the French authorities through Ambassador Henri, who in turn cautioned Governor General Catroux to accept Japanese terms lest the colony be occupied by force. The Governor first sought Washington's assistance but received no encouragement, and the Pétain government was in no position to direct the course of events in French Indo-China. Acting on his own authority, the Governor finally decided to yield.

The Japanese military observers group was composed of forty members drawn from the War, Navy, and Foreign Offices, and was headed by Major General Nishihara. It arrived in Hanoi on June 29, and immediately took up positions at the border. The Governor further agreed that for one month starting July 7 all shipments of goods to China would be ceased. Thus Japan gained the first victory in its quest for cessation of foreign aid to China.

By then Catroux apparently felt that it was expedient to appease the Japanese demands. On his own responsibility, he suggested to General Nishihara that French Indo-China was willing to enter into a mutual defense pact with Japan provided the territorial integrity of the colony would be respected. However, while the Yonai Cabinet was still drafting the text of a possible agreement with Indo-China it was forced out of office and succeeded by the Konoye Cabinet.

In assuming his office, Foreign Minister Matsuoka declared that his policy would be different from his predecessors and would cease to be all things to all men—in Japanese terms, *Happo Bijin*, a beauty who had a smile for everyone approaching from eight different directions. Just what he meant by abandonment of *Happo Bijin* was clearly shown in his action towards French Indo-China. On August 1, he handed Ambassador Henri an *aide-memoire* demanding the rights of transit for Japanese forces through Indo-China, of construction and use of air fields, and of stationing Japanese troops to guard military installations. Henri told Matsuoka that these demands amounted to asking France to declare war against China, which Japan itself had not done.[1]

Vichy procrastinated with hopes that the delay might bring about Washington's intervention. Admiral Jean Decoux, who was newly appointed as Governor General of Indo-China to succeed M. Catroux, submitted figures showing that French Indo-China could defend itself. General Weygand, the Minister of Defense, also favored out-and-out resistance. However, their views were challenged by M. Lémery, the Minister of Colonies, and M. Baudouin, the Minister of Foreign Affairs. It was obvious that the French Army stationed in Indo-China was no match for the Japanese Canton Army which was clamoring for action. Furthermore, U. S. intervention never materialized and Japan already occupied several strategic points north of the border as well as the Hainan Island. From the Hainan Island, the Japanese Air Force and Navy could strike the French colony at any time they chose. All-out resistance might mean a total loss of the colony. This being the case, the Pétain government decided to acceed to the Japanese demands.[2]

On August 30, with an exchange of notes, Matsuoka and Henri reached a political accord. It stipulated that Vichy was to recognize Japan's superior political and economic interests in the Far East, in return for Tokyo's recognition of the "paramount French interests in Indo-China." France was to grant Japanese citizens in French Indo-China most favored nation treatment, and to permit the Japanese Army the rights to pass, station, transport war materials, and use air fields in Tongking. These terms were to be implemented by military and economic agreements to be negotiated locally at Hanoi.

But military accord was slow in coming. Both Governor General Decoux and General Martin, the Commander of the French Army in Indo-China, claimed they lacked power to negotiate on the matter.

While they stalled, Vichy made another approach to Washington for aid. It also requested from Berlin permission to employ the planes immobilized aboard the carrier *Béarn* at Martinique. The Germans rejected this but told Vichy that they would not object to French Indo-China receiving arms from the United States. By September 14 Japan became so concerned about the French Indo-Chinese situation that the matter was brought to the Emperor for immediate decision. Marquis Kido thought any further delay would "only allow England and the United States a chance to work out their designs and align with French Indo-China." So there was no other recourse but to resort to a stronger policy.

On September 20 General Nishihara delivered an ultimatum to Governor General Decoux, stating that the Japanese Army would cross the border at midnight September 22 with or without a military agreement. Hastily the Governor General agreed to sign a military convention making the Japanese entry legal. By September 23 Japanese occupation of Northern French Indo-China was complete.

The reaction in Washington was one of open hostility. Three days later the Roosevelt Administration placed all types of iron and steel scrap under embargo, clearly aiming at Japan.

Mediation of Thai-French Indo-Chinese Dispute. One sequel to the French Indo-Chinese embroilment was the upsurge of nationalism in Thailand. The Matsuoka-Henri agreement provided Thailand with the golden opportunity to recover its lost territory. On September 13 the Thai government handed an *aide-memoire* to the French government, asserting that the situation in Indo-China was not based on equity, and a revision of the existing boundary would become necessary suggesting that the Mekong River constitute the new border. The acceptance of these conditions by the French would have meant retroceding all the territories won by France since the Siamese crisis of 1893. The Thai government further suggested that Laos and Cambodia be ceded to it if France should desire to relinquish its sovereignty in Indo-China. All of these conditions were presented as the *sine qua non* of a successful conclusion to a pending non-aggression pact. The French, while rejecting these conditions, nevertheless agreed to set up an international commission for the purpose of delimiting the disputed boundary along the Mekong River.

Japan's occupation of Northern French Indo-China did not produce the results Thai expected. The occupation was confined to the northern part and did not cover the territories desired by Thailand. Furthermore at least on paper, the Japanese guaranteed territorial integrity of French Indo-China and could not openly support the Thai claims. Hoping Indo-China would be thrown into turmoil, Thai concentrated its troops on the border ready to march into the Indo-Chinese territory. The French also gathered their troops to defend the border, and Thai was militarily in no position to take independent action. Japan did not give any encouragement to Thai's cause, since it was more concerned with its impending economic convention with French Indo-China and did not desire to aggrieve further the victim of its military occupation.

During September and October Thai sent a mission to Tokyo headed

by its Vice Minister of Defense to sound out the possibility of concluding an alliance with Japan and enlisting the latter's support in
regaining its *terra irredenta*. As far as Japan was concerned, the mission
originated in Thailand, and had no official support of the Japanese
Government. It thus gave lukewarm answers to the questions raised
by the mission and brushed aside any talk of an alliance.

On November 5, the Japanese Cabinet came to a different conclusion. It was incensed by the activities of the British and American
Ministers in Bangkok who were trying to draw Thailand to the western
column. Though the Prime Minister of Thailand denied existence
of negotiations with western powers for an alliance, the matter was
of grave concern to Tokyo. Should the British succeed in concluding
an alliance with Thailand, Japan would counteract by occupying
Saigon in Southern French Indo-China, Vice Foreign Minister Ohashi
declared.[*]

Late in the month two cruisers were sent to Saigon for "a friendly
visit." This served a dual purpose—first, to notify the French Indo-
Chinese authorities that the occupation of Southern Indo-China might
be in the offing, and second, to impress the Thai government of the
might of Japan.

The heavy concentration of armed forces on both sides of the
border finally ended in a series of skirmishes at the end of November.
Matsuoka took this occasion to find out if the French desired mediation.
Ambassador Henri declined, saying that his country would maintain
the integrity of its territory and had no intention of altering the existing
boundary. Matsuoka, who was annoyed by Thai's excessive demands,
let the matter rest there.

In January 1941, the Thai Navy suffered a crushing defeat at the
hands of the French Indo-Chinese Navy. The French Navy sank a
Japanese-made Thai warship, entered deep into the mouth of the
Menam River and took position ready to bombard Bangkok, Thai's
capital city. In a way, this was an exact replica of the situation existing at the time of the Siamese crisis of 1893, and Thailand was thrust
into great confusion. The Japanese Government feared the British
would take advantage of the situation to intervene in order to keep
Thailand under their constant surveillance. The Navy in the South
China Sea was partially mobilized and conducted a demonstration
aimed at the French Indo-Chinese authorities. On January 18 the
military observers group gave Governor General Decoux a statement
tantamount to an ultimatum, saying that if the truce as Japan demanded
were not carried out Japan might be forced to occupy Southern French

Indo-China.   On January 20 Matsuoka formally made an offer of
mediation to the two countries which was accepted by Vichy two
days later.

French Indo-China was placed in a rather precarious position.
Despite its victory at sea, it could not expect any reinforcement from
the battle-torn mother country.   Japan had on several occasions
explained to Berlin that a successful attack on Singapore hinged on
securing a military base in Thailand, and asked Berlin either to
prevail on Vichy to accept Japanese terms, or else, at least to prevent
Vichy from sending any reinforcement to French Indo-China.   Under
the terms of the truce Vichy was obligated to ask permission from
Berlin for the movement of any of its armed forces.   Accordingly it
requested Berlin to grant permission to send several contingents of its
Foreign Legion to Indo-China, but this was unceremoniously rejected.
Even if Berlin had agreed to Vichy's proposition, it was doubtful that
it could have secured necessary means to transport the troops to the
Far East in a short period of time.   Japan already had one-half of
Indo-China, and the latter could do nothing but accept Japan's forced
mediation.

The attempt for mediation started at the request of the Thai government, and did not originate in Tokyo.   It gave Japan an opportunity
to put into effect one of its basic southward advance policy assump-
tions.   This called for applying pressure whenever feasible, and for
employing force against French Indo-China, if necessary.   The Liaison
Conference which met on January 30 further elaborated on this
basic approach.   In essence, Japan was to give Thailand a bait in the
form of the return of its lost territory in order to prevent it from
joining the western camp.   To this end persuasion and pressure, but
not actual military force, were to be applied.   As to French Indo-China,
Japan would eventually occupy the entire territory.   In the meantime, Japan would demand an agreement with France pledging that
the latter would not enter into any military or political convention
affecting the future of Indo-China.   This agreement was to include
provisions stating that Indo-China would not lease any of its air
bases, harbors, and other transportation facilities to a third power and
would permit stationing of the Japanese Army in parts of the territory
that had not been occupied.   A punitive action would be taken if
French Indo-China should refuse Japan's mediation.

The truce was signed aboard a Japanese cruiser anchored near
Saigon, and negotiations followed in Tokyo.   Thailand first welcomed
the mediation as a face-saving device as well as the means to ac-

complish what it sought. However, when it realized that it had
actually won on land, it suddenly stiffened its demands. The battles
were fought mostly in remote jungle areas where no facilities for
telecommunication existed. The reports from the front were slow in
coming, and the news of Thai's victory in a series of skirmishes over
the border did not reach the Thai capital until after the truce was
signed. Thai was elated at the news and asked that the entire territories of Cambodia and Laos be ceded to it. More than once, Thai's
unreasonableness coupled with its obstinacy almost wrecked the
conference. Finally, on March 6 a joint communique was issued,
which was followed by the signing of a treaty between France and
Thailand. Thai got what it had asked, but at the price of subjugating
the country under the fiat of imperial Japan.

With the success of the mediation, the first stage of southward
advance was complete. The April meeting of the Supreme Command
Conference noted with satisfaction that henceforth Japan's South
Sea policies should be directed towards the solidification of Japan's
relation with French Indo-China and Thailand, and towards a closer
economic tie with the Dutch East Indies. The success gave Japan
a moment to pause, and the Foreign Minister left for Berlin and
Moscow.

The subjugation of French Indo-China and Thailand placed Japan
in a stronger position to attack and overtake Singapore. This was the
subject often discussed, and the fears expressed in Washington and
London were not necessarily unfounded. Yet there was no indication
that an attack on Singapore had ever been taken up as an official
policy. Matsuoka's reluctance to make a definite commitment after
giving an elaborate plan for an attack suggests that the Japanese
Cabinet was by no means unanimous in its policy towards Singapore.

Dr. Schmidt, who recorded the conversations between Matsuoka and
German leaders, related Matsuoka's position. "Matsuoka then began
to speak of Singapore again. The Japanese were not worried on
account of the British Navy. But there were Japanese circles which
viewed a conflict with America with great misgivings, since they
assumed that this would involve a five or ten-year war with the
United States. He would readily admit that America would not risk
its fleet in a war against Japan, but for that very reason these Japanese
circles were worried because under these circumstances the war
would last for years."[4] In other words, Japan was not ready to risk
a war with the United States on account of Singapore. Hereafter

increasingly its attention was directed towards "peaceful" pentration of the Dutch East Indies.

Oil and the Dutch East Indies. "A drop of oil is a drop of blood" was the slogan in Japan throughout the war years. It was quite necessary for Japan to acquire oil for its war efforts. The Dutch East Indies were rich in oil, and thus became the prime target of Japanese southward expansion. The problems Japan had to face were, however, dissimilar to those which confronted it in Indo-China. In Indo-China occupation was primarilly for strategic reasons. The land was contiguous to South China and occupation did not present a particular problem in military movement. The resources Japan sought from Indo-China were rice and minerals which were not vastly important to Japanese economy. The destruction of the land as the result of military operation would still be compensated by the strategic advantages Japan would gain from the move—namely, cessation of aid to Chiang Kai-shek, and acquisition of a strategic base from which Japan could attack Singapore.

In contrast, what Japan sought from the Dutch East Indies was oil. Any hasty military action taken by Japan would probably mean destruction of oil wells and refineries. Occupation of the Indies would also necessitate a large scale naval operation which, if taken, might involve Japan in a war against the United States. It was apparent to the Japanese policy-makers that the United States would readily come to the defense of the Indies, while it would not enjoin Japan from taking a "punitive" action against French Indo-China. Vichy was distrusted by the western powers, while the Dutch Government in Exile in London was not.

Both France and the Netherlands were overrun by German armed forces. While Germany could prevail on Vichy to accept Japanese terms, it could not do so with the Dutch, since there was no government in existence that would take orders from Germany, and the East Indies' government remained loyal to the Government in Exile in London. All these factors led Japan to take an entirely different course towards the Indies. Prince Fushimi, Chief of Naval Operations, remarked that the Navy did not desire an early attack on the Indies or Singapore. "We need at least eight months to prepare for combat readiness," said Prince Fushimi, "and we should like to delay the war as long as possible."

Japan's cautious approach towards the Dutch East Indies was also reflected in replacing the head of its economic mission to the Indies.

Originally General Koiso was slated to take the job but was dropped when he requested that he be sent in a battleship and that he be granted power to bombard Batavia. His replacement was Ichizo Kobayashi, a businessman presently serving as Minister of Commerce and Industry.

Kobayashi arrived in Batavia on September 12, 1940. Already on the scene was Haruo Mukai, Chairman of the Board of the Mitsui Corporation, who headed a non-official mission to conduct a business deal with the Dutch East Indies authorities. He was instructed to acquire prospecting rights for Japanese concerns to drill oil wells and to purchase oil in as large a quantity as possible.

The oil industry in the Dutch East Indies was controlled by three companies. The first was the Bataafsche Petroleum Maatschappij (BPM), a subsidiary of the Royal Dutch and the Shell Oil Companies which controlled well over seventy per cent of the oil produced in the Indies. The next was the Nederlandsche Koloniale Petroleum Maatschappij (NKPM), a subsidiary of the Standard Oil Company of New Jersey which controlled about twenty-five per cent of the total output. The third was the Nederlandsche-Indische Aarodolie Maatschappij (NIAM) which was jointly owned by BPM and the Dutch government.

Annually Japan was purchasing 650,000 tons of oil from the East Indies. Pressure mounted in Japan to increase this amount outright to 3,150,000 tons annually. The reason for Japan's anxiety to gain an adequate supply from the Dutch East Indies is readily understood when viewed in the light of the paucity of oil in Japan. Both the Army and Navy had stockpiled oil which would sustain Japan for one and one-half to two years of military operation. Without oil it would be completely stranded while engaged in an all-out war. The United States remained the major supplier of oil for Japan during the first three years of conflict in China. But on July 26, 1940, when the Roosevelt Administration decided to include high aviation gasolines in the list of those commodities which could not be exported without license, the Japanese Government saw the handwriting on the wall. The commercial treaty with the United States had already expired. Despite an oral assurance from the State Department that the lack of a treaty itself would not affect the existing trade relations, it was clear that Japan could not get what it sought from the United States. Having in fact lost the major supplier, Japan had to turn elsewhere to fulfill its needs.

From the outset Kobayashi's mission was doomed to failure. There were no concrete instructions from Tokyo, and the East Indies authorities were not accommodating. "The Governor General," said Kobayashi in his telegram to Tokyo, "does not show a bit of interest in what I have to say about Japan's intent towards the Dutch East Indies. I fear that it is almost impossible to negotiate with this gentleman. It seems to me that I have made this trip in vain."[5]

After nearly two weeks of delay, the Dutch authorities finally agreed to open formal negotiations. Commissioner for Economic Affairs of the colony, Hubert van Mook was appointed the plenipotentiary. Kobayashi immediately presented van Mook with the demand of 3,150,-000 tons annual shipment for five years.

Not long after the negotiations began, Japan's alignment with Germany was announced. The text of the Axis Pact called for German recognition and respect for Japan's leadership in East Asia. This clause caused much disturbance among the Dutch authorities. They could subscribe neither to Japan's policy of establishing the Greater East Asia Co-Prosperity Area nor to what the language of the pact implied. They would agree to continue negotiations only if Japan would not demand leadership over the Dutch East Indies, and with the understanding that Japan entertained no hostile intent against the Indies. Van Mook also clearly indicated his fear that any export made to Japan from the East Indies might directly or indirectly aid Germany who occupied his homeland.

On October 16 Kobayashi and van Mook issued a joint communique stating that the friendly relations between the Netherlands and Japan would not be altered by the conclusion of the Tripartite Pact. It further noted that the impending item on the agenda for negotiations was the matter of oil, and the Commissioner of Mining had given a careful explanation of the oil situation to the Japanese representative. In other words, the Dutch representatives were noncommittal and were employing delay tactics. This caused Mr. Mukai, the unofficial negotiator, to request a new set of instructions from Tokyo that would reduce the Japanese demand to the bare essentials.

So far, Kobayashi had been negotiating in generalities, hoping that he might be able to agree to a pact essentially similar to the one Japan hoped to secure from French Indo-China. Like many other Japanese negotiators, Kobayashi lacked specific instructions, and often found himself in the embarrassing position of not being able to define Japan's own terms. Nothing concrete came from one month of negotiations.

On October 21, Kobayashi left for Tokyo to "attend the celebration of the 2,600th anniversary of the founding of the Empire," leaving the unfinished business in Mr. Mukai's hands. Meanwhile Tokyo doubted the wisdom of permitting Mukai to continue the negotiations. Matsuoka thought it might be more desirable if the talks were transferred to Tokyo.

The failure of the Kobayashi mission caused the Konoye Cabinet to make a radical shift in Japan's policy towards the East Indies. On October 25, the Cabinet decided that the East Indies should be forced to sever its economic ties with the United States and Britain and join the East Asian economic bloc. Implicit in this decision was that the cajoling of the East Indies had to be abandoned and replaced by a "get tough" policy. The Cabinet's blueprint for the East Indies' cooperation included the following features: that the Indies repeal any restrictions imposed on Japanese economic activities; develop resources on a joint investment basis; accept Japanese economic advisers; grant Japan special rights for transportation and communication facilities; suppress anti-Japanese activities; and permit publication of Japanese papers. These conditions were reminiscent of the ones imposed on Wang Ching-wei. In this instance, though, Japan would not insist that the East Indies join the Yen bloc.

Concurrent with the Cabinet decision, the inspired Japanese press began to print the so-called ABCD encirclement, meaning that America, Britain, China, and the Dutch East Indies were working hand-in-glove to prevent Japan's legitimate expansion. The papers also blamed the stubbornness of the Dutch authorities for the breakdown of the negotiations.

On October 29 the Dutch authorities informed Mukai that they would permit shipment of 1,306,500 tons of oil to Japan for the coming year. This took the form of a private contract between Mukai and the two major oil producers, BPM and NKPM. It did not have the force of a commercial treaty and was to run for only six months. This feature was hardly pleasing to the Japanese Government which was bent on a long-term commitment from the East Indies. Mukai was also offered some prospecting rights in Borneo, Celebes and New Guinea—rights of dubious economic value.

In the meantime another agreement was entered in Tokyo which provided for purchase by Japan of 490,000 tons of oil. The two agreements would have given Japan the right to purchase a combined total of 1,796,500 tons, representing more than one half of Japan's original request. This was a qualified success. Yet the news was completely suppressed. The Government apparently felt it was desirable to create an impression that the East Indies stood in Japan's way of establishing the East Asia Co-Prosperity Area. Japan's attitude was not overlooked by the Dutch government. On November 15, General Pabst quietly handed Vice Minister Ohashi an *aide memoire* suggesting that the negotiations be terminated.

The Second Konoye Cabinet was publicly committed to the policy of southward advance, and it was forced to continue the negotiations. As a face-saving device following General Pabst's rebuff, the Cabinet quickly appointed former Foreign Minister Kenkichi Yoshizawa to head a new economic mission.

Yoshizawa arrived in Batavia at the end of the year. His demands ranged from relaxation of the immigration law to a guaranteed supply of oil, rubber, tin and other raw materials. In raw materials, the demands included: 3,800,000 tons of oil, 1,000,000 tons of tin, 400,000 tons of bauxite, 180,000 tons of nickel, 30,000 tons of coco-oil, 30,000 tons of rubber, 10,000 tons of sugar, and an unspecified amount of scrap iron and other materials. These demands reflected the ones decided at the October 25 meeting of the Cabinet. Van Mook remarked that the excessive demands for raw materials were conclusive evidence that Japan was intent on re-exporting them to Germany. Again, as in the past, the Dutch authorities resorted to delay tactics. Matsuoka's speech at the Diet declaring that the Dutch East Indies were clearly within the confines of the Greater East Asia Co-Prosperity Area gave the Dutch authorities an excellent excuse to postpone the negotiations. They were not resumed until February 17.

Yoshizawa, a seasoned negotiator, saw no point in stressing trivial matters such as relaxation of the immigration law, and counseled that they be dropped in order to concentrate on the question of obtaining raw materials. But Tokyo was inflexible. It had adopted an all-or-nothing approach, and was ready to break off the negotiations on its own accord. Matsuoka himself was in sympathy with the course advocated by Yoshizawa, but domestic pressure would not allow it. In an impromptu interview with Privy Councillor Fukai, Matsuoka remarked: "If I had followed that course, the Cabinet would certainly have fallen. Then what next?"[6]

The negotiations were allowed to stagger along. The armed services found the delay advisable, since it would permit their military experts' stay in the Indies a little while longer enabling them to gather more military information. The Foreign Office was counting on a shift in the international relations which would be favorable to Japan, citing the possibility of a non-aggression pact with Russia and better relations with the United States. If these were accomplished, the Dutch authorities might become more amenable to the Japanese terms.

Leaving matters at this point, Matsuoka left on his European journey. Yoshizawa disputed the Foreign Office's premises, and requested his own recall. Tokyo persuaded him to stay at least until the return of Matsuoka. Yoshizawa recommended that Japan should accede to the Dutch demand that none of the materials purchased from the Indies be re-exported to Germany. This Tokyo was not willing to do. The only change Tokyo allowed was a slight reduction in the amount Japan would demand from the Indies.

On May 14, 1941, Yoshizawa presented his second demand which was a modified version of the first one. Despite the less comprehensive nature of the second version, the Dutch stood fast. They asked for Japan's assurance that not only the materials imported from the Indies but also similar materials imported from Thailand and French Indo-China would not be shipped to Germany. They contended that the East Indies could not subsidize directly or indirectly the need of its enemy, Germany.

Japanese papers again proceeded to criticize the "insincerity" of the Dutch East Indies government. On June 3 and 4 Yoshizawa held the last meetings with the Governor General; on June 6, the Dutch reply was handed to him. The Dutch made minor concessions but most of the Japanese demands were either ignored or sharply curtailed. The recall of the entire delegation was then ordered, and only an unofficial negotiator, Mr. Ito, who took Mukai's place, was left to carry out the unfinished business. The Army wanted its military experts to remain with Ito, but the Dutch government refused. With Yoshizawa's departure from Batavia on June 17, Japan's dream of economic penetration into the Dutch East Indies abruptly ended.

The failure of the Kobayashi and Yoshizawa missions to achieve their goals had wide repercussions in Tokyo. Matsuoka privately conceded that the Dutch government could have taken no other course, and that the world opinion would support them. It gave the *coup de grâce* to the idea of peaceful penetration to the South Sea regions. The militarists found in the failure a prime example of the uselessness of diplomacy. Agitation for more direct action followed, which culminated later in the military occupation of Southern French Indo-China.

Chapter XI

NEGOTIATING WITH THE UNITED STATES

Nomura Appointed Ambassador. The setback in the Dutch East Indies brought to the foreground the question of adjusting relations with the United States. There was a growing realization that once Japan persuaded the United States to agree to a new commercial treaty—to take the place of the one that had expired January 26, 1940—the need for quick settlement with the East Indies would largely be obviated. The United States had been the most important single supplier of goods to Japan, providing 33.6% of Japan's total import in 1937, 34.4% in 1938, and 34.3% in 1939.[1]

The lack of a treaty in itself did not single the end of normal trade relations. The United States had been rather cautious in applying trade restrictions against Japan. When the licensing system was first introduced in July 1940, conspicuously absent from the list were crude oil and scrap iron, the two items Japan desired most from the United States. However, these two items were placed under embargo on September 26, 1940, following Japan's occupation of Northern French Indo-China. The embargo was imposed ostensibly to conserve essential resources for Hemisphere defense, and did not specify Japan as its object. Nor did the supply of these items cease to flow to Japan at that time. Yet the implication was that Japan could not take aggressive steps which were displeasing to Washington. The issues presented were: (1) should Japan submit to the economic power of the United States and abandon its expansionist policies; or (2) should Japan continue its policies and negotiate with the United States from the "position of strength."

The first course had been previously ruled out as being impractical, and it was on the second one that the Foreign Office laid its hope of success. In a sense, the southward advance policy was aimed at gaining such a "position of strength" for Japan. A memorandum prepared by the Foreign Office on March 3, 1940, five weeks after the commercial treaty expired, contained the following recommendation: "The most urgent measure which Japan should take is the policy of establishing our economic system not threatened by the attitude of the United States by eliminating the extreme reliance upon America as at present.

There is no doubt that the establishment of such a system itslf has a great effect in making America reconsider."[2]

Yet once Japan embarked on a southward advance policy, it was bound to meet American opposition. The Philippine Islands stood between Japan and the Dutch East Indies, shielding the latter from Japan's penetration. Previous to the European war, Singapore posed another threat to Japan's ambitions. However, as the Japanese statesmen saw it, the British power was on the decline, and the end of the empire might be in sight. Singapore would be dangerous to Japan only if the United States should use it as its naval base. Thus it was the United States and not Great Britain that stood in Japan's path. Furthermore, the U.S. Pacific Fleet was safely anchored in Pearl Harbor. Thus Japan's success in the conquest of the South Sea regions could still be met with opposition from the U. S. Navy.

Aside from economic and strategic considerations, there was the China question. The conquest Japan had made since 1931 would be nullified if the United States and other western powers would unite in their opposition. The Stimson Doctrine was a reminder to Japan that this possibility existed and could be translated into reality at a future date. The European war had neutralized British influence in China, but the United States replaced Great Britain as guardian of foreign rights and champion of China's territorial integrity. Everywhere Japan turned it was greeted by talks of quarantine, moral embargo, sanctity of international law, open door, and the like. Japan's answer to these public pronouncements by Washington was the Monroe Doctrine for East Asia, which implied that the United States should recognize Japan's domination over China.

In short, what Japan sought from the United States were: a new and favorable commercial treaty; and acquiescence in Japan's present and future gains both in China and in the South Sea regions. Since the success of the Konoye Cabinet's other policies hinged on the attainment of these two objectives, negotiations with the United States were pursued with great determination.

The negotiations with the United States officially started with the appointment of Admiral Nomura as Ambassador to Washington. He had known President Roosevelt as the Assistant Secretary of Navy while he himself was a Naval Attaché in Washington during the First World War. It was hoped that his excellent connection in Washington might help thaw out the U.S.-Japanese relations which were described as "cold as ice," and create a more suitable atmosphere in which the two countries could iron out their differences.

The position was offered to Nomura as early as August 27, 1940, but his acceptance did not come until November 7, following Konoye's assurances that no major policy decisions would be kept from him and that the Cabinet was willing to review its China and South Sea advance policies.

Despite Konoye's assurance that Japan would reconsider its basic approach towards the United States, Matsuoka showed no inkling of proceeding in that direction. Normura accepted the Tripartite Pact as a national policy, but was not slow in pointing out the inconsistency between having an alliance with Germany and endeavoring to improve relations with the United States. He urged Matsuoka to play down the Tripartite Pact in order to facilitate his mission, but the advice was not heeded. At the December 18 meeting of the Japan-America Society in Tokyo, held in honor of the new Ambassador, Matsuoka spoke of the Tripartite Pact as constituting Japan's basic policy. "Japan is," declared the Foreign Minister, "and will remain, loyal to its allies."

Referring to the establishment of the Great East Asia Co-Prosperity Area, Matsuoka remarked for the ostensible benefit of Washington: "It seems to me that this world of ours is too wide politically and too narrow economically. While economic activities should be world-wide and should suffer no limitation, our political efforts had better be restricted to only those spheres in which we are vitally interested, and not be extended to other people's domains. If regional peace is effectively secured through regional understanding, the world will, by its aggregation, be able to enjoy a universal peace. . . . The recent Havana Conference is a case in point, being an attempt to ensure peace and order in the Western Hemisphere through a regional cooperation."³ As to the Chinese problem, the Foreign Minister chided the American attitude toward China as "largely a question of sentiment," while it "constitutes a truly vital issue affecting the very existence of our Empire."

On January 23, 1941, the Admiral left Tokyo for Washington, carrying with him Matsuoka's instructions containing much the same points the Foreign Minister raised at the Japan-America Society luncheon.

The American public was hardly in the mood to welcome the new Japanese Ambassador. With overwhelming enthusiasm it had just accepted President Roosevelt's declaration that America would never "acquiesce in a peace dictated by aggressors and sponsored by appeasers." When Nomura arrived in Washington on February 11, Congress was engaged in a hot debate over the Lend-Lease legislation.

Nomura's public announcement was paraphrazed by the *Time* Magazine in Pidgin English. It was in this atmosphere of unfriendliness that the first meeting between the President and Nomura took place.

On February 14 Nomura presented his credentials to the President. There he thought he had a meeting of minds with Mr. Roosevelt, the "naval person." The President was reported to have said that there was room in the Pacific for everyone. Nomura was further encouraged by the President's assurance that he was a friend of Japan, and the Admiral being a friend of the United States, the two could get together to talk things over with utmost frankness. After the meeting, Nomura told the Japanese Foreign Office that Japan should not be too crafty in its approach but should take a statesmanlike attitude. The Japanese Cabinet Information Bureau also exhorted Japanese citizens in the United States to be calm, and engage in their daily occupations as usual, reasoning that while the relations between the two countries had deteriorated, there was no likelihood of war. All in all, there seemed to be dim hope that somehow the situation might become brighter.[4]

Secretary of State Cordell Hull, who was present at the meeting, did not share Nomura's optimism. He thought Nomura simply dwelled on diplomatic niceties and could not grasp what was actually taking place.

The first extended conversation between Hull and Nomura took place in the evening of March 8 in Mr. Hull's apartment at the Carlton Hotel. The meeting, one of some forty such meetings before Pearl Harbor, was conducted on an informal basis, and both spoke off the record. There Hull gave a long lecture on reciprocal trade agreements, his favorite subject. Nomura's suggestion that normal trade relations between the two countries be restored was not heeded. Hull continued by saying Japan's new order resembled Hitler's aggrandizement, and was a form of military conquest. To this, Nomura countered, saying that Japan concluded a pact with Wang Ching-wei on the basis of equality. What Japan desired from China were: good-will, economic cooperation and defense against Communism. These basic desires in no way hindered third nations from establishing normal trade relations with China and from aiding the latter's economic development. Yet Japan would require priority in China's iron and coal supplies. It would not tolerate third nations to have large military establishments in China. Beyond these Nomura had no concrete suggestions to offer. On the question of combining the Chungking and Nanking governments, Nomura was conspicuously lacking in precise terms. Neither could he clarify his government's position on the Tripartite Pact with regard to the United States. The meeting ended with Hull expressing grave concern over the prospect of Matsuoka's forthcoming visit to Berlin and Moscow.[5]

On March 14 Nomura received a confidential cable from the Navy Ministry signed by Vice Minister Toyoda. It consisted of four points. elaborating Matsuoka's foreign policy as of that time. The first contained Matsuoka's assurance that he would not commit Japan to the conquest of the South Sea regions by force, even if Germany should request so. The second explained that Japan was not ready to fight against the United States. "In fact, such a suggestion violates the basic principles of the Tripartite Pact," continued the telegram. It went on to say that peaceful means would be employed in Japan's economic penetration towards French Indo-China and Thailand, and that Japan would make its foreign policy goals to attain peace and to reach a rapprochement with the Soviet Union. The telegram added very little to what was already known about Japan's intentions. However, it served to clarify the issues at hand. It was apparent that Matsuoka still felt the Tripartite Pact was the best instrument for restraining the United States from intervening in the European war, and by the same token, the best means to bring back better relations between the United States and Japan.

The meeting Nomura had with President Roosevelt on that same day proved Matsuoka to be wrong. President Roosevelt told Nomura that the pact had upset the American people to no end, and expressed fear that Japan might collaborate with Germany and attack Singapore and the Dutch East Indies while Germany and Italy pushed their way to the Suez Canal. The implication that the pact stood in the way of better understanding between the two countries did not escape Admiral Nomura. The President again emphasized that the problems existing between the two governments could be solved amicably without a military clash. But in this and in the subsequent meetings, the representatives of the two countries endlessly restated their respective positions. Neither side was willing to yield on such fundamental issues as the Axis Alliance, China policy, and trade problems.[6]

Progress was slow. In the meantime, Matsuoka left for Europe, after forcing French Indo-China and Thailand to accept his mediation. In Matsuoka's absence a cabinet reorganization took place. Admiral Teijiro Toyoda, heretofore Vice Minister of Navy, became Minister of Commerce and Industry. Mr. Shozo Ogura, the Osaka industrialist, became Minister without Portfolio. General Teiji Suzuki, former President of the China Board, became President of the Government Planning Board with the rank of Minister without Portfolio. Mr. Ogura headed the great industrial concern of Sumitomo and had cooperated with the government in his private capacity to expand Japan's military industry. His civic activities included the presidency of the Kansai chapter of the Japan-America Society, and he was privately known as pro-American. Admiral Toyoda was the unanimous choice of the Army and Navy for the post because of his exceptional executive ability, having served previously as head of the naval procurement program. The revamping was apparently engineered by Baron Hiranuma to give strength to the Cabinet. It suggested that the government needed more than ever the cooperation of the private industry in pursuing its economic policies. The reorganization also implied that the Cabinet was contemplating a gradual shift in foreign policy. Ambassador Grew remarked that the result should be healthy and "we may expect to see a restraining influence on the hothead extremists." He was convinced that there were "symptoms of at least a slight cooling off of pro-Axis-sentiment."

The Wikawa-Drought Conversations. Ambassador Grew had good reasons for being optimistic. Since November of 1940, informal talks had been carried out by two Catholic priests and Japanese militarists and businessmen with Prince Konoye's and Washington's knowledge. The talks seemed to bear some fruit in the spring of 1941.

Back in November 29, 1940, Tadao Wikawa, a trustee of the Central Board of the Cooperative Bank of Japan, received a letter from a Catholic priest named James M. Drought asking to meet with him on the matter of bettering U.S.-Japanese relations. Enclosed in the communication was a letter of introduction by Lewis Strauss of Kuhn and Loeb of New York, the firm that helped to float Japanese bonds in Wall Street during the Russo-Japanese War. Wikawa was a former Treasury official and knew Konoye personally. On December 7 he wrote to Konoye:

"Enclosed is a letter from an American named Drought, whom I met the other day. I gathered that he wished to sound out our intentions with regard to adjusting relations with the United States especially on the matter of economic cooperation...

"He told me that Mr. Strauss wanted him to maintain close contact with me and talk business with me only. This may end up in nothing. But at least we can learn from him the opinion of one of the most influencial financial concerns which perhaps controls one-half of the financial world in the United States ... '"

Wikawa added that he had cleared the matter with General Muto,

Director of the Central Bureau of Military Affairs, and Colonel Iwakuro, his assistant, before meeting with the Catholic priest.

Father Drought also gave Wikawa a paper entitled "Practical Analysis of Our Position and Policy in the Far East with Special Emphasis on Our Relations with the United States," which was written as if the author were a Japanese. The calibre of the paper impressed Wikawa who thought it could not have been written by the priest alone. Concluding that the paper had had some official backing, Wikawa turned the paper over to Prince Konoye for his attention. This was on December 14, 1940.

In brief, Father Drought maintained that American public opinion of Japan and sentiment against Japan were so pronounced that they could drag the United States into an unwanted war with Japan. Aside from the calamity the war would inflict on the two nations, it was undesirable because the United States would no longer be able to take a unified action against Germany. For the good of the United States and of Japan, the two countries ought to come to some mutually satisfactory solutions to their problems.

Father Drought then analyzed Japan's geographical, military, and economic positions, and expounded the idea of the "Monroe Doctrine" for the Far East under which Japan would become the bulwark against European imperialism. If the two nations could work together on this basis in the years to come, the importance of Europe would eventually be minimized. Furthermore, the cooperation of the two nations would have the effect of preventing the spread of the European War to the Far East, and strengthening the two countries' respective positions against the Soviet Union. A treaty of friendship with the United States would also help Japan to check the advance of either Germany or Great Britain if one should emerge victorious from the current conflict.

Without sacrificing the positions already gained, Japan could still recognize the principle of the "open door." Since the United States was concerned with the security of the Philippines, Japan could invite it to sign a security pact. By informal conversations, the two countries should be able to resolve the questions relating to the Dutch East Indies or French Indo-China. As to the question of China, Japan should recognize a political system more acceptable to the American public opinion without radically altering the *fait accompli*. If the United States should insist on "preservation of territory" it might still be possible to exclude Manchuria from the application of this principle. If not, Japan should demand that the United States give some concrete method through which China's territorial integrity could be preserved and yet meet Japan's minimum demands—e.g., assurance that the country would not be divided by internal strife, that the country would be free from threat of Communism and maintain peace, order and prosperity.

In order to implement what he had suggested, Father Drought thought the heads of the two governments should meet either in Tokyo or in Honolulu, preferably the former. To prepare the way for the "leaders' meeting" first the Prime Minister or the Foreign Minister should make a public pronouncement appealing to the Americans for mutual understanding, and this should be done before Ambassador Nomura reached Washington, and preferably around December 20, when the Christmas spirit prevailed. The statement should denounce the Stimson Doctrine, advocate the creation of a Pan-Asian defense system, and give warning of the inherent danger in the present American policy which would force Japan to create a new "non-capitalistic" system in East Asia. The price of non-cooperation would be the total exclusion of American capital from this area. On the other hand, if the two countries cooperated, its beneficial effects would at once be felt by the American capital.[8]

General Muto and Colonel Iwakuro of the Central Military Affairs Bureau literally embraced Father Drought's suggestions. The paper embodied most of the concessions sought by the Japanese militarists in the past, without requiring Japan to provide substantial *quid pro quo.* Father Drought was later joined by Bishop James Edward Walsh, Superior General of the Catholic Mission Society at Maryknoll, New York. Bishop Walsh was a close friend of Postmaster General Walker, a prominent Catholic layman. The fact that the bishop had such excellent connections in Washington convinced some Japanese officials that something might indeed come out of this *démarche.* Encouraged by the initial response, the two priests went as far as to suggest that Matsuoka adopt the text of a speech prepared by them for delivery at the Japan-America Society meeting honoring Ambassador Nomura. Vice Minister Ohashi turned down the suggestion in disgust.

After holding lengthy conversations with General Muto on December 27, the two clerics left for Washington. In mid-January they were in the U.S. capital and took the matter up with Postmaster General Walker. The latter in turn consulted Secretary Hull. On January 20, a telegram was sent to Wikawa informing him that the talks were proceeding satisfactorily. Then on the next day another telegram told Wikawa that the matter was under consideration by the President him-

self, and that all preliminary preparation had been completed. On
January 23, the two priests had an interview with the President which
lasted for more than two hours. Confident that their White House
meeting had opened the door for further discussions, the two priests
cabled that Wikawa should come to Washington.

Both Bishop Walsh and Father Drought apparently overestimated
their own influence. The White House was perturbed by Bishop
Walsh's secret memorandum which contained many of the points
raised in Father Drought's paper. These points were radically different
from the Administration's position. Yet the Administration decided
to allow the two clerics to continue their informal contact with the
Japanese Embassy and report back their findings through Mr. Walker. Mr. Hull however preferred that the matter be held in abeyance
pending the arrival of the new Ambassador. This constituted the background of Mr. Hull's suggestion to Nomura when the two first
met, that he and Nomura should be the ones to conduct the talks.°

Mr. Wikawa arrived in the United States about the same time Admiral Nomura did; he immediatly started to lay ground for private
conversations. In February Colonel Iwakuro was relieved of his duty
as department head in the Central Military Affairs Bureau in order
to permit him to devote his full time to the pending negotiations.
Iwakuro had been a proponent of the Tripartite Pact, but was convinced that a war with the United States would be futile. He was
satisfiied to find that those who advocated war with the United States
were still in the minority within the Army, and the Navy was asking
for moderation. In the latter part of March Iwakuro joined Wikawa
in New York.

Proposal for Understanding. A "proposal for understanding" was
first drafted by Father Drought and the two Japanese representatives in
the early part of April. It was then submitted to Mr. Hull and to
Nomura. Despite the feeling that the document contained all that the
Japanese militarists could desire, Mr. Hull felt that some points
could be accepted as they stood and that still others could be agreed
to if modified. In any event, it was worth some exploration. On
April 14, he invited Ambassador Nomura to his Wardman Park Hotel
apartment to discuss the program with him. He inquired if the Ambassador were conversant with the content of the documents, and
whether his government wished to present that document officially to
the U.S. government as a basis for negotiations.

Even after this meeting Ambassador Nomura did not forward

the full text of the "Proposal for Understanding" to his government. He thought it was necessary first to prepare his superiors psychologically for its acceptance. On April 16 Secretary Hull and Ambassador Nomura met again. Hull pressed for a definite assurance in advance from Japan that it had the willingness and ability to go forward with a plan for settlement, and that it would abandon its "present doctrine of military conquest by force." Hull then presented the four principles he had long cherished as the basis of good relations between the nations. They were: (1) respect for the territorial integrity and the sovereignty of each and all nations; (2) support of the principle of noninterference in the internal affairs of other countries; (3) support of the principle of equality, including equality of commercial opportunity and (4) nondisturbance of the status quo in the Pacific except as the status quo may be altered by peaceful means. The Secretary also took the caution of informing Nomura that the two countries had not reached the stage of formal negotiations, and the two countries were merely engaged in preliminary informal conversation.[10]

After the meeting the Ambassador promptly cabled Tokyo the Drought-Wikawa-Iwakuro draft and Mr. Hull's four principles, but he failed to mention that the two countries had not reached the stage of formal negotiations. Nor did he take pains to point out that the draft was strictly informal and did not represent the views of the U.S. Government.

"It looks as though the document could change the course of history," was the comment of Vice Foreign Minister Ohashi when he reported to Konoye the content of Nomura's telegram. An emergency session of the Liaison Conference was called to discuss the government's position. The "Proposal for Understanding" which excited the Japanese ruling circles consisted of the following:

1. The concepts of the United States and of Japan respecting international relations and the character of nations.

2. The attitudes of both governments toward the European War.

3. The relations of both nations toward the China Affair.

4. Naval, aerial and mercantile marine relations in the Pacific.

5. Commerce between both nations and their financial cooperation.

6. Economic activity of both nations in the Southwestern Pacific area.

7. The policies of both nations affecting political stabilization in the Pacific.

The heart of the proposal was in point 3. It provided that the President of the United States would request Chiang Kai-shek to accept peace, if certain conditions were guaranteed by Japan. And if Chiang rejected Mr. Roosevelt's mediation offer, American aid to the former would be stopped.

Other points included a declaration by Japan that its "military obligation under the Axis Alliance comes into force only when one of the parties of the Alliance is aggressively attacked by a power not at present involved in the European War." On economic cooperation it was proposed that "both governments further consent to take necessary steps to the resumption of normal trade relations as formerly established under the Treaty of Navigation and Commerce between the United States and Japan."

These conditions were unmistakably favorable to Japan. But there were several conditions which the Japanese would consider restrictive of Japan's freedom of action. These conditions included: (1) As a pre-requisite for American economic cooperation, Japan would guarantee that its activities in the Southwestern Pacific area would be carried on by peaceful means: (2) the two powers would not recognize future transfer of territories within the Far East and in the Southwestern Pacific area to a European power; (3) the two nations would mutually pledge that they would not resort to such disposition of their naval forces and aerial forces as to menace each other, and (4) as soon as the first ray of hope for the settlement of the China Incident arose, the Japanese Government would agree to use its good offices to release for contract by Americans a certain percentage of Japan's total tonnage of merchant vessels, chiefly for the Pacific service. This would have permitted the United States to divert part of its merchant marine then in the Pacific service to the Atlantic to aid the British war efforts. In addition, the Proposal also contained provisions calling for a summit meeting by the heads of the governments.[11]

The Liaison Conference was overwhelmingly in favor of accepting the Proposal as a basis for negotiations. It found in the Proposal the best and fastest way of settling the China Incident. The Wang regime proved to be nothing but a deep disappointment, and direct negotiations with Chungking seemed almost impossible. Since Chungking relied heavily on the United States for support, Japan had no other choice but to accept the U. S. mediation. Furthermore, it was generally recognized that Japan's power was on the wane and its essential natural resources were at the exhausting point. Some strategists in the Supreme Command frankly admitted that Japan needed a period of recovery before it could undertake a vigorous southward advance program. At least for the time being, it seemed expedient to shake hands with the United States, in order to acquire the needed resources and to stockpile them.

Beneath the cool calculation, there was deep-seated distrust of the United States, a fear that the United States might circumvent and thwart Japan's efforts in East Asia. This prompted Prince Konoye, in his capacity as Acting Foreign Minister to ask Nomura's opinion: "Once we enter into an agreement with the United States, there might be a temporary breathing spell, but suppose Germany emerged victorious. Would it not make our future position untenable? Or suppose Great Britain and the United States should win the war, would there be any assurance that the two countries would honor their agreement with us? Would they not put pressure on us as they did after the First World War?"

Keeping "good faith" with Germany was Konoye's overriding consideration because of his unshakable belief that Germany would win the war. A meeting Konoye had with Kido in the Imperial Palace about that time underscores this sentiment. There the two officials were discussing new instructions to be sent to Ambassador Nomura. They agreed that Japan's basic position was to "bend every effort to keep good faith with Germany and Italy and at the same time to realize the establishment of a new order in the Greater East Asia Co-Prosperity Area."[12]

In the meantime, Tokyo's attitude drifted from one of enthusiasm to one of doubt. A meeting attended by officers of the Central Bureau of Military Affairs and the Central Bureau of Naval Affairs on April 21 was marked by its lack of sympathy with an out-and-out reconciliation with the United States. The officers were realistic in recognizing that the Tripartite Pact and the proposed agreement with the United States were mutually exclusive of each other. They wanted to accept the proposal, and wanted the talks in Washington to go on, not because they trusted the United States, but because they wanted to "outwit" it. A report prepared by them read in part: "The United States is taking advantage of our weakness in offering this proposal. It aims to forestall our positive southward expansion, and at the same time, is trying to gain time in order to strengthen its aid program for Great Britain. In so doing it hopes to weaken the Tripartite Pact, eliminate its foreign and domestic difficulties, complete its armament, and then attain leadership in world affairs."

The report warned against the danger of betraying the trust the nation had placed in the Tripartite Pact. As to Hull's four principles, hardly any attention was paid to them. In General Tojo's words, the Japanese placed much more emphasis on "the practical solution of existing problems than on a statement of general principles."[13]

On his way back from his European journey Matsuoka was in Dairen on April 20. Konoye phoned him about the Proposal for Understanding and urged his immediate return. Matsuoka was jubilant. "As he put down the receiver Matsouka was beaming," Toshikazu Kase, his aide, recalled. "The conversation with Steinhardt had borne fruit! After his return to Tokyo . . . he would soon fly to the United States to complete his peace program. He had brought about a rapprochement with Russia. He would restore friendship with China. This would be followed by conciliation with the United States. Together Japan and America would bring peace back to Europe. Such was his dream!"[14]

Matsuoka Blocks the "Proposal." Matsuoka returned to Tokyo on April 22. The Liaison Conference, eager to know what the Foreign Minister thought of the Proposal, had been in session since eight in the evening patiently awaiting his arrival. However, Matsuoka learned that the Proposal did not emanate from his conversations with Steinhardt and chose not to attend. He remarked to Vice Minister Ohashi that only a fool could accept such a proposal and then went to the Imperial Palace for an audience with the Emperor. After a frenzied search by Konoye, Matsuoka finally appeared at the meeting late in the evening. He evaded the questions posed to him but concentrated on talking about his visits with Mr. Hitler, Mr. Ciano, Mr. Stalin and the like. When pressed by Konoye he said flatly that even if the Army and Navy decided to accept, he could not agree to such "a weak proposition." He spoke of Japan's responsibility toward its allies, and cited the example of the Lansing-Ishii agreement during the First World War. In his own words, this agreement "permitted the United States to enter the war without fear of being attacked from the rear, and gave Japan the dirty work. Yet after the war it revoked the agrement." He continued to contend that the proposal was 70% out of bad will and 30% out of good will. He wanted to have two weeks, and better still, a month, to consider the matter carefully. Only a resolute Japan could ward off the danger of an open conflict with the United States, he declared.

Generals Tojo and Muto were for the acceptance of the proposal to "outwit" the United States, but they lacked diplomatic perceptives. While becoming weary and increasingly annoyed by Matsuoka's attitude they felt it best to yield on the matter. Repeated efforts were applied by the War and Navy Ministers as well as by the Prime Minister to persuade Matsuoka to accept. There was also talk of removing Matsuoka from his office if he persisted. But the Foreign Minister still wielded strong support from young officers and a cross section of the country. Matsuoka pretended illness and remained in his private residence for a week. Konoye also became ill and no meeting of the Liaison Conference was held until May 3. In the intervening week, Matsuoka still held the key to the future of the "Proposal for Understanding."

Matsuoka's reluctance to accept the Proposal was partly due to the fact that the conversations had been inaugurated without his knowledge, and partly due to political considerations. Home Minister Baron Hiranuma and Matsuoka were rivals in the Konoye Cabinet, and were often at odds with one another. When the true nature of the Proposal from the United States was first conveyed to Matsuoka, he suspected that Hiranuma was the one who started this in order to circumvent Matsuoka's authority as Foreign Minister. He recalled that it was Hiranuma who had suggested that he go to Europe. Thus, at a welcoming rally at the Hibiya Hall, Matsuoka spoke of the impotence and indecisiveness characteristic of Japanese leaders. His particular object being Baron Hiranuma. For Matsuoka to acquiesce to a project originated by Hiranuma would be tantamount to mortgaging his political life under Hiranuma's influence.

For some time, Matsuoka had been planning for a Cabinet of his own and his close friend Minister of Overseas Affairs Akita was actively engaged in this scheme. Having seen Hitler, Mussolini, and Stalin, and concluded a successful diplomatic journey, Matsuoka was on the crest of popularity. There was also considerable following among the youth of the nation. It was felt that another dramatic step such as flying across the Pacific and meeting with President Roosevelt would have assured the premiership for him. He dreamed of this, and for this reason he declined an offer from the United Press' Roy Howard to come to the United States while he was still in Berlin. At that time a specially chartered plane was waiting for him at Lisbon to take him to Washington for a confidential meeting with Mr. Roosevelt. His political ambition also dictated that the negotiations should be carried on solely by himself as in the case of the Tripartite Pact.

After the war both in Japan and in the United States, several theories were advanced to ascertain that the Drought-Wikawa-Iwakuro conversations were initiated by Prince Konoye. Matsuoka's journey to

Europe was supposedly a maneuver to get Matsuoka out of the way, so the Prince could exercise more direct control over the negotiations with the United States.[15] This hypothesis is not supported by evidence now available in the Japanese Foreign Office Archives. It was true that Prince Konoye had given his blessings to Wikawa's mission. But he did not go further. He was rather anxious to have the counsel of his Foreign Minister. In fact he had been instrumental in delaying the instructions to Ambassador Nomura pending Matsuoka's return to Tokyo. As Acting Foreign Minister in Matsuoka's absence, and also as Prime Minister, he had been in the position to issue instructions if he saw fit. He had chosen not to do so. His patience in dealing with Matsuoka also proves that the Prince was in essential agreement with his enigmatic Foreign Minister.

The questionnaire Prince Konoye sent to Ambassador Nomura on April 19 shows the similarity of thought between the Prince and the Foreign Minister on basic issues. Where Konoye inquired of a possible "chilling" effect on Japanese relations with Germany, Matsuoka spoke of faithfulness to the agreement made with the Nazis. When the Prince sounded off his distrust of the United States intentions, there was an echo in Matsuoka's talk about the "breach of faith" committed by the United States after the First World War.

Contrary to popular belief, the amendments Matsuoka presented to the Liaison Conference on May 3 after two weeks' delay, were strikingly similar in content to the ones prepared by the Foreign Office while it was still under Prince Konoye's guidance. Konoye read these suggested amendments, made certain concurring remarks on the margin, and approved all of them. It is hard to conceive that Prince Konoye could have changed his mind in a fortnight.[16] Matsuoka's sin was not in differing on policy matters but in his procrastination, and not so much in his procrastination as in his inability to find a better alternative to the common problem.

The amendments as approved by the Liaison Conference on May 3, and later presented to Mr. Hull on May 12 with oral explanations, contained some important departures from the original "Proposal for Understanding." They reflected the views of Matsuoka and a majority of the Army and Navy. Under these amendments the Government of Japan would declare that the purpose of the Tripartite Pact was and would be defensive and was designed to prevent participation in the European War by nations not presently involved in it. On the other hand, the Government of the United States would declare that its attitude toward the European War was not dictated by such aggressive measures as to assist any one nation against another.

As to economic activities of both nations in the Southwestern Pacific area, Japan would declare that it would pursue its activities by peaceful means and would require the United States to cooperate in the production and procurement of natural resources—e.g., oil, rubber, tin, nickel, etc.—from this area. There was no qualifying phrase "without resorting to arms" as in the original "Proposal for Understanding." Matsuoka insisted that "the peaceful policy of the Japanese Government has been made clear on many occasions in various statements made both by the Premier and by the Foreign Minister," and regarded their prior statements as sufficient guarantee.

On the critical issue of cessation of hostilities in China, the amendments stripped off all the conditions attached and substituted instead that American proposals to Chiang Kai-shek for peace should be based on the Konoye Statement of January 1938, the basic treaty with Nanking of November 1940, and the joint declaration by Japan, Manchukuo and Wang Ching-wei of the same date. Matsuoka justified these changes on the ground that the three principles enunciated by Prince Konoye—i.e., neighborly friendship, joint defense against communism and economic cooperation—were sufficient to encompass the conditions originally set forth in the Proposal.

The original Proposal also provided for a summit conference to be held at Honolulu between President Roosevelt and Prince Konoye. Matsuoka dropped this provision, stating that he did not want the matter to be contained in a formal agreement. However, he would agree to an informal exchange of notes setting forth the procedures for such a meeting.[17]

The majority at the May 3 meeting favored new instructions embodying the amendments to be sent immediately to Nomura in Washington. But Matsuoka persuaded them first to accept his version of a neutrality pact between the United States and Japan as a trial balloon. He prevailed on the Conference to rely on his "diplomatic skills" in the question of informing the Germans about the existence of current U. S.-Japanese talks. The day of "total reliance on Matsuoka" was not over yet, and the conference granted him the *carte blanche*. After the meeting, Matsuoka sent two telegrams to Washington, one asking Ambassador Nomura to proffer a neutrality pact to the United States "on his own initiative," and the other containing Matsuoka's tentative reply to be presented as an oral statement.

On the next day the Foreign Minister boarded a train westward to

Ise to worship at the shrine of the Emperor's ancestors. This was calculated to gain popular support, since Matsuoka's presence always drew a large crowd in the western part of the country. In his absence, Mr. Sakamoto, head of the European and Asian Affairs Bureau, was sent to the German and Italian Ambassadors to inform them of the pending negotiations with the United States. The battle was on. Matsuoka made full use of the time given him by the Liaison Conference to sway young officers in the armed services to his views. On April 6, after returning from Ise, Matsuoka confided to the German Ambassador that his handling of the American proposal would probably strain his relations with the financial circles, but he would conduct the negotiations in his own way. He would therefore appreciate having Ribbentrop's views on this matter for Japan's "domestic" consumption.

Matsuoka also told the Emperor that Japan should stand on the side of Germany and Italy if the United States entered the war. Above all, an attack on Singapore would become necessary. He also predicted that the war might spread and involve the Soviet Union. In that case, Japan should also fight in Siberia and discard the Neutrality Pact. He cautioned that the adjustment of relations with the United States would become useless in such contingencies. Japan should not court America's favor, forgetting about its obligations to Germany and Italy.

Trusting Prince Konoye would go along with his views, Matsuoka confided in him on what had taken place at the Imperial Palace. The perturbed Prince secretly discussed with the War and Navy Ministers what could be done about this unpredictable Foreign Minister. The next day, through Kido, the Emperor suggested that Konoye might seriously consider removing Matsuoka.

Konoye's reluctance to fire Matsuoka stemmed from his personal weakness as well as from political considerations. The advantage of having a rapprochement with the United States had to be carefully equated with the possible domestic repercussions. Japan could well be torn into two bitterly dissenting camps if Germany openly voiced its disagreement, or if the United States radically amended the plan Japan suggested or entered the war after reaching an agreement. The Prince was not willing to take the gamble and could only promise the Emperor that he would do his best to bring about an early solution to the problem.

Matsuoka's temporary reply and offer of a neutrality pact were presented on May 7 to Secretary Hull, who simply brushed them aside.

"As I see it," Ambassador Nomura cabled, "the tense international situation and the attitude of the United States no longer allow us to engage in propaganda, bluff, and guesswork. For the greater good of our country, I beg of you to show your statesmanship, and make a great stride toward adjusting our relations with the United States." The Ambassador later commented that unless Japan wanted to commit a love suicide with Germany, there was no reason for its foreign policy to be so inflexible.

The confusion in Tokyo was accelerated when Ambassador Oshima in Berlin heard of what was going on between Tokyo and Washington and asked "if there were any secret negotiations?" The Military Attaché in Berlin threatened that the entire Embassy staff in Berlin would resign *en masse* in protest.

On May 11 Colonel Iwakuro reported that the great debate on providing American naval protection of supplies intended for Britain was almost over. Mr. Roosevelt was expected to make a speech on May 14 proclaiming the use of convoys. With Iwakuro's telegram in hand, Konoye finally succeeded in persuading Matsuoka to authorize Nomura to submit to Secretary Hull the amendments agreed to by the Liaison Conference of May 3. This was to be done with or without a reply from Germany.

Nomura's two meetings with Mr. Hull on May 12 and 14 hardly shed a "ray of hope" for understanding between the two countries. Secretary Hull carefully reminded Nomura that the meetings between the two were still in the stage of "talks" and there was as yet no question of "negotiations." The future discussions were to be conducted on a similar basis.

Just after Matsuoka had instructed Nomura to communicate the amendments to Secretary Hull, the eagerly awaited reply from Ribbentrop reached Tokyo. Ribbentrop warned that the policy of the American Government was to let the Axis powers fire the first shot, while it continued its unneutral actions without declaring war. He suggested that Japan consider American proposals only if the United States abstained from the convoy system or similar actions. This note was followed by a strongly-worded protest submitted on May 17, reminding Matsuoka of Japan's obligations under the Tripartite Pact and insisting he make them the basis of an agreement with the United States.

In Tokyo two meetings of the Liaison Conference were held on May 15 and 22. The meetings did not exceed the realm of exchanging opinions and news. Matsuoka apparently made the most of the

German reaction in his fight against his colleagues. He contended that only through strength could Japan hope to come to terms with the United States.

On May 23 Matsuoka found out that the first proposal was made from Nomura and not from Hull. The Japanese Cabinet as a whole had believed that the "Proposal for Understanding" represented the official view of the United States Government. Only Matsuoka at times had suspected that this was not the case. Furthermore, the Navy deciphered a telegram sent by Lord Halifax in Washington to the British Foreign Office. It said that Mr. Hull was of the opinion that while all the responsible persons in the Japanese Government wanted a rapprochement with the United States, Mr. Matsuoka was the only one opposing it. A strongly worded telegram was sent to Nomura asking him to proceed immediately to clear the misunderstanding with Mr. Hull. Nomura had just sent a telegram to Matsuoka requesting greater authority and latitude in negotiating with the American Secretary of State. The latter was ignored with an irate note on the margin, "that Nomura, a fool," apparently in Matsuoka's own handwriting.

By this time, however, Matsuoka was fast losing ground. General Tojo, who had been a close friend of the Foreign Minister since their Manchurian days, no longer supported his views. The political coalition that guided the Second Konoye Cabinet was at a breaking point. The so-called Niki-Sansuke—the two Ki's and three Suke's—the five men who owed their prominence to their prior activities in Manchuria no longer worked as a unit.[18] No one had so far openly challenged Matsuoka's authority as Foreign Minister. But the undercurrent was already visible, and Matsuoka unabashedly hinted that he would resign if the Emperor so desired.

Despite the enthusiasm Konoye and Tojo had shown in the proposal, it is extremely doubtful that the agreement could have ever been reached between the two countries on such shaky grounds. Mr. Hull had been skeptical of the usefulness of the original "Proposal for Understanding" submitted to him through Postmaster General Walker. Furthermore, the four principles of Mr. Hull which he insisted as "a basis for starting conversations" would have nullified most of the gains Japan had attained in the past. The confusion which accompanied the transmission of these documents between Washington and Tokyo also indicated that a rapprochement was still far out of reach. In a sense Matsuoka's amendments represented what the Japanese militarists sought from the United States. The Japanese who had thought that the Proposal originated in Washington were not prepared to retreat from the position they had taken in the Matsuoka amendments.

There was a false conception of the balance of power which dominated the minds of Japanese statesmen. It was true that Japan was not strong enough to face the United States alone. But together with the might of Germany and Italy, Japan could challenge the United States effectively. The Axis alliance seemed to have provided an invincible defensive shield for the security of Japan. The Japanese were not willing to discard this alliance, and no matter how disagreeable the attitude of the Foreign Minister had been, they had to follow his lead. In his person, Matsuoka represented the *alter ego* of other Japanese statesmen. When others were content in their garbs of Dr. Jeykell, Matsuoka recklessly showed them how they could become Mr. Hyde.

There were several conversations between Ambassador Nomura and Secretary Hull in Washington in the ensuing weeks. There were some interim proposals, but they were simply restatements of past positions.[19]

The talks were at a standstill; the Cabinet found no solution. Matsuoka and Konoye, while outwardly cordial, showed no inclination of yielding to one another. Only some superior force or radical change in the international situation could rescue Japan from this predicament.

Chapter XII

COLLAPSE OF MATSUOKA'S DIPLOMACY

Quandary over the Nazi-Soviet War. News of the war between Germany and Soviet Russia reached Tokyo on the early morning of June 22. "Japan is in a quandary as a result of the German-Soviet war," observed Ambassador Grew.

When Japan first concluded the Tripartite Pact, it was done on the premises that the close association of Germany and Soviet Russia would continue for some time—at least two or three years—and that an alignment with these two powerful nations would insure Japan's place in the sun. Matsuoka did not discount the possibility of an eventual conflict between the two countries, but he hoped that during the two or three years he could bring about a rapprochement with the United States, end the conflict in China, and solidify Japan's claims to the South Sea regions. The German-Soviet conflict rendered a *coup de grâce* to all these fond dreams.

The General Staff and the Foreign Office were kept informed of German intentions. During Matsuoka's visit to Berlin, Ribbentrop made it clear to Matsuoka that the relations between the Reich and the Soviet Union were deteriorating, and both he and Hitler indicated that the German Army was prepared to crush Soviet resistance at any time if Russia chose to betray Germany. Moreover, in his telegram of May 18, Ambassador Oshima stated in unmistakable terms that war between Germany and Russia was expected momentarily.[1]

Matsuoka was in no particular hurry to ascertain German intentions. But he was constrained to wire Ribbentrop some advice in his personal capacity "as a friend." He requested that the German Government refrain from attacking Soviet Russia for the common good of Germany and Japan, but preferred to let the matter rest there. Ribbentrop replied that the result of the war would be beneficial to Japan, and predicted that the war would end within two or three weeks. Oshima was also told by the German High Command that the war would be concluded within four weeks. It would be a police action, since it could hardly constitute a war.

On June 4 Oshima was invited to Hitler's retreat at Berchtesgaden and heard directly from the Führer that Germany would attack Soviet Russia "to eliminate communism . . . for the sake of humanity." The Liaison Conference which convened to study Hitler's implicit invitation to join the war decided that the chance of war was remote. Matsuoka expounded a theory that odds against the war were about six to four. Germany was either camouflaging its intent to attack Great Britain during the coming summer or using military pressure to gain more favorable terms from Soviet Russia. General Tojo agreed with Matsuoka.

Within the next ten days Matsuoka had a serious second thought. To the Privy Councillors, he informally said the danger of war had increased to eighty per cent according to the latest available information. Yet the tense situation might not result in war, since Stalin would be likely to accept whatever conditions Hitler would impose on him. So great was Matsuoka's belief in Hitler's ability to force his terms without resorting to war that he could regard the possible German-Soviet clash as of secondary importance in his agenda. His primary concern at that time was to entertain the visiting head of the Nanking regime, Wang Ching-wei. The day Germany attacked Russia, Matsuoka was found in the Tokyo Kabuki Theater, in the company of Wang Ching-wei.[2]

The German action was such an affront to Japan that Prince Konoye thought the resignation of his Cabinet *en masse* inevitable. Hitler had betrayed the confidence of Japan and destroyed the basis of the Tripartite Pact. He then toyed with the idea of withdrawing from the Axis partnership. "The policy which was proper in the fall of 1940 became a dangerous one in the summer of 1941," recalled the Prince in his memoirs. "This is so because as a result of the outbreak of war between Germany and Russia, the hope of an accord between Japan, Germany and Soviet Russia was dashed, and Soviet Russia was driven into the British-American camp. It became a dangerous policy for us to stick with the alliance with Germany."[3]

Yet to Foreign Minister Matsuoka, the war represented an entirely new challenge and opportunity. For him the German move meant only one thing, that Japan ought to follow the steps of its ally and declare war on the Soviet Union. By-passing Prince Konoye—as he had previously done so often—Matsuoka went to the Imperial Palace expounding the thesis that Japan had no other choice but to stand on the side of Germany, lest Japan be faced with the possibility of fighting against Soviet Russia, the United States, and Great Britain all at the same time. He thought the southward advance could be dropped temporarily. The Emperor was interested in knowing if

Matsuoka's policy would bring about the "positive penetration of the Japanese Navy and Army both in the South and the North," and if Japan had enough national power to meet such "a preponderant military operation." Konoye later assured the Emperor that Matsuoka was only projecting his policy for the future and was not necessarily intending to go into action immediately.

Here again Matsuoka's inordinate passion for power exceeded his better judgment as a diplomat. It was recalled that Matsuoka was the one who told Hitler: "Open fire, and the Nation will then be united." He was apparently counting on the support of the powerful Army group headed by Generals Araki and Ishihara who consistently advocated that Japan could never feel safe until it had taken Vladivostok and the Maritime Provinces. This group which drew its members from the discredited Kodoha represented a potential threat to the preeminence enjoyed by the China group centered around the War Office now headed by General Tojo. Resurgence of the Araki-Ishihara group would be assured if Japan declared war on Russia, and in all likelihood Matsuoka would be entrusted with the premiership replacing Prince Konoye.

Theoretically Japan was at a point where it could radically revise its foreign policy and withdraw from the Tripartite Pact. Prince Konoye favored this course. Yet Matsuoka and the Army were reluctant to follow this advice, since German success had been so spectacular. The only policy to be decided was in effect narrowed down to the question of whether Japan should immediately open fire on Soviet Russia or delay it.

The speedy elimination of Soviet Russia, counselled Ribbentrop, would "probably be the best way to convince the United States of the absolute futility of entering into the war on the side of England, then completely isolated and facing the most powerful alliance on earth." However, the memory of the severe setbacks which the Japanese Kwantung Army suffered in 1938 and 1939 at the hands of the Soviet Far Eastern Army was not forgotten. Despite the damages it sustained in the western front, Russia moved none of its active forces from the Far East. The Army General Staff was realistic in estimating its own strength, and hoped that the Germans would soon defeat the Soviet forces and compel the Kremlin to withdraw its Far Eastern Army to Europe. If this should happen it would provide a more favorable opportunity for Japan to enter the war. In the meantime the bulk of the Japanese Army was still in the China theater, and the combat-ready troops were concentrated in South China and in

French Indo-China for southward operation. Furthermore the much needed oil and other raw materials were not found in Siberia. If the war lasted more than two years the supply of oil would be completely exhausted. It seemed quite illogical for Japan to abandon its southward expansion in favor of a rather dubious prize in the North.

Inter-service rivalry also entered the picture. If war against Russia should materialize, it would chiefly be the Army's task and the Navy would be assigned the thankless task of anti-submarine operation. This would imply that the equal distribution of the defense budget as agreed in 1936 would probably be discarded in favor of the Army. On the other hand, in southward expansion the Navy would be given a major role.

An Imperial Conference held on July 2 was a clear indication that a compromise had been reached between one extreme which advocated the outright cancellation of the Tripartite Pact and the other extreme which urged an immediate participation in the war. The decisions restated Japan's basic policies to be in (1) the establishment of the Greater East Asia Co-Prosperity Area, (2) an early settlement of the China Incident, and (3) the security and preservation of the nation, including the southward advance and, if feasible, a settlement of the Soviet question. As to how these decisions could be implemented, the Conference supplied these clues:

"Though the spirit of the Tripartite Pact will form the keynote of our attitude toward the German-Soviet War, we shall not intervene for a while, but shall steadily proceed with military preparations against the Soviet Union and decide our final attitude independently. At the same time, we shall continue carefully correlated activities in the diplomatic field.

"In case the German-Soviet War should develop to our advantage, we will make use of our military strength, settle the Soviet question, and guarantee the safety of our northern borders."[4]

In other words, the Tokyo government decided to adopt a wait-and-see policy. Meanwhile the Kwantung Army was steadily reinforced in anticipation of a possible attack on Siberia.

The July 2 Conference also touched on the question of the U. S.-Japanese relations. It clearly foresaw the possibility of an armed conflict with the United States if Japan forced its way deeper into the South Sea regions: "In case the diplomatic negotiations break down, preparations for war with the United States and England will also be carried forward. First of all, the plans that have been laid with reference to French Indo-China and Thai will be prosecuted, with a view to consolidating our position in the southern territories. In carrying out the plans outlined in the foregoing article, we will not be deterred by the possibility of being involved in a war with the United States and England." The tone of this decision is not more bellicose than the ones in the decisions of July 26 and 27, 1940, reached almost a year earlier. However, in order to understand the full significance of the July 2, 1941 decision, it will be necessary to return to the narrative of the U. S.-Japanese negotiations.

Matsuoka: Persona Non Grata. It was not until June 21 that Secretary Hull handed to Ambassador Nomura his reply to the Matsuoka amendments delivered to the Secretary on May 12. This note was marked "unofficial, exploratory and without commitment." However, it was actually the culmination of the past few months' conversations between Secretary Hull and Ambassador Nomura and their aides, and represented the most comprehensive statement of the American position on outstanding issues. It was accompanied by an oral statement which was highly critical of Foreign Minister Matsuoka.[5]

The note contained a lengthy statement of the basic concepts of the United States with respect to international relations; and the American positions in regard to the European war, peaceful settlement of the China Incident, commercial and economic relations of both countries in the Pacific area, and neutralization of the Philippine Islands. Several annexes and proposed letters were attached to the main document. One of these would give the United States freedom to choose its course of action toward Germany, while neutralizing Japan as far as the Tripartite Pact was concerned. The other would provide specific terms of settlement of the China Incident, and still another would restrict the flow of commodities between the two countries "in amounts up to the figures of usual or pre-war trade, except, in the case of each commodity which it needs for its own purposes of security and self-defense." Should Japan accept the June 21 note it would have to modify radically its relations with Germany, and settle the China Incident on less favorable terms without having the assurance of resumption of normal trade relations with the United States. The note must have sounded unduly harsh to Ambassador Nomura, coming just a day after the United States announced a ban on the export of oil from Atlantic and Gulf coast ports to all countries, except Great Britain and the Latin American Republics.

In delivering the note, Secretary Hull did not hide his suspicion of the intent of the Japanese Government, and of its Foreign Minister in particular. He told Nomura orally a point he had made on the Tripartite Pact: "At a time when Nazi Germany has invaded some fifteen or so countries, the Japanese Minister for Foreign Affairs is declaring in effect that measures of resistance by countries not already actually invaded would call for action by Japan under the Tripartite Pact. This is like saying that, if a tiger should break loose in the countryside and if a villager living a mile or so away from where the tiger is committing depredations and killing neighbors should go out and attack the tiger in order to protect his family, his action would constitute aggression."[6]

Under these circumstances further conversations would be futile, the Secretary added. This was put in unequivocal terms in his oral statement which also made it crystal clear that the stationing of Japanese troops in China "as a measure of cooperation with China in resisting Communistic activities" affected the sovereign rights of a third country, and was counter to the "liberal policies to which the United States is committed."

Before communicating all of these points raised by the Secretary, Ambassador Nomura did his utmost to convince the Secretary that several of the points were unacceptable to Japan, and it was better if those objectionable sections were deleted or not communicated to Tokyo at all. Yet on June 23, he obligingly telegraphed the entire content of the note which arrived in Tokyo the next day. By then Ambassador Nomura was a seasoned observer of Washington's mood. He took this occasion to impress on his superiors that unless Japan reached an understanding with the United States, the alternative would be the latter's freezing Japanese assets. He also cautioned Tokyo that there would be no further hope of adjusting relations with the United States if Japan expanded further to the South.

The Imperial Conference of July 2 was primarily concerned with the attitude to be taken toward the German-Russian War, and there was no visible evidence that the U. S. note of June 21 had materially affected its outcome. According to Prince Konoye, the Japanese Government decided to occupy Southern French Indo-China in order to appease the activists who were agitating a fight against Russia. On the other hand, Matsuoka's supporters vehemently argued that it was precisely for the reverse reason that Matsuoka advocated northward expansion. By having the Army happily occupied in attacking Russia, Matsuoka hoped to cool off the desire of those who wanted to expand southward. Southern French Indo-China occupied a strategic position in its relation to Singapore and the Dutch East Indies. He regarded any move toward this direction as further endangering Japan's relations with the United States.

The fact that the decision was taken at all suggests that neither Prince Konoye nor his colleagues felt the danger of an outright break with the United States was imminent. It was Tokyo's view that the United States was not ready to fight yet, and as long as this condition persisted, Japan could expand without incurring retaliatory measures from the United States. Among other factors that influenced the decision were (1) the failure to reach an agreement with the Dutch East Indies for extensive commercial commitments in recent months, and (2) the incapacity of the Soviet Union to strike at Japan as the result of the German-Soviet War.

To placate Matsuoka's hurt feelings, on July 4, Prince Konoye wrote a personal letter to the Foreign Minister, seeking his cooperation in bringing about an understanding with the United States. Pointing to the danger of a two-front war against Soviet Russia and the United States, the Prince stated the occupation of Southern French Indo-China might be postponed, "unless the Soviet question is solved." He also suggested that Japan should go ahead with its plan of a rapprochement with the United States even though it would incur the wrath of Germany. He added that the Emperor was gravely concerned about the U. S.-Japanese relations.

Matsuoka, son of a Choshu samurai, was apparently moved by the Emperor's concern. He phoned the Prince the same night, and conferred with Konoye on the morrow, offering to resign if his policy became a hindrance to an amicable settlement of outstanding issues with the United States.

In the meantime, President Roosevelt sent a personal message to Prince Konoye which was delivered to the latter through Ambassador Grew on July 6. It was a plea to the Prince for Japan not to intervene in the Nazi-Soviet war on the side of Germany. The message was addressed to Prince Konoye, but the latter felt that he should not attend to the matter alone and referred it to Matsuoka. At Matsuoka's suggestion, different versions of the reply were drafted by staff members of the Foreign Office and the Cabinet Secretary. But in the end Matsuoka drafted his own, ignoring what the Prince wanted to state in the other versions. In his reply, Matsuoka assured the President that the Japanese Government had "not so far considered the possibility of joining the hostilities against the Soviet Union," but inquired "whether it is really the intention of the President . . . to intervene in the European War?"

By this time, the United States intelligence had finally succeeded in deciphering the Japanese diplomatic code, and the substance of the July 2 decision was already known to Washington.[7] As a result, the U. S. attitude became visibly stiffened. Ambassador Nomura was unaware of the existence of the "magic," the deciphering technique employed by the U. S. Navy, but could not help noticing the changed attitude in Washington. There was no sign that the United States would capitulate or yield to Japanese demands, even if Japan should adopt a tougher line, the Ambassador cautioned. He asked Tokyo to reconsider its stand, and requested instructions.

Nomura's request prompted another meeting of the Liaison Conference on July 10. Matsuoka was accompanied by his adviser Saito, and both insisted that the American proposal of June 21 was nothing but a scheme to subjugate Japan, and the only matter that could be discussed at the Conference was how the negotiations could best be broken off. After the meeting Matsuoka, in a strongly-worded telegram, reprimanded Ambassador Nomura for his handling of the negotiations and for his use of "associates," not duly accredited diplomats and not authorized by him.

Meanwhile, disturbed by the attitude of the Foreign Minister, Konoye secretly met with the War, Navy, and Home Ministers. The presence of Home Minister Hiranuma was noteworthy in that Hiranuma and Matsuoka were political enemies of long-standing. By then Konoye was obviously on the side of those who opposed the Foreign Minister. The subject of their discussion was whether they could continue the present negotiations with the United States without the Foreign Minister, and if so, on what basis. Ironically enough the meeting ended with the participants realizing that they were in essential agreement with the Foreign Minister on basic issues.

At the July 12 meeting of the Liaison Conference, the substance of what had been discussed in the meeting two days earlier by the four ministers was restated. The War and Navy Ministers made it clear that they were not willing to accept the American terms as contained in the June 21 note. Nor would they agree to scrap the Tripartite Pact. On the Chinese question, they would allow the United States to make peace overtures to Chiang Kai-shek, but would not permit the United States to set forth the conditions for a settlement. They were nevertheless anxious to continue the negotiations so Japan could occupy Southern French Indo-China without opposition.

On the basis of the July 12 decision, Matsuoka agreed to draft a counter-proposal, and referred the matter to his adviser Saito, Chief of American Bureau Terasaki, Cabinet Secretary Tomida, Military Affairs Bureau Chief General Muto, and Naval Affairs Bureau Chief Admiral Oka. Matsuoka himself did not participate in the discussion. He pretended illness but received German Ambassador Ott on various occasions.

On July 14, Matsuoka approved a draft which modified the June 21 note on several points. The draft included a clause stating that "in case the European War unfortunately extends, the Government of Japan maintains that its attitude will be determined solely by the considerations of the fulfillment of its treaty obligations and of the defense of its own national welfare and security." The draft also eliminated from the American note any mention of the conditions to be offered to the Chungking Government.[8]

While it was the understanding of the Liaison Conference that the counter-proposal finally agreed upon would be immediately despatched to Washington, Matsuoka insisted that Hull's "oral statement" should be rejected first. In his view, the oral statement was an intolerable attempt on the United States' part to interfere in Japan's domestic affairs and could be interpreted as a demand for Matsuoka's dismissal. Citing the Delcassé affair during the Algiers crisis of 1905, Matsuoka termed the document "impolite and improper." Konoye feared that the outright rejection of the "oral statement" without an accompanying counter-proposal to soften the impact might worsen the already strained relations between the two countries. He stressed that the rejection and the counter-proposal should be despatched to Washington simultaneously. At eight in the evening of July 14 Dr. Saito was at Konoye's private residence. This gave Konoye the opportunity to urge him to send the telegrams. Saito promised that he would do his best. At midnight Konoye wanted to be certain, and called Mr. Terasaki, Chief of the American Bureau, on the phone. To his surprise, Terasaki found that the rejection of the oral statement was already sent to Washington by Dr. Saito's order without Terasaki's knowledge. The telegram had been set on code since eight o'clock. On the other hand, the counter-proposal had not even reached the stage of being coded.

Matsuoka was absent from his office the following day. Terasaki waited for Vice Minister Ohashi to come to the office and got his signature in order to send the new instructions containing the counter-proposal to Ambassador Nomura. It was also learned on that day that Matsuoka had already ordered Chief of Euro-Asian Bureau Sakamoto to inform the German Foreign Office of the content of the counter-proposal.

Mr. Hull expressed surprise that his oral statement was interpreted in that manner and agreed to have it recalled. It otherwise caused no difficulty, but Ambassador Nomura decided to tender his resignation.

In the meantime, incensed by Matsuoka's obstinacy, General Tojo demanded Matsuoka's dismissal at a meeting he had with Prince Konoye and the Home and Navy Ministers. He suggested that either Matsuoka should be fired, or the Cabinet resign *en bloc* and then form a new one without Matsuoka. Prince Konoye was cool to both of these suggestions. It was he who had insisted on the selection of Matsuoka with the hope of having him conduct foreign policies without interference from the Army. He felt that Matsuoka's failure was his own making, and wanted to take the responsibility by resigning himself. He thought Baron Hiranuma would have made an excellent Premier to succeed him. Konoye would submit his resignation "in order to facilitate the nation in accomplishing the aims of the holy war." Lord Privy Seal Kido thought the proposed reason for resignation too evasive. The Emperor also inquired whether it was not possible to fire Matsuoka alone. But Konoye persisted so Japan could avoid giving the appearance of yielding to American pressure. The formal action was taken the next day in a surprise Cabinet meeting. Matsuoka was absent, having been confined to bed by illness. On July 17 the elder statesmen unanimously approved formation of another cabinet by Prince Konoye which was completed by July 18.

The Third Konoye Cabinet. The most conspicuous change in the Third Konoye Cabinet was the absence of Matsuoka and his replacement by Admiral Toyoda. The Admiral previously held the posts of Vice Minister of Navy and Minister of Commerce and Industry in the Second Konoye Cabinet. As a naval officer, Toyoda was well versed in the Navy's sentiment that there should be no war against the United States, and as a former Minister of Commerce and Industry, he had first-hand knowledge of Japan's acute need for raw materials. Lately he had been advocating that a clash between the United States and Japan should be avoided at all cost.. It was Prince Konoye's hope that the new Foreign Minister would carry through negotiations with the United States to a satisfactory conclusion. Vainly he hoped that the new Cabinet would make a good impression on Washington and facilitate future negotiations.

In Washington, Ambassador Nomura did not communicate to Secretary Hull Matsuoka's July 15 counter-proposal. He found the document evasive, since it did not touch on the vital issues of the rights of self-defense, of stationing troops in North China and Mongolia, and of a non-discriminatory commercial policy in China. Since the Cabinet had just been reorganized, he thought it prudent to ask for new instructions.

The Ambassador's request was quietly turned down, with Admiral Toyoda stating that there had been no change in Japan's foreign policy: "As successor of former Foreign Minister Matsuoka," wrote Toyoda, "I intend to continue his foreign policy and to strengthen even more the close unity of Japan, Germany, and Italy, and march forward in the common spirit."[9] This statement was merely a reflection of what the militarists wanted of the Third Konoye Cabinet. Indeed Toyoda's appointment as Foreign Minister was conditioned on the following three points, imposed by the Army High Command:

"1. The basic policies decided on July 2 should be upheld, and military occupation of Southern French Indo-China should be carried out according to the time table previously agreed upon.

"2. No delay should be allowed for preparation of the northward and southward expansion.

"3. Negotiations with the United States should be conducted in the manner previously agreed upon, and should not be carried out in a way contradictory to the spirit of the Tripartite Pact."[10]

In plainer language, the military served notice that no change in the foreign policy would be tolerated, and if the Konoye Cabinet chose to depart from the agreed-upon policies, it would run the risk of being overthrown by the military. Such an overt threat had not been employed against the Second Konoye Cabinet. During that period, Foreign Minister Matsuoka generally had a free hand in determining what procedures should be followed in carrying out policies decided by the Liaison Conference. This had lasted until the conclusion of the Neutrality Pact with Soviet Russia.

The Army's renewed interest in placing itself at the driver's seat in foreign policy questions, both in substantive matters and procedural matters, indicated that the Army was bent on implementing its expansionist policies without interference by the civilian branch of the government. In this instance its primary objective was the occupation of Southern French Indo-China.

Freezing Order Follows Southern Indo-China Occupation.   Conspicuously absent from Japan's Southern French Indo-China policy was the force of moderation. In the past, the Navy represented such a force and successfully tempered the Army's inordinate ambitions. However, in regard to French Indo-China, the Navy was an advocate of military occupation. In fact, as early as April 1941, the Navy had already contemplated the use of force against French Indo-China and Thailand if encirclement by America, Britain, China, and the Dutch East Indies (the ABCD encirclement) developed to such a degree that it constituted a threat to national security.

The decision to occupy Southern French Indo-China in July was directly influenced by the failure of the talks in the Dutch East Indies. The Army and Navy High Command attributed this to the obstructionist tactics of the United States and Great Britain. They also noted that Japan encountered difficulties in acquiring a sufficient amount of rubber and rice since the breakdown of the talks in Batavia. They reasoned that these countries were fearful of losing their economic ties with the western powers. Japan's occupation of Southern French Indo-China would have the advantages of (1) allowing Japan to gain a foothold in the "strategic defense line" running from Southern China to Thailand, Burma and the Malayan Peninsula, and (3) consolidating Japan's political gains resulting from the mediation of the past spring. The possibility of the United States resorting to arms was ever present. But the High Command chose to minimize it, contending that Japan's inaction would make it possible for the appearance of an American Indo-China after the fall of Britain.[11]

At that time Matsuoka was the only Cabinet member who opposed the High Command's occupation plan. At the Liaison Conference of June 30, he requested the postponement of its implementation for at least another six months. Navy Minister Oikawa consented and asked the Army for its opinion. Not only the Army Chief of General Staff, but also the Chief of Naval Operations opposed the postponement.

Again at the Imperial Conference of July 2 Matsuoka asked for reconsideration, pleading that the move would jeopardize any chance of success for negotiations with the United States. The request was turned down unceremoniously. The decision became final and irrevocable as the imperial sanction was granted.

Ironically, one of Matsuoka's last official acts was to instruct Japan's Ambassador in Vichy, Mr. Kato, to open formal negotiations for peaceful occupation of Southern French Indo-China. It took place on July 14, and two days later, Matsuoka was forced to resign from his post. In brief, the Japanese demands contained the following pro-visions: Vichy was to permit Japan to despatch the "necessary" land, sea and air forces to Southern Indo-China in order to forestall inter-ference by the British, American or Gaullists troops; allow Japan to occupy eight air and two naval bases in the same region; recognize freedom of movement for Japanese forces in Southern Indo-China; and withdraw French garrisons from the places to be occupied by the Japanese. The demands were to be met by July 20, giving the Vichy Government less than one week's time.

Ambassador Kato's note was followed almost immediately by Prince Konoye's personal message to Marshal Pétain assuring him that the territorial integrity of Indo-China and the sovereignty of France would be respected. He explained that the new demands were due to "the inevitable necessity of self-preservation and defense of Japan and maintenance of its position in the Greater East Asia Sphere." Con-currently, Vice Minister Ohashi solicited Berlin's aid in securing a favorable reply from Vichy.

Washington was secretly informed of the Japanese designs by Admiral Darlan. Chief of the Far East Division Hamilton and Coun-selor Ballantine visited Ambassador Nomura to ascertain the correct-ness of the news. The Ambassador first denied any knowledge of it, but hinted that the occupation was within the realm of possibility, im-plying that it was not different from the actions the United States might take with regard to the Azores.

On July 21 Under Secretary Welles warned Japanese Minister Waka-sugi, who served under Nomura, that the proposed Japanese occupa-tion of Southern French Indo-China would definitely jeopardize the American-Japanese conversations. Nomura was vacationing in Maine but hurried back to Washington to meet with Mr. Welles on July 23. There the Acting Secretary warned that Mr. Hull could not see any basis for the pursuit of the conversations if Japan occupied Southern French Indo-China, and suggested that the conversations be tempo-rarily suspended. Taking this to mean that the United States might sever diplomatic relations, Nomura telegraphed Tokyo that there was a growing feeling in Washington that the negotiations he was carry-ing on were merely a cloak to shield Japan's southward advance, and that many high officials were convinced of that possibility. Mr. Hull himself had once remarked that Nomura's effort in Washington would be torpedoed by Tokyo. Thus it was essential that the new Foreign Minister confer with Mr. Grew to clarify Japan's stand. He again re-quested that a new set of instructions be sent to him so he could know where the new Cabinet stood in its relations toward the United States.

Toyoda saw Ambassador Grew twice on July 25, and explained to him that the occupation was to avoid encirclement, and there was no territorial design on Japan's part. He termed the entire operation merely a "precautionary measure." Yet these two meetings failed to impress the Ambassador.

The local agreement was concluded on July 23, following the Mutual Security Pact of July 21 signed in Vichy. On July 24 Washington had full information of what had transpired. On that day Ambassador Nomura secured an appointment with President Roosevelt through Admiral Stark. Mr. Roosevelt, while expressing sympathy for Japan's problem in obtaining natural resources, also hinted that an oil embargo might be imposed upon it, if Japan proceeded to occupy Southern French Indo-China. On the other hand:

"If the Japanese Government would refrain from occupying Indo-China with its military and naval forces or, had such steps actually been commenced, if the Japanese Government would withdraw such forces, the President could assure the Japanese Government that he would do everything within his power to obtain from the Governments of China, Great Britain, the Netherlands, and of course the United States itself, a binding and solemn declaration, provided Japan would undertake the same commitment, to regard Indo-China as a neutralized country . . . . He would further endeavor to procure from Great Britain and the other pertinent powers a guarantee that so long as the present emergency continued, the local French authorities in Indo-China would remain in control of the territory and would not be confronted with attempts to dislodge them on the part of de Gaullist or French agents or forces." [12]

In suggesting neutralization of French Indo-China, the President was apparently hoping to dispel Japan's fear of encirclement, as well as U. S. fear of Japanese penetration in the South Sea regions, including the Dutch East Indies, the Philippines, and Singapore. Yet the Ambassador, preoccupied by the possible imposition of economic sanctions, failed to grasp the President's proposal. He reported to Tokyo in such a manner that none in the Foreign Office or the Cabinet was able to understand the implication of the President's suggestions. The substance of Mr. Roosevelt's remarks was known to Tokyo only through Mr. Grew who met with Toyoda July 27. This was one day after the Japanese Government announced its decision to occupy Southern French Indo-China.

Japan's determination to push through its scheme of southward expansion despite the U. S. warnings precipitated the greatest crisis yet to occur before Pearl Harbor. Soon after he heard Japan's public announcement that it was ready to occupy Southern French Indo-China, Mr. Roosevelt, by an executive order, froze all Japanese assets and funds in the United States. Great Britain took a similar action respecting Japanese assets in that country. Two days later the Dutch East Indies followed suit. All armed forces in the Philippine Islands were reorganized and placed under the control of the United States, with General Douglas MacArthur becoming Commander-in-Chief of the Far East. In China, an American Military Advisory Group was established, and a volunteers' air regiment was formed under General Chennault to fight against Japanese fighter and bomber planes. The gravity of the situation forced Prince Konoye to ask the Chief Police Inspector to add extra guards for the safety of the American Embassy in Tokyo. On August 1 the United States further announced that a total embargo would be imposed with regard to Japan. Only cotton and food were excepted. Thus Japan was cut off entirely from its major sources of oil supply.

With some misgivings, the Privy Council approved the Japanese French Mutual Security Pact for ratification on July 28. The next day, in Vichy, Admiral Darlan and Ambassador Kato exchanged notes to confirm its ratification. Simultaneously the Japanese troops marched on to Southern French Indo-China. Foreign Minister Toyoda explained to the Privy Councillors that the imposition of the freezing order was anticipated for some time, and it would have come even if Japan refrained from occupying Southern French Indo-China.[13]

The lack of oil posed a very grave problem. Stockpiling of oil in the past had not been too successful, and the Navy's oil reserves were expected to run out in about two years, or within a year-and-a-half if engaged in a full-scale fight. Oil allocated for civilian use— already highly rationed—would last for less than a year. The synthetic oil program was not expected to reach the stage of mass production for some time. As a result, Japan's war potential was severely curtailed. Moderates in the Navy were turning into activists, insisting on immediate action.

On July 31 Admiral Nagano, Chief of Naval Operations, had an audience with the Emperor. Nagano claimed that he was at heart against a war with the United States, but thought it was better to strike quickly than to wait, in view of the ominous oil situation. He would have preferred an understanding with the United States, but this was impossible because of the Tripartite Pact. And without a rapprochement with the United States, no oil could be secured.

The foreign policy implication of the Navy's changed attitude was that Prince Konoye could no longer count on the Navy to exercise its moderating influence. The peace party was in a shakier position than before, since the Navy became as outspoken as the Army in favoring war.[14]

Marquis Kido was present at the audience Nagano had with the Emperor, and was "filled with trepidation by the Imperial anxiety over the danger of having to wage a desperate war." On August 7 Kido saw Konoye and urged the latter to do all he could to avoid that catastrophe. "It is almost impossible to carry a two-front war against the United States and Soviet Russia," said Kido. He wanted the Prime Minister to work closely with the Army and Navy High Command to effect a unified peaceful policy. As for the outlook on war, the lack of oil would certainly deter Japan from winning. Aside from the United States, Japan could get oil from the Dutch East Indies, and in a limited scale from Northern Sakhalin. But suppose Japan wanted to occupy the Dutch East Indies, it had to occupy Singapore and the Philippine Islands first. And while Japan took military actions against Singapore and the Philippines, the oil wells in the Indies might be destroyed, and could not be restored for production before Japan's oil reserves were exhausted. Even if Japan succeeded in occupying the oil-rich Indies, would there be any guarantee that the oil could be transported safely to Japan? He thus urged the Prime Minister to wait for at least ten years before Japan should again embark on any positive step toward expansion. For the moment, the Government should strive for a successful conclusion of the conversations with the United States, and work toward further industrialization of the country. In uttering these words, Kido was apparently speaking for the Emperor.[15]

Yet Kido's counsel of caution carried very little weight among the military circles. The Iwakuro-Wikawa team saw the worsening of the situation, and asked to be recalled for consultation. Leaving Washington for Tokyo on July 31, they hoped to convince the Tokyo Government of the folly of fighting against the United States. Iwakuro spoke to his military superiors, and Wikawa to civilian members of the Cabinet. Iwakuro was also given a chance to address the Liaison Conference. But Sugiyama and Tojo were unimpressed. They told Iwakuro that the "grace of the Emperor" and the "Japanese spirit" were much stronger than America's phenomenal productive power.

Soon after his return to Tokyo, Iwakuro was "promoted" from his all-powerful position of the head of a department in the Military Affairs Bureau to a commander of a regiment in French Indo-China. Iwakuro, who was a past master of military intrigue took the matter with dispassionate abandonment. "The prevailing sentiment in the Army had been for war," he recalled. "And they had no room for me in Tokyo."

CHAPTER XIII

THE LIGHT OF A FALSE DAWN

Gazing Up to the Summit. There was still a ray of hope left for the peace party. Mr. Roosevelt's proposals as conveyed through Ambassador Grew—for which Mr. Grew thanked his stars—opened the way for the neutralization of French Indo-China. This was an entirely new approach, and on its basis resumption of conversations seemed possible. Thus on August 4 the Liaison Conference reached a decision to submit a new set of proposals to the United States.

These proposals were drafted as answers to Mr. Roosevelt's suggestions, and were squarely aimed at the resumption of the temporarily halted conversations in Washington. They included the following conditions:

"1. Japan would promise not to send troops into territories other than Indo-China.

"2. Japan would withdraw its troops from Indo-China after a settlement had been reached between Japan and China, but the United States would have to recognize Japan's special position in Indo-China even after the withdrawal, and had to exercise its good offices to bring about direct negotiations between Japan and China. Furthermore, if Chiang Kai-shek did not agree to negotiate, America would have to discontinue aid to China.

"3. Japan would guarantee neutrality of the Philippine Islands.

"4. The United States would suspend its military measures in the Southwest Pacific area, and advise the British and Netherlands Governments to do likewise.

"5. The United States should remove its restrictions upon trade with Japan, and also cooperate with Japan in securing necessary raw materials from the Dutch East Indies."

Omitted from the proposals were the mention of neutralizing French Indo-China as suggested by Mr. Roosevelt, withdrawal of Japanese troops from China upon termination of hostilities, Japanese stand on the open door policy, and the conditions Japan would impose on Chiang Kai-shek for settling the China Incident.[1]

The proposals were presented to Secretary Hull on August 6, two days after he returned from White Sulphur Springs. The Secretary was visibly disappointed, commenting that Tokyo had moved even further away from possible negotiations. Nomura reported to Tokyo that he saw no hope for further conversations as long as Japan continued its policy of conquest by force.

Evidently the proposals did not satisfy Prince Konoye, and without waiting to hear from Ambassador Nomura, he charted a new course. This came in a proposal for a leaders' conference between himself and President Roosevelt.

In essence Prince Konoye wanted to establish a *point d'appui* through personal contact, and share the desire of the American President to "leave no stone unturned." Konoye was sincere in his approach, and post-war evidence discloses that he did not intend the proposed meeting to be a cover-up for Japan's expansionist movement. In fact, he was ready to make several concessions which were politically unpopular in Japan.[2]

Konoye recognized Japan's aim in establishing the East Asian Co-Prosperity Area and the Nine Power Treaty as mutually incompatible, but thought there was still room for compromise. Citing the doctrine of *rebus sic stantibus*, Konoye felt changed conditions would justify revision of the Nine Power Treaty. Furthermore, the United States had often expressed that it was not averse to modifying existing treaties through legal means. On the other hand, Japan lacked the power to establish the East Asian Co-Prosperity Area in the manner it desired. Thus Japan could offer certain concessions on this matter. There would always be a possibility of give and take and "if the two sides would base their talks on a statesman-like attitude, we could always find a satisfactory solution."

When asked their opinions about the proposed leaders' conference, Navy Minister Oikawa reported that he was in favor of it, but War Minister Tojo was exceedingly cautious and skeptical. He brought back his answer a day or two later in a written statement, presumably after consulting with his subordinates in the War Ministry.

Tojo thought the proposed meeting "would inevitably weaken Japan's present foreign policy based on the Tripartite Pact, and give unfavorable domestic repercussions." The Army would go along with the plan only if the Prime Minister would not retreat from the basic position agreed upon at the August 4 meeting of the Liaison Conference, and in the event the talks should fail, Prince Konoye would not resign his post, but would take responsibility for leading the nation into war.[3]

Tojo's conditional acceptance enabled Konoye to call another meeting of the Liaison Conference on August 7 which duly approved his plan. Konoye had the solid backing of the Navy and the elder statesmen. He also received some encouragement from the Emperor. The Army, on the other hand, remained cool, and appeared ready to torpedo the plan if it should prove to be adverse to Japan's interest. Instructions were sent to Nomura that night, asking him to sound out Washington's reaction to the proposed leaders' conference.

The Japanese proposal could not have come at a worse time. Since the U. S. Navy had succeeded in breaking the Japanese code, every move Japan made was regarded by Mr. Hull and the rest of Washington as a mere cover-up of its expansionist policies. Japan was seen as a militarist nation eager to move into the British, Dutch, and American possessions in the Far East. Ambassador Nomura's task was further complicated by the absence of Mr. Roosevelt from Washington when the important proposal arrived.

On August 13 Secretary Hull gave Nomura a document containing instances of Japanese infringement of American rights in China. Naturally Nomura saw very little hope in the proposed Roosevelt-Konoye meeting. But he was consoled by the fact that the Secretary inquired whether he would be in Washington for the weekend, giving the impression that an important proposal might come from the Roosevelt Administration.

Mr. Hull's inquiry was made at the behest of President Roosevelt, who was attending the Atlantic Conference with Prime Minister Churchill. A wireless message sent from the *Augusta* on August 12 asked the Secretary to alert Ambassador Nomura to be ready to come to the White House Saturday or Sunday of that week.

Japan was one of the main topics discussed at the Atlantic Conference by the two statesmen. On August 9, after the two parties first met, and after President Roosevelt finished inspecting the *Prince of Wales*, Sumner Welles and Sir Alexander Cadogan, British Permanent Under Secretary of State for Foreign Affairs, conferred on a document prepared by the British Government. This was to constitute "parallel communications" by the two governments to the Japanese Government that "any further encroachment by Japan in the Southwestern Pacific" might compel the United States Government to declare war on Japan.

The President apparently wavered between a firmer position and a softer one, but finally decided to take a somewhat milder course by committing himself to hand a warning to Nomura along the line of the proposed joint communications but would continue the conversations with him provided the Japanese Government would give the commitment that it "will not further station its troops in the Southern Pacific areas, except Indo-China, and that the Japanese troops now stationed in French Indo-China will be withdrawn." If Japan refused this procedure and took further steps in the nature of military expansion, the President would warn that "the taking of such measures might result in war between the United States and Japan."[4]

In Churchill's words, the President's idea was to negotiate about these unacceptable conditions and thus procure a moratorium of about thirty days during which Great Britain could improve its position in Singapore. While these negotiations showed little chance of success, the President considered that a month gained would be valuable.[5]

The eight-point declaration containing the war and peace aims of the United States and Great Britain, known as the Atlantic Charter, was made public on August 14. When Tokyo received its full text, the daily papers attacked the inconsistency between Point Three which said "They respect the right of all peoples to choose the form of government under which they live," and the subjugation of the peoples of India, Burma, Malaya, and Indonesia. As usual, the Tokyo press chose to show its affinity with the military. Meanwhile two attempts were made on Baron Hiranuma's life which cast a dark shadow over the political stability of the Konoye Cabinet.

Although August 17 was on a Sunday, Ambassador Nomura was called to the White House to meet with President Roosevelt. Nomura drew out of his pocket instructions he had received from his government in which Prince Konoye stated that he felt so urgent about preserving peaceful relations between the two countries that he would be disposed to meet with the President. Mr. Roosevelt, without making reference to Nomura's proposal, started to make some observations which contained much of the warning he and Churchill agreed upon at the Atlantic Conference and modified by the State Department. He pointed out that notwithstanding his efforts, "Japan has continued its military activities, . . . and has occupied Indo-China." He agreed to the resumption of talks with Japan, but added that the United States could not think of reopening the conversations if Japan were to continue its present movement of force and conquest supported by its bitter press campaign against the United States.

On the other hand Nomura was encouraged by the President in the matter of the proposed leaders' conference. The President told him that despite his admonition he was not averse to the idea of meeting with Prince Konoye, and suggested that Juneau, Alaska could be chosen as a possible site for a meeting to be held some time in mid-October.[6]

The President's admonition left a deep imprint on Nomura's mind. To Foreign Minister Toyoda he telegraphed: "Today we are at the crossroads of peace and war and the country is divided. My sympathy is with you in all the difficulties that you have to face." Admiral Toyoda was a junior in point of service in the Navy and Nomura could talk to him candidly without hesitation. After reviewing the war in Europe, he pointed out that German victory was not likely, and Japan should pursue an independent foreign policy, implicitly suggesting that Japan should either scuttle or minimize the present alignment with Germany.

It was not until August 26 that Tokyo could agree on the language of Konoye's personal message to President Roosevelt and the government's official reply to the American note of August 17. Meanwhile, the Japanese public learned for the first time the existence of negotiations between Japan and the United States through Churchill's Empire broadcast. The Churchill statement was at once denounced as "lies, fraud, bluff, gibberish, and ridiculous" by the Tokyo press. The German Embassy issued a statement warning that "brazen-faced Churchill is merely trying to split the Axis in order to divide and rule." This was echoed by the Tokyo press which thought the Churchill statement represented the desire of the ABCD powers to "destroy the work of the reorganization of East Asia, of which Japan is the central sponsor."[7]

The press generally spoke for the Army and for the expansionists, and as it might have been expected, the mere agreement on the language of the message to be sent to the United States did not mean that the Liaison Conference finally reached an accord. On August 19, German Ambassador Ott visited the new Vice Minister, Mr. Amau, complaining that Japan was permitting American tankers sailing for Vladivostok to pass through Japan's contiguous waters. On the very next day, the Supreme Command saw fit to draft a tentative plan to attack the Soviet Far East after the fashion of the Siberian expedition. "In the event of the collapse of the Stalin regime, Japan must take certain preventive measures to insure against Siberia falling under a third power's influence," said the plan. It also gave a detailed blueprint for strengthening the military forces in Manchuria and for attacking Siberia.[8] This document was termed "Discussion Materials on the North Chinese Questions," which was of course quite inappropriate. The notation to it read that the document could be used by Ambassador Nomura in exchanging opinions with the U. S. Government. Coming at that particular time, the document served as an unveiled warning to Prince Konoye that the Army must have a place to expand regardless of whether the Government succeeded in reaching an agreement with the United States.

The text of the Konoye message was marked with cordiality. In contrast, the accompanying note, in response to Mr. Roosevelt's August 17 remarks, was sharply worded. The note stated that when a have-not nation was obstructed in the path of its natural and peaceful development, it was the duty of that nation to take defensive measures. And this was "the motivating policy of the Japanese Government." It proceeded to ridicule America's strict adherence to its interests and principles: "With admirable modesty of mind, the Government of the United States has seemed frequently unaware that its words and policies are automatically weighted with the immense power of America's accomplished facts, natural endowment and potential might. The President of the United States, and the Secretary of State, in their own unquestioning adherence to the ways of peaceful procedures, might find it difficult to believe that other nations, anywhere, could consider themselves threatened by the United States." •

On the other hand, the Konoye message assured that "the Japanese Government has no intention of using, without provocation, military force against any neighboring nation." Written in a conciliatory spirit, the message urged a meeting of the responsible heads of the two Governments which would "confirm and give such sanction to our purposes that peace in the Pacific would be instituted by that meeting." As to the procedure, the Konoye message simply added that the two leaders "should meet first to discuss from a broad standpoint all important problems between Japan and America covering the entire Pacific area, and to explore the possibility of saving the situation." The Japanese would prefer "adjustment of minor items" to be left to "negotiations between competent officials of the two countries," following the meeting.

Neither the note nor the message contained a paragraph embodying Japan's demand to acquire necessary raw materials. The text, which was agreed upon at the Liaison Conference but was left out by the Foreign Office as too bellicose, read as follows: "The Imperial Government deems it the prime requisite of a true peace that a have-power which is endowed with rich natural resources, and is militarily, politically, and economically placed in a much more advantageous position than others, should cooperate with have-not-powers in the matter of distributing resources on an equitable basis. As to a nation which does not possess sufficient resources, its demands for such resources from neighboring nations should be deemed as inevitable and proper, and its need should be adjusted sufficiently on a mutually satisfactory manner."[10]

Nomura presented Konoye's message and the accompanying note to the President on August 28. There the reaction was mixed. President Roosevelt complimented Konoye on the spirit of his communication. According to Nomura, the President jokingly remarked that though he was looking forward to meeting with Prince Konoye, he wondered "whether invasion of Thailand can be expected during these conversations just as an invasion of Indo-China occurred during Secretary Hull's conversations with your Excellency." Mr. Roosevelt thought he could meet with Prince Konoye for three days but objected to the selection of Hawaii. He again suggested Juneau, Alaska as a possible site. Nomura asked the President for an early date, but the latter avoided giving a definite date.

That evening Nomura was invited to Secretary Hull's apartment to discuss the proposed meeting of the two leaders. The Secretary promptly started to throw cold water on Prince Konoye's pet project. "Serious consequences from the viewpoint of both Governments," said the Secretary, "would ensue if the meeting failed to result in an agreement. The meeting should therefore have as its purpose the ratification of essential points already agreed to in principle." This was exactly counter to Prince Konoye's intention. As conditions precedent to a general agreement, Mr. Hull suggested that Japan indicate its intention of withdrawing from the Axis pact, abandon retention of Japanese troops in North China and Inner Mongolia, and clarify the application of the principle of nondiscrimination in international commercial relations. Nomura asked if other pending questions between Japan and the United States could be settled without mentioning the China question. This procedure would enable the two countries to tide over a critical situation in their relations, the Ambassador contended. Mr. Hull rejected Nomura's suggestion emphasizing that the China question was "one of the pivotal ones." If it remained unsettled to the satisfaction of all, "the roots of future instability and trouble would remain."

Nomura's report on his meetings with the President and the Secretary of State arrived in Tokyo on August 29 and 30. The Government was partly optimistic, and partly pessimistic, but decided to prepare for the meeting. Konoye got several of his confidants together to map up a plan—which incidentally was superseded by a Foreign Office plan—and began to select members of the mission from the War, Navy, and Foreign Ministries. "Perhaps this was the moment the two nations were closest to an agreement," remarked the Prime Minister. Foreign Minister Toyoda was enthusiastic. He felt that the "statesmanlike" attitude of the President would finally prevail over Mr. Hull's "traditional" line.

Konoye's position was considerably worsened when news leaked out that he had sent a message to the President. In leaving the White House on August 28, Ambassador Nomura inadvertently told reporters that he had just delivered a message from Prince Konoye to President Roosevelt. The Cabinet News Bureau was forced to make a brief announcement confirming that such a move had been taken. On August 29 and 30, the Italian and German Ambassadors made strong representations. Tokyo explained that the message was sent to ease the existing tensions, and that the Tripartite Pact would not be affected. When Ambassador Oshima from Berlin also protested, Toyoda sharply reprimanded him, stating that the Japanese Government had adhered to the purpose of the Tripartite Pact to keep the United States out of war.

Several threats were made on Prince Konoye's life. The Japanese Foreign Office, however, decided to turn this mishap into a political fortune. Terasaki, chief of the Bureau of American Affairs, was hurriedly sent to Mr. Grew. Teresaki told Mr. Grew that the meeting between the two responsible heads of the governments should take place without delay. He asserted that the revelation of the Prince's message had stirred up considerable resentment among the public, especially the pro-Axis element, since they were indignant at the steps taken by the American Government, including the freezing order. He felt that the message was consequently of direct advantage to the extremists and pro-Axis elements in Japan.

On September 2 the *New York Herald Tribune* carried an article stating that Konoye had proposed to the President a meeting on a warship in the Pacific. It prompted the White House press secretary, Stephen Early, to issue a denial: "The President has no invitation. ... The only plan the President has involving a trip on the water in the immediate future is a cruise (starting) from Annapolis on the Chesapeake Bay and on the Potomac River." Tokyo seized this opportunity to suggest, whether it might not have been better if a joint communique were issued from Tokyo and Washington simultaneously to create a more favorable atmosphere for the pending Roosevelt-Konoye meeting.

Mr. Hull's suspicion of the Japanese grew as days passed. On September 1 he had another occasion to meet with Admiral Nomura. Criticising the agitation of the Japanese press for a policy of conquest and anti-American campaign, he emphasized that if the Japanese Government found it difficult to influence the Japanese public opinion, "there's no assurance that your Government could obtain public support for any such settlement after it had been concluded—and then a new political crisis in Japan might occur."

The Secretary's skepticism was later shared by the President himself who received Nomura on September 3 to hand his reply to the Japanese note of August 28: " . . . . I cannot avoid taking cognizance of indications of the existence in some quarters in Japan of concepts which, if widely entertained, would seem capable of raising obstacles to successful collaboration between you and me along the line which I am sure we both earnestly desire to follow." The President therefore suggested that both the United States and Japan "take precaution, toward assuring that our proposed meeting shall prove a success, by endeavoring to enter immediately upon preliminary discussion of the fundamental and essential questions on which we seek agreement."

In the accompanying note Mr. Hull chose not to answer directly Japan's persistent proposals for the Roosevelt-Konoye meeting. Instead he reiterated the fundamental principles with which the Japanese had said they were in basic agreement but had betrayed by their actions. Mr. Hull made it known that before considering negotiations with Japan affecting China, the United States would discuss the entire subject with China, Britain, the Netherlands, and Australia. Any dim hope that Prince Konoye might have had on the meeting was practically wiped out by Mr. Hull's high moral sounding note.

Meanwhile, independently of the Hull note, the Japanese Foreign Office devised a seven-point program to serve as an agenda for the proposed leaders' meeting. The program was communicated to Mr. Hull through Ambassador Grew in Tokyo and Ambassador Nomura in Washington. One of the points in the program reaffirmed "that the attitudes of Japan and the United States toward the European War will be decided by the concepts of protection and self-defense, and in case the United States should participate in the European War, the interpretation and execution of the Tripartite Pact by Japan shall be independently established." The very ambiguity of this provision again pointed to the divergence of opinion in Japan's ruling circles. It was a compromise between those who favored withdrawal from the Tripartite Pact and those who advocated continued adherence to it. Yet America's right to defend itself against Nazi provocation was tacitly recognized; this represented Japan's major concession.

The program as transmitted to Washington was silent on the matter of stationing of troops in China except to say that Japan would withdraw its troops after the resumption of normal relations between Japan and China. The proceedings of the Liaison Conference, on the other hand, revealed that after the formal withdrawal, Japan would still insist on the right to station troops "in order to preserve peace, in accordance with an agreement to be entered into between the two nations." Japan was willing to have the United States serve as a mediator between Japan and China, but would request the United States to abstain from measures prejudicial to Japan's efforts to reach a settlement with China. The United States was also to resume the commercial relations between the United States and Japan on a non-discriminatory basis. In essence the program was an old song with the same refrain. Even if it had reached Mr. Hull before the latter's note was delivered to Nomura on September 3, it was extremely doubtful that the program would have been accepted by the American Secretary.[11]

At the Crossroads of War and Peace. In Tokyo, Konoye's plan was confronted by a familiar obstacle. General Tojo had given his assent to the plan reluctantly. Now that the plan showed no sign of quick success, he was determined to press for a complete review of Japan's foreign policy. Representatives of the War, Navy, and Foreign Ministries, General Muto, Admiral Oka, and Mr. Imamoto were called ostensibly for the purpose of mapping out the concrete proposals to the United States on the China question. As it turned out, they were charged with the task of preparing an agenda for one of the most important Imperial Conferences to be held before Pearl Harbor.[12]

The Imperial Conference of September 6 was convened to settle once for all the issue of war or peace. Its decision, an "Outline for the Execution of the National Policy," was inflexibly followed thereafter, and is thus worthy of reproduction:

"Determined not to be deterred by the possibility of being involved in a war with America (and England and Holland) in order to secure our national existence, we will proceed with war preparations so that they can be completed approximately toward the end of October.

"At the same time we will endeavor by every possible diplomatic means to have our demands agreed to by America and England. Japan's minimum demands in these negotiations with America (and England), together with the Empire's maximum concessions, are embodied in the attached document.

"If by the early part of October there is no reasonable hope of having our demands agreed to in the diplomatic negotiations mentioned above, we will immediately make up our minds to get ready for war against America (and England and Holland)."

General Tojo later explained that the decision was adopted in view of the tense international situation—e.g., economic sanctions imposed by the United States, England and Holland, the ABCD encirclement, American and British preparations for war, difficulties in the negotiations with the United States, and no visible means of settling the China Incident. It was therefore necessary to prepare for war and yet continue the conversations, even though the problem of regulating diplomacy and strategy was rather intricate. The deadline for the negotiations was set because November would be the best month for landing operations. December would be possible but difficult, January would be impossible because of the northeast monsoons.[13]

In brief, Japan's minimum demands and maximum concessions were as follows: (1) The United States and Britain should not interfere in a settlement of the China Incident by Japan. They should close the Burma Road and cease all military, political or economic aid to the Chiang Kai-shek government. Meanwhile Japan would adhere rigidly to its plan of stationing troops in specified areas of China. (2) The United States and Britain should not establish any military bases in Thailand, the Dutch East Indies, China and Far Eastern Russia, and they should not increase their forces in the Far East beyond the existing strength. (3) The United States and Britain should cooperate with Japan in its attempt to secure needed raw materials, restoring trade relations with Japan and supplying raw materials from their colonies in the Southwestern Pacific area.

If the above demands were met: (1) Japan would not use French Indo-China as a base for operations against any neighboring country except China. (2) Japan would withdraw troops from Indo-China as soon as a just peace was established in the Far East. (3) Japan would guarantee the neutrality of the Philippine Islands. (4) With regard to Soviet Russia, Japan would abide by the Neutrality Pact, unless there was a violation of the spirit of the Pact by Russia.

As to the Axis Pact, Japan would independently decide its own obligations, if the United States should become involved in the European War. This was, however, not to be interpreted that there would be any change in the execution of its obligations under the pact. In essence these conditions were a restatement of Japan's basic terms. However, they represented the stiffening of Japan's attitude, harsher in terms than those pronounced by former Foreign Minister Matsuoka.

On September 5, a day before the Imperial Conference was convened, Prince Konoye had an audience with the Emperor who was distressed by the fact that the outline of policy decisions submitted to him seemed to put military preparation first and diplomatic negotiations second. He asked Konoye whether it was proper to ask the opinions of the Chiefs of Staff of the Army and Navy at the Imperial Conference. At Konoye's suggestion the two Chiefs were called in immediately. They, like Prince Konoye, answered that the Government would strive to effect a diplomatic settlement first, and only after diplomatic means were exhausted would the Government prepare for war. No significance should be attached to the mere fact that military preparations appeared first in the document.

When the Imperial Conference met on September 6, the Emperor greatly desired to continue his questions further, but delegated the task to Mr. Hara, the Privy Council President. Mr. Hara accordingly posed the same questions the Emperor had raised the day before. Minister of Navy Oikawa answered but the two Chiefs of General Staff remained silent. The Emperor then took the floor, expressing his regret that no one from the Supreme Command had answered the questions posed by Mr. Hara. He took a sheet of paper out of his pocket and started to read a poem by Emperor Meiji, his grandfather. The poem spoke in allegorical terms of His Majesty's concern over the shrieking gales and roaring waves that disturbed the calm of the sea, inasmuch as the Emperor had regarded the inhabitants of all Four Seas his brothers. Emperor Hirohito explained that he read this poem often in order to cultivate the love for peace as his grandfather had. "Everyone was struck with awe," was Prince Konoye's recollection, "and there was silence throughout the hall." Admiral Nagano saved the situation by explaining that the Minister of Navy spoke for the Supreme Command as well as for the Government, and assured the Emperor that the Supreme Command considered diplomacy as the primary means.

Prince Konoye was satisfied with the Emperor's intervention. While the outline still insisted on preparing for war, the Emperor's firm stand made it possible to continue negotiations with the United States much easier than before. He also found encouragement in the fact that the outline itself as adopted was a modification of the original version the Army wanted to impose. Previously the outline contained the phrase, "by the early part of October, if our demands are not met, we will immediately make up our minds to get ready for war against America." This was changed to include the following words, "If ... there is no reasonable hope of having our demands agreed to," at the insistence of Navy Minister Oikawa. It allowed a certain leeway for the Government before it would be required to take the last plunge. Prince Konoye was confident that he still had a better than even chance to negotiate with the United States.

With the approval of the War, Navy and Foreign Ministers, Prince Konoye ventured his personal diplomacy. On the night of September 6, after the fateful Imperial Conference was concluded, he secretly met with Ambassador Grew for several hours. Hopefully the Prince told Mr. Grew that the Minister of War had promised to send a full General to accompany him, and the Minister of the Navy had agreed to send a full Admiral, possibly former Minister of Navy Admiral Yoshida, to accompany him to the meeting. In addition the Vice Chiefs of the General Staff and other high-ranking officers of the armed forces would go with him. Since he had the full support of the responsible chiefs of the Supreme Command, it would be possible for him to put down and control any opposition which might develop among these elements.

According to Mr. Grew, Prince Konoye "conclusively and wholeheartedly" agreed with the four principles enunciated by the Secretary of State as a basis for the rehabilitation of relations between the United States and Japan. Prince Konoye, however, recorded that he agreed to the Hull pronouncement in principle, but maintained that in its implementation several problems would arise. Therefore it was imperative to meet with the President. At any rate, the private meeting encouraged Mr. Grew, who in transmitting Prince Konoye's statement to the President, remarked that the telegram might become the most important one since he began his diplomatic career.

Fall of the Konoye Cabinet. Japan's September 4 proposal embodying the seven-point agenda for the proposed leaders' conference was handed to Secretary Hull on September 6. Mr. Hull thought the new proposals contained only "an evasive formula," and termed it much narrower in scope than the assurances given in the statement communicated to the President on August 28. On September 9, Mr. Hull cabled to Ambassador Grew a series of questions to be submitted to Foreign Minister Toyoda regarding the intentions of the Japanese

Government in offering some of the proposals, especially those relating to China. A few days later Nomura also telegraphed Tokyo urging a clear-cut decision on the question of stationing troops in China. By then all the outstanding issues gradually narrowed down to one central issue, the China question.

On September 13 another meeting of the Liaison Conference was called to discuss the question of peace terms with China. The key phrases in the decision of that day were as follows:

"The stationing of Japanese Army units for a necessary period in prescribed areas in Inner Mongolia and North China for the above purpose, as well as the placing of Japanese warships and units for a necessary period in Hainan Island, Amoy, and other localities on the basis of previous agreements and practices.

"Withdrawal of troops: The Army units which have been sent to China for the prosecution of the China Incident shall, with the exception of those mentioned in the preceding item, be withdrawn attendant upon the settlement of the Incident."[14]

Other conditions, such as economic cooperation of the two nations, the merger of the Wang and Chiang regimes, were essentially restatements of older ones and hardly merit further elaboration. It must be noted, however, when the terms were handed to Ambassador Grew they represented a certain modification. This was effected by not faithfully translating the original version, and by transmitting only the doctored-up English version to the Ambassador. Foreign Minister Toyoda hoped that this procedure would make the English version less offensive and help future negotiations. He was supported in his decision by General Muto and Admiral Oka, respectively Chiefs of the Military Affairs and Naval Affairs Bureaus in the War and Navy Ministries.

Prince Konoye was taken aback when he emerged from the Liaison Conference. "In respect to the stationing of troops," recalled the Prince. "There were times when the Army seemed to hold the moderate view that pretext and form were of no importance, but at the very next moment one would come up against a firm resolution not to give in on any account."[15] Yet Prince Konoye felt that he could still count on the support of the moderate element in the Army.

By mid-September the Foreign Office had completed all the necessary preparations for the proposed leaders' conference. It thought any agreements reached should be put in the form of exchange of notes. They would have a similar effect as treaties and need not be ratified by and with the consent of the Privy Council. Prince Konoye would be endowed with full power, and the Emperor would be notified of any decisions to be reached at the conference through telegrams sent from the warship. The Emperor would be in the position to sanction all the moves taken by the Prince. As a further safeguard, the Prince would be accompanied by high-ranking responsible Army and Navy officers.[10]

The Foreign Office was confident that once the question of the stationing of troops was solved there would be no difficulties in reaching an agreement at the forthcoming conference. It felt that the United States would finally agree to some form of stationing of troops in North China, but feared that China would oppose this step strenuously. On the other hand China might not be averse to the stationing of troops in South China. Strategically speaking, the latter move would be primarily against the United States and Britain, and the United States would likely oppose this plan while it was offering its good offices to effect a settlement. The Foreign Office, nonetheless thought a compromise could be worked out by allowing Japan to use airfields in China, without otherwise permitting stationing of Japanese troops. If this stand would not gain acceptance, another alternative was to agree on direct negotiations with China.

Ambassador Nomura had been cabling from Washington that the United States interpreted Japan's every move as a mere subterfuge, first yielding and then resorting to force. The Military Attaché there candidly stated that it was time for Japan to decide either to sacrifice the issue of stationing troops in China or to terminate the negotiations entirely. He also believed that the question of the Tripartite Pact could be squared off against the U.S. insistence on self-defense. The key to the success or failure of the problem was solely in the question of the stationing of troops.

While the proponents of withdrawal of troops from China were gaining some support, the military High Command took a decisive action to silence such moves. The deadline it had set for ending the negotiations was near, and the High Command pressed for another meeting of the Liaison Conference to review all the pertinent policy questions. The September 20 Conference adopted a new formula for negotiations which reaffirmed Japan's prior position that the troops were to stay in certain areas of China for the purpose of "preventing Communistic and other subversive activities which may constitute a menace to the security of both countries." Admiral Toyoda by this time was converted to the view of complete withdrawal of Japanese troops from China, if necessary, in order to bring about a rapprochement with the United States. But he was powerless. In his new instructions to Ambassador Nomura he had to state reluctantly that Japan could not yield on this basic issue. Furthermore, if the United States proposed patrolling the demilitarized areas with international troops, Japan would be irrevocably opposed to it.

On two separate occasions, September 22 and 25, Admiral Toyoda gave Ambasador Grew a gist of the new terms the Liaison Conference had agreed upon September 20, with an urgent plea that the proposed leaders' conference not be delayed any longer. Ambassador Grew was sympathetically inclined to the idea of such a conference. In a personal letter dated September 22 to President Roosevelt, he referred to his conversations with Premier Konoye who the Ambassador said, "in the face of bitter antagonism from extremist and pro-Axis elements in the country is courageously working for an improvement in Japan's relations with the United States. . . . In spite of all the evidence of Japan's bad faith in times past in failing to live up to her commitments, I believe that there is a better chance of the present Government implementing whatever commitments it may now undertake than has been the case in recent years. . . . The alternative to reaching a settlement now would be the greatly increased probability of war. . . . "

Ambassador Grew again met with Foreign Minister Toyoda on September 27, the first anniversary of the Tripartite Pact which was marked by the Japanese public's coolness to the Pact. Two days later the Ambassador cabled a long report to Secretary Hull cautioning the Secretary that the proposed Roosevelt-Konoye meeting should not be lightly brushed aside: "Should the United States expect or await agreement by the Japanese Government in the present preliminary conversations ... almost certainly the conversations will drag along indefinitely and unproductively until the Konoye Cabinet and its supporting elements desiring *rapprochement* with the United States will come to the conclusion that the outlook for an agreement is hopeless and that the United States Government is only playing for time. . . . *The logical outcome of this will be the downfall of the Konoye Cabinet and the formation of a military dictatorship which will lack either the disposition or the temperament to avoid colliding headon with the United States.* There is a question that such a situation may prove to be more serious even than the failure to produce an entirely satisfactory agreement through the proposed meeting between President Roosevelt and Prince Konoye, should it take place as planned."[17]

Mr. Hull was hardly in a receptive mood. Despite his due deference to Mr. Grew's "admirable understanding of the Japanese situation," the Secretary felt that the Ambassador was not in a position to "estimate the over-all world situation as we could in Washington." His feeling was if the proposed meeting did not produce an agreement, the Japanese military leaders would then be in a position to declare that the United States was responsible for the failure of the meeting. Furthermore any suggestion of a meeting between the President and Prince Konoye would have a critically discouraging effect upon Chiang Kai-shek.

Secretary Hull's feelings were shared by his colleague, Secretary of War Stimson who in approving a staff report calling for "forceful diplomacy vis-à-vis Japan," noted that "during the next three months while we are rearming the Philippines great care must be exercised to avoid an explosion by the Japanese Army. Put concretely this means, that while I approve of stringing out negotiations during that period, they should not be allowed to ripen into a personal conference between the President and P. M. (Prime Minister Konoye)."

Thus when the formal American reply was completed on October 2 it left no mistake about where the United States stood in its relations with Japan. In short, the note complained that Japan constantly made application of the broad principles set forth by Washington in narrower and more restrictive terms. While the President still earnestly desired to hold the meeting, all the uncertainties about the application of the general principles had to be dispelled first.

The note reached Tokyo on October 4. Despite Ambassador Nomura's assurance that "the United States worded their memorandum in such a way as to permit a ray of hope to penetrate through," both Prime Minister Konoye and Foreign Minister Toyoda realized that their policy had failed. Foreign Minister Toyoda had already engaged a steamship, and Konoye's aides were prepared to leave at a moment's notice. Furthermore, the Foreign Office had prepared a document giving a definite date for the withdrawal of troops from China and from Indo-China. A plan was also worked out so that in case of internal upheaval, the Tokyo Metropolitan police would be mobilized to its fullest strength. But all of these preparations seemed to lose their meaning after the note came from Washington.

What Japan sought from the United States was an expression of its views regarding the three major points of differences between the two governments, namely, (1) the withdrawal of troops from China, (2) Japan's obligations under the Tripartite Pact, and (3) nondiscrimination in international trade. If Japan evaded specific commitments on all major issues, so did the United States. In the Japanese eyes, the United States Government was not willing to give any specific answers Japan was looking for. Thus in the early part of October, negotiations were going round and round in circles.

As a last resort, Prime Minister Konoye suggested to War Minister Tojo to agree to the withdrawal of troops from China with the understanding that some arrangement would be made for the stationing of troops at certain key localities later on. Tojo rejected this outright. The Army High Command held a conference of its own on October 6, confirming the policy that the Army "shall not change an iota with regard to the problem of stationing our troops in China, in form as well as in substance."[18]

Chief of Naval Operations Admiral Nagano also felt that any further prolongation of the negotiations useless. Only Navy Minister Oikawa was still opposed to a war with the United States.

The political situation was getting out of hand. At the insistence of General Tojo, an emergency session of the long-defunct Four Ministers' Conference was held on Sunday, October 12. General Suzuki, President of the Government Planning Board, also participated. The meeting lasted for more than four hours. Toyoda pointed out that there was no chance of success in Washington negotiations unless Japan made concessions on the matter of stationing troops in China. He also suggested if Japan deferred sending troops to Northern French Indo-China, it would help the matter considerably. Tojo held that the stationing of troops in China was the very life of the Army itself and he could not yield on this point. As to the sending of reinforcement into French Indo-China, the Army was simply carrying out the decision of the Imperial Conference and it was therefore irrevocable. Oikawa's request for a clear cut decision on war or continued negotiations was left unanswered with Konoye evading the issue.[19]   The Conference ended up in adopting Tojo's recommendations that the negotiations be carried out only if they did not change the policy with regard to the stationing of troops in China, and if they did not hinder the settlement of the China Incident. The full-dress Cabinet meeting of October 14 failed to change the situation.

On the night of October 14 Tojo sent General Suzuki as his messenger to Konoye proposing that the whole Cabinet resign in favor of one formed under Prince Higashikuni. He reasoned that only a prince of royal blood could overcome the oppositions of the Army and Navy and adopt a policy independently of the Imperial Conference decision of September 6. This idea appealed to Konoye, who was ready to throw off the burden of his office at any moment. Furthermore he felt that Prince Higashikuni would carry out his policy of reconciliation, and continue negotiations with the United States. Konoye appealed to the Throne on October 15 on this matter. By implication, the Emperor approved Konoye's forthcoming resignation and the appointment of Prince Higashikuni as his successor. Kido, however, had certain reservations and met with Konoye and General Suzuki in private. Kido instructed Suzuki to find out from Tojo whether the Army would abide by the decisions Prince Higashikuni might make. Suzuki reported back that Tojo did not have any confidence in controlling the Army if the Government decided for peace, and would prefer a royal prince to unite the nation. Kido sensed that Tojo abhorred the responsibilities, and wanted Prince Higashikuni to attend to all the unfinished tasks. Konoye privately broached Prince Higashikuni on the subject and asked his help in avoiding the war. Prince Higashikuni made no commitment.

By the morning of October 16 Kido definitely decided against a possible Higashikuni Cabinet, fearing that the politically inexperienced royal prince might fall an easy prey to the Army's intrigues. He might become their puppet to lead the nation into war. It was not advisable to have a member of the royal family assume responsibility for a national disaster.

On October 16 Prince Konoye tendered his resignation, submitting a long letter explaining in detail the chain of events that led to his resignation. He blamed the Army's stand on the stationing of troops as costing him a successful conclusion of the negotiations with the United States and his premiership.

By this time Marquis Kido's choice of Konoye's successor narrowed down to either Navy Minister Oikawa or War Minister Tojo. He favored the Navy Minister, since the Navy did not want war. But he shuddered at the thought of the Army revolting against Oikawa's cabinet. On the other hand, if Tojo were appointed, there would be a possibility of his continuing the negotiations. He would be in the position to exercise strong control over the Army, and would have to assume the responsibility whether he succeeded or failed in the negotiations. Otherwise no mention was made of the possible effect on the U.S.-Japanese relations as the result of appointing General Tojo. On October 17 the Senior Statesmen met in conference. There were suggestions of appointing General Ugaki, whose prior attempt to form a cabinet was foiled by the Army. Prince Higashikuni's name was again mentioned. But Kido's argument that the royal family should not be exposed to the rigidity of practical politics prevailed. Finally the fear of internal dissention and revolt overrode the resentment against General Tojo. After an unusually heated session, the Senior Statesmen approved the choice of Tojo.

At 3:30 p.m. Tojo received the imperial mandate to form a cabinet. The Emperor gave a command to Admiral Oikawa, the outgoing Navy Minister, that the Navy should cooperate fully with the Army in order to cope with the difficult international situation.

Prince Konoye concluded his official act by writing a letter to Ambassador Grew urging the United States not to be unduly alarmed by the appointment of General Tojo. He assured Washington that the Tojo Government would continue his policy and do its utmost to carry the conversations to a successful conclusion.

CHAPTER XIV

THE LAST PLUNGE

Tojo's Advent to Power. "In deciding the national policy, you are instructed not to be bound by the decision of the Imperial Conference of September 6, but to study broadly and intensively the domestic and foreign situations, and apply cautious re-evaluation of all the problems present," so Marquis Kido informed Premier-designate, Lieutenant General Hideki Tojo of the Emperor's intentions.

Without the imperial command that all major issues ought to be reconsidered *de novo*, the General might not have accepted the imperial mandate. By this time, he was well aware of the inadequacy of the country's resources for a major war and of the fact that the Navy was opposed to a conflict with the United States. Reversing himself somewhat, he had even come to a point of thinking the country should be prepared for peace as well as for war during the period the policy was being re-examined. He decided to hold his former position as Minister of War and in addition assume the post of Home Minister. This latter position, he said, was essential since he feared that internal confusion would result if peace was decided upon instead of war. "To meet such a state of affairs, I felt I should make myself answerable as Home Minister as well as War Minister."

After leaving the Imperial Palace he wandered around and worshiped at the shrines of Emperor Meiji, Admiral Togo, and the War Dead in order to get "divine inspiration." Naoki Hoshino was invited to become the Cabinet Secretary to assist in the formation of the cabinet. Hoshino had been a member of the second Konoye Cabinet, and a former colleague of Tojo in Manchuria. By evening, Ministers of Education, Justice, Agriculture, Health and Welfare, and Commerce and Industry as well as President of the Government Planning Board were chosen, all accepting their posts over the phone.

Only Shigenori Togo, former Ambassador to Germany and Russia, and Okinori Kaya, former Finance Minister, inquired whether the new Cabinet would continue conversations with Washington. Upon receiving a satisfactory answer, both consented to join the Cabinet. Kaya was persuaded by Prince Konoye to remain in the Tojo Cabinet so that the new Cabinet could retain some of the characteristics of

Prince Konoye's cabinet. Togo consented to become the Foreign Minister only after Tojo had assured him that the new Cabinet would not object to reviewing the question of stationing troops in China as well as other major issues that stood in the way of better relations with the United States. On the next day Admiral Shimada, who lacked previous administrative experience, reluctantly assumed the post of Navy Minister. The investure ceremony took place the same afternoon, October 18, and the Tojo Cabinet was thus established.[1]

Almost overnight Tojo became the most powerful man in Japan. He was also promoted to the rank of a full general, and was retained on the active list. In his hands the political, military, and police powers were concentrated. In contrast, the cabinet ministers were drawn mostly from bureaucrats and career servicemen who lacked political experience. To the outside world, this move was intended to demonstrate that the new Premier, unlike his predecessors, would wield sufficient authority to carry through any policy which would be decided upon, whether for peace or for war. "Actions, not words" would be his motto, said the Premier. "The national policy calls for a successful settlement of the China Incident and the establishment of the Greater East Asia Co-Prosperity Sphere. The Government intends, externally to promote amicable relations with friendly powers, and internally to perfect national defense, and thus under the august virtue of His Majesty, the Emperor, go forward toward the accomplishment of the holy task with a united nation. Given the trust and cooperation of the entire nation, I hope to promote the prosperity and welfare of the nation, and to glorify the nation's three-thousand-year history."

Otto Tolischus, the *New York Times* correspondent in Tokyo, thought Tojo's invocation of Japan's "holy mission" was tantamount to a declaration that the "armed diplomacy" which Japan had used heretofore against China and French Indo-China would be applied on a grander scale against the United States and Great Britain.[2]

Washington's reaction to Tojo was one of cool sarcasm. "Little good as we had to expect from the Konoye Cabinet, we had even less to expect from the Cabinet headed by Premier General Hideki Tojo," Secretary Hull related. His opinion of Tojo was "a typical Japanese officer, with a small-bore, straight-laced, one-track mind. He was stubborn and self-willed, rather stupid, hard-working, and possessed a quantity of drive."[3]

Only Ambassador Grew viewed the shift in a different light, expecting that "General Tojo, in retaining his active work in the Army," might as a result be in a position to exercise "a larger degree of control over Army extremist groups." Two weeks later, however, the Ambassador himself had to revise his own statement and sound out a war warning to Washington:

"Japan may go all-out in a do-or-die effort to render herself invulnerable to foreign economic pressure, even to the extent of committing national hara-kiri, and that those of us who are in direct touch with the atmosphere from day to day realize that this is not only possible *but probable;* . . . . that we would be lacking in perspicacity if we were to disregard or underestimate Japan's preparations for war in case its alternative program for peace should fail or if we were to regard these preparations merely as bluff designed to reinforce Japan's diplomacy; and that war between Japan and the United States may come with *dangerous and dramatic suddenness."*[4]

Tout ça change, tout c'est la même chose. Grew was correct. On October 23, at the insistence of the Supreme Command, a meeting of the Liaison Conference was held, the first one since Tojo had assumed power. At this meeting Tojo was surprised to see the impatience of Admiral Nagano who demanded that the Government make a clear cut decision for war or peace immediately. He explained that for each hour the Navy waited for a decision it consumed 400 tons of oil, and it could not long withstand the drain on its oil reserves. Tojo could detect that neither Admiral Nagano nor General Sugiyama was interested in the continuation of negotiations with the United States. They were not in sympathy with the Emperor's command that all major issues be re-examined *de novo.* Instead, they showed every sign of adhering to the decision of the September 6 Imperial Conference. General Tojo suddenly realized he was placed in a position similar to his predecessor Prince Konoye. On October 27 Tojo secured from General Sugiyama an assurance that the deadline could be extended to a future date which would be determined later. In the meantime, diplomatic negotiations would be allowed to continue, and the task was given to Foreign Minister Togo.

Togo was obsessed by the fact that "the Third Konoye Cabinet had retired leaving behind it the bomb of the Japanese negotiations with fuse alight." Unable to find a new formula acceptable to both the Army and the United States, he decided to concentrate his energy on the solution of the most crucial issue, the withdrawal of troops from China. Judging from Nomura's telegram of October 3, he believed that a tacit understanding had been reached with regard to the Tripartite Pact as well as on the question of no discrimination in Chinese trade.

Togo's own program was that Japanese troops stationed in China, including those in the special areas of North China and elsewhere, should be withdrawn within five years, and that Japan should with-draw its troops from Indo-China to demonstrate that it had no aggres-sive intent in the Southwestern Pacific.[5]

Whatever dream Togo might have had for the successful consum-mation of negotiations with the United States, it was destroyed by the attitude of the Army High Command which insisted that war preparations should take precedence over negotiations, especially after the early part of October in accordance with the terms set forth in the September 6 Imperial Conference decision. From Washington, Admiral Nomura requested his recall, declaring that he could no longer bear "this hypothetical existence, deceiving myself as well as others."

When the Liaison Conference met again on October 29 it was the sixth time within the week beginning October 23. All those present agreed that there was little chance of success in the current negotia-tions so long as Japan maintained its position. The debate thus centered on the question whether Japan could make any further concessions. General Sugiyama insisted that the Army could not alter its prior position with regard to the Tripartite Pact. Nor could it permit withdrawal of troops from French Indo-China. As to the question of stationing troops in China, Japan would not make any definite commitment to the United States. However, if asked, it could answer that it intended to station its troops for a period of twenty-five years. These conditions were stringent, and set the tone for the day. In principle, Japan would agree to Hull's four principles, "pro-vided certain other conditions were met." As to nondiscriminatory treatment in trade, Japan would agree to its application in China, if that "principle would be made applicable throughout the world." Foreign Minister Togo registered his protest. But the rest of the Conference approved the stiffer conditions and decided to reject the American note of October 2, lest Japan become a third-rate power.[6]

Debate in the Liaison Conference reached its height of intensity on November 1. The meeting itself lasted from nine in the morning to one-thirty the next morning. Before this meeting Tojo had a private meeting with General Sugiyama sounding him out for three possible alternatives. They were: (1) Japan should be prepared to go through thick and thin in order to avoid war. (2) Japan should immediately decide for war and concentrate its efforts on preparation for war. (3) Japan would decide for war and prepare for it. But in the meantime, negotiations should be continued, and if possible, bring them to a successful conclusion.

The Conference discussed all the possible choices exhaustively. The first alternative that Japan should avoid war at all cost was rejected outright without any dissenting voice. The question thus narrowed down to whether Japan should decide for war immediately or for the continuation of the negotiations. Sugiyama argued that without delay Japan should decide for war which should start in the early part of December. He would agree to the continuation of the conversations in Washington only if they would conceal Japan's true intent while engaging in the preparation for war. Admiral Nagano reviewed the depletion of oil reserves and also pressed for war. The Army High Command suggested that the deadline should be set at November 15 to end all diplomatic negotiations. The Navy would give another week for them, but otherwise agreed to Sugiyama's stand. Both the Army and Navy agreed that the longer Japan waited, the poorer it would become. Steadily the situation would worsen and the Empire would collapse eventually without war. No one was sure Japan could win the war. But for at least two years the Army and Navy could achieve a reasonable degree of success. If Japan could occupy the South Sea regions during this period, and secure the needed natural resources, it would be in a stronger position and the total collapse might be avoided. Togo and Kaya strenuously objected to this line of reasoning; they urged that the negotiations be continued without a deadline imposed on them.

At this point the meeting deadlocked, and Premier Tojo adjourned the meeting in order to confer privately with the Chiefs of Staff. When the meeting was resumed, the Conference adopted the third alternative and decided to continue the conversations while preparing for war. The deadline was extended until midnight, November 30. Togo was then allowed the opportunity of explaining to his colleagues his Proposal B as a *modus vivendi* to be used as a last resort in arriving at an agreement on a few items essential for averting war. This was to be presented to the United States only if his Proposal A did not bring about a solution. Sugiyama objected to Proposal B because in his opinion its provisions on China were far from being adequate. Tojo persuaded Sugiyama to accept it, reasoning that its rejection might cause the resignation of the Foreign Minister, which might in turn bring about another cabinet crisis.[7]

Togo's Proposal A contained the following three points relaxing somewhat Japan's September 25 proposal:

"1. Nondiscriminatory Treatment in Trade.

"Our position on this subject will be modified to provide that the Japanese Government agrees to its application to the entire Pacific area, including China, of the principle of nondiscrimination, if that principle be applied throughout the world.

"2. Interpretation and Implementation of the Tripartite Pact.

"3. Withdrawal of Troops.

"a. Withdrawal from China.

"Troops will be stationed in designated areas of North China and in Inner Mongolia and Hainan Island for a necessary period after the establishment of peace between Japan and China, and all other troops will be withdrawn within two years.

"b. Withdrawal from French Indo-China."

Proposal B consisted of the following five points and two accompanying notes:

"1. The Governments of Japan and the United States undertake to make no military advance into any of the regions, excepting French Indo-China, of Southeastern Asia and the Southern Pacific area.

"2. The Governments of Japan and the United States shall cooperate with a view to acquisition of those goods and commodities which the two countries require from the Netherlands East Indies.

"3. The Governments of Japan and the United States shall mutually undertake to restore their commercial relations to those prevailing prior to the freezing of assets.

"4. The Government of the United States undertakes to refrain from measures and actions prejudicial to the endeavor for restoration of general peace between Japan and China.

"5. The Government of Japan undertakes to withdraw troops now stationed in French Indo-China upon either the restoration of peace between Japan and China or the establishment of an equitable peace in the Pacific area.

"The Government of Japan declares that it is prepared upon conclusion of the present agreement to remove its troops now stationed in the southern part of French Indo-China to the northern part thereof.

"Notes:

"1. It may if necessary be promised at the conclusion of this agreement to withdraw the Japanese troops upon either the restoration of peace between Japan and China or the establishment of an equitable peace in the Pacific area.

"2. The provisions of Proposal A concerning nondiscriminatory treatment in trade and the interpretation and implementation of the Tripartite Pact may if necessary be added to this agreemnt."[8]

On November 4 Ambassador Nomura was instructed to proceed on the basis of Proposal A as soon as the Imperial Conference, scheduled to be held on November 5, approved it. "The present negotiations are our final effort," said Togo in his telegram. Claiming that Japan had already yielded enough and that there was a limit to Japan's forebearance, Togo continued. "If speedy conclusion of the negotiations is not to be attained even on the basis of these proposals, their breakdown is unavoidable, however regrettable it may be." Nomura was ordered to abide strictly by his instruction, and was given "no room for discretion."

Togo was dissatisfied with the way in which Ambassador Nomura was conducting his conversations in Washington. However, the situation had already reached such a critical stage that it was no longer practical to replace him by a professional diplomat. Togo's solution was to despatch Ambassador Saburo Kurusu, former Ambassador to Berlin, to Washington to assist Nomura.

Late on the night of November 3 Kurusu was summoned from his bed to Togo's official residence, and was asked to go to Washington. The two and the staff members of the Foreign Office thoroughly discussed Proposals A and B. Kurusu asked whether he could take an entirely new proposal to Washington that could be presented to Mr. Roosevelt at the psychological moment of their first meeting. Togo told him that time was running short and necessary instructions would be sent through telegrams. Through Ambassador Grew, the Foreign Office secured two seats in a trans-Pacific Clipper which was held up in Hong Kong for two days waiting for Kurusu and his secretary, Mr. Yuki. Within twenty hours from the time he was requested to go to Washington, Kurusu was already on his way.[9]

Things were then moving at a rapid pace. The Imperial Conference of November 5 formally ratified the prior decisions that Japan would open war on the United States and Great Britain in the early part of December if the negotiations failed. For the purpose of military operations, the time limit for the consummation of diplomatic negotiations was irrevocably set at November 25.

In sanctioning the despatch of Kurusu, Premier Tojo seemed to have entertained some hope for the success of the negotiations. But this feeling was not shared by the Supreme Command. On November 5, without the knowledge of General Tojo, an order was sent from Admiral Nagano to Admiral Yamamoto, Commander-in-Chief of the Combined Fleet, that the fleet be prepared for war with the Netherlands, the U.S., and England at a moment's notice. In so ordering Admiral Nagano also accepted Admiral Yamamoto's plan for a surprise attack on Pearl Harbor. On the next day, the Army set up a Southern Expeditionary Force and named General Terauchi as its Supreme Commander. On November 7 Admiral Yamamoto ordered all of his task forces to assemble at the Hitocup Bay in the Kuriles by November 22 to be refueled and to await further orders. Three days later Admiral Nagumo, Commander of the special task force, ordered all telecommunications cut off, and gave instructions to his top aides that preparation for combat-readiness should be completed by November 20. December 8 (Japanese time) was tentatively fixed as the day to start operations.[10]

Ambassador Nomura visited Secretary Hull in his apartment in the evening of November 7 and handed him two of the three points covered in Proposal A. Hull was unimpressed since he already knew through the "magic" Japan's deadline for cutting off negotiations.

The intercepted messages were not the only warnings that had come to Mr. Hull. There was Ambassador Grew's prediction that Japan might "resort to measures which might (make) war with the United States come with dramatic and dangerous suddenness." Generalissimo Chiang Kai-shek also reported to Washington and London excessive concentration of Japanese troops at Haiphong on the coast of Northern French Indo-China. Fearing that these moves were preliminary to an all-out attack of Kunming, the Generalissimo requested the United States and Great Britain to take arms to defend his country and supply needed military equipment.

The War Plans Division of the War and Navy Departments opposed the movement and employment of U. S. military forces in support of Chiang Kai-shek, and urged that the State Department make an arrangement with Japan to tide the situation over for the next several months. In this the War Plans Division was following the same policy that was decided at the Atlantic Conference—namely, that the primary objective was the defeat of Germany, and the principal objective in the Far East was to keep Japan out of war. However, in its report to the President on November 5, the War Plans Division urged the United States to go to war against Japan if either one of the following events occured.

"(1) A direct act of war by Japanese armed forces against the territory or mandated territory of the United States, the British Commonwealth, or the Netherlands East Indies.

"(2) The movement of Japanese forces into Thailand to the west of 100° East or south of 10° North; or into Portuguese Timore, New Caledonia, or the Loyalty Islands."[11]

It was against this background that the Cabinet meeting of November 7 took place. It preceded Mr. Hull's meeting with Nomura by a few hours. Mr. Hull warned the President and his cabinet colleagues that the relations with Japan were "extremely critical," and that the United States "should be on the lookout for a military attack by Japan anywhere at any time." To Mr. Hull, Japan's Proposal A was merely "rewordings of the previous Japanese points," and "contained nothing basically new, nor did they offer any real concessions." It was not surprising, therefore, that the Cabinet could tell the President that it was their unanimous opinion that the American people would support the Administration if it should decide to strike at Japan, in case Japan should attack England in Malaya or the Dutch in East Indies.

Togo greeted the news of Hull's apparent rejection of the parts of his Proposal A with mixed feelings. Hull's indifference seemed to cast a dark shadow over the future of the negotiations. Yet there was an encouraging note. "Suppose," the Secretary of State had told the Japanese Ambassador, "the Chinese were now to say that they desired a real friendship with Japan and would do everything in their power to work together with Japan along peaceful ways. Would this not be a wonderful opportunity for Japan to launch forth on a real new order, an order in which Japan would gain real moral leadership in the Far East?" Togo thought this would open the way for Japan to enter into direct negotiations with Chiang Kai-shek with the good offices of the United States. It was the formula the Foreign Office had been after for some time. Togo welcomed the suggestions.

On November 10 Togo hopefully telegraphed Nomura: "By making use of Mr. Hull's suggestion, we may even be able to exclude the question of stationing troops in China from the present negotiations. This would greatly aid the successful conclusion of the negotiations." It was a premature bud. When Ambassador Nomura, accompanied by Minister Wakasugi, visited the White House on the same day (though it was November 11 in Tokyo), Mr. Roosevelt mentioned nothing of the sort. Nomura pressed for quick decisions of the three main issues separating Japan from the United States—namely, Japanese troops in China, the Tripartite Alliance, and the principle of nondiscrimination in trade. The President saw fit to interject that "nations must think one hundred years ahead, especially during the age through which the world is passing." He told the Japanese Ambassador that in discussing a solution to the U. S.-Japanese relations, patience was necessary and that the United States did not want a temporary agreement.[12]

On November 15 a formal rejection of Proposal A was given to the Japanese Ambassador. On this occasion, Mr. Hull reiterated that there was no existence of "negotiations," contending that only after the two countries had reached agreement on basic principles would it be possible to begin formal negotiations.

In Tokyo, Togo made a half-hearted effort to convince the British Ambassador, Sir Robert Craigie, that the negotiations with the United States had reached their final stage, and hinted through Ambassador Grew that Japan would like to have the British Government conclude an agreement simultaneously with the United States. At this late stage Tokyo was still hoping that London would prove to be more accommodating, and possibly serve as an intermediary in convincing Washington of the futility of forcing unacceptable issues upon Tokyo.

In this instance London was not accommodating. In the course of his address at the annual Guildhall banquet, Winston Churchill warned that if the United States became involved in war with Japan, "the British declaration will follow within the hour." The *Prince of Wales* and the *Repulse* were already sent to the Far Eastern waters. Indeed, "every preparation to defend British interests in the Far East, and to defend the common cause" had been and was being made. The British would not permit Japan's bluff to force them into an appeasement.

Togo's diplomatic talks, whatever they were worth, were only a sideline in this already tense last month. On November 11 the Liaison Conference completed its draft of the reasons to be published in the event of war against the United States and Great Britain. Two days later the Liaison Conference discussed the matter of German participation in the common war against the United States. In the past Japan and Germany had gone separate ways in pursuing their foreign policy goals, and at this late date, Japan was still uncertain of Germany's participation. It was fearful that Germany might press for Japanese participation in the war against Soviet Russia as an equitable *quid pro quo*. On this, the Liaison Conference decided that Japan should not participate in the war against Russia even if it would have meant delay in German participation in the war against the United

States. Official notification of the decision for war would be given
Germany some time after November 25, the deadline set by the
Supreme Command for breaking off the negotiations.

While Japan was uncertain of Germany's intention its victory in the
war would largely depend on Germany's ability to subdue Great
Britain. The same Liaison Conference of November 15 discussed in
detail the prospect of war. It concluded that the United States would
lose its will to fight, if any of the following situations developed:
(1) If Japan firmly established self-sufficiency, and lasted through the
prolonged war without suffering defeat. (2) If Japan could subdue
Chiang Kai-shek with positive and incisive action. (3) If Great
Britain sued for peace as the result of Japanese-German cooperation.
The Liaison Conference believed that Germany could accomplish the
last mentioned objective, and on that ground calculated the war
could be won, despite the fact that Japan's national power could
not match that of the United States.

In order to insure German victory over Great Britain, the Liaison
Conference actively considered the possibility of mediating between
Germany and Soviet Russia, and of Soviet Russia eventually fighting
on the side of the Axis, its prizes being India and Iran. However,
this did not go beyond the stage of wishful thinking. The Japanese
military leaders could not trust their northern neighbor. In fact, the
combat strength in Manchuria was not reduced at all. Instead, the
Army High Command drafted a plan to shift troops from the South
Sea regions as soon as practicable to Manchuria in order to prepare
for any unforeseen attack from the Soviet Union.

By the time the Liaison Conference of November 15 was held Togo
had in his possession a telegram from Nomura, dated November 14,
warning that the American Government would stop any further
Japanese advances at all costs:

"If we carry out a venture southward for the sake of our existence
and our lives, it naturally follows that we will have to fight England
and the United States, and chances are also great that the Soviet Union
will participate. It is inevitable that this war will be long, and this
little victory or that little victory, or this little defeat or that little
defeat do not amount to much, and it is not hard to see that whoever
can hold out till the end will be the victor . . . . I had expected in the
past that should the United States start warlike activities in the Atlantic, there would be considerable feeling for a compromise in the
Pacific, but there has been no evidence of such an inclination as yet.
There are even now many arguments against war with Germany as

opposed to internal questions, but there is not the slightest opposition to war in the Pacific. It is being thought more than ever that participation will be carried out through the Pacific area."

Nomura then urged that the Japanese Government be patient for a while in order to get a clearer view of the world situation, maintaining that in the long run Japan could win in the negotiations.

This was out of question as far as Tokyo was concerned. The Foreign Office's preoccupation was to find out a workable solution before the inflexible military deadline came. In a reply dated November 15 Togo told Nomura that there would be no change in the date set for reaching a settlement. Nomura was not to "allow the United States to diversify the issues and delay the negotiations any further . . . ."[13]

At this point, Togo was ready to negotiate on the basis of his proposal B and necessary instructions were sent to Nomura.

Mr. Kurusu in Washington. Kurusu arrived in Washington on Saturday, November 15. Two days later he had his first meeting with President Roosevelt and Secretary Hull. In trying to do his "touchdown" the special envoy had no better luck than Nomura. For one thing, prejudiced by Kurusu's part in the signing of the Tripartite Pact, Hull intensely disliked the new emissary. "His only recommendation in my eyes was that he spoke excellent English, having married his American secretary," commented Mr. Hull. "Nevertheless, I found that Nomura, despite his faulty English, understood the points I made much better than did Kurusu, whose mentality was such that he could not appreciate our views."[14] For another thing, Kurusu lacked any new proposals to offer, even though he had made an arrangement with Togo to be the one to submit proposal B to Washington at the "psychological moment" of his first meeting with the President.

Significantly, Kurusu's first meeting with President Roosevelt was marked with lack of constructive proposals. Kurusu chose not to present Proposal B fearing that its usefulness was limited. Instead, he was satisfied with presenting Japan's case on the issues of evacuating troops from China and of Japan's obligations under the Tripartite Pact.

At the end of the day, after meeting with Mr. Hull, the two Ambassadors paid a call to a certain cabinet member, presumably Postmaster General Walker. The latter told his visitors that the President was desirous of an understanding with Japan which could be reached if "Japan would now do something real, such as evacuating French Indo-China, showing its peaceful intentions, the way would be open for us to furnish you with oil and it would probably lead to the reestablishment of normal trade relations." The two visitors took the hint. On November 18, in their meeting with Secretary Hull, they suggested a limited agreement involving a return to the *status quo* prior to July 24. This would have meant withdrawal of Japanese troops from Southern French Indo-China, rescinding of American freezing order, and supplying of a limited amount of oil to Japan by the United States.

In communicating their informal suggestions for return to the *status quo* prior to July 24, the two Ambassadors stressed that they regarded their suggestions as the only means to success in the negotiations. As surmised by Ambassador Nomura, their position was:

" . . . . looking at it from a practical point of view, we are of the opinion that prior to presenting proposal B it would be more advisable to reach a practical settlement, principally on the questions of the acquisition of goods and the cancellation of the freezing legislation mentioned in Proposal B, and then to try to proceed with the resolution of other questions on this basis. Unless we follow this course we are convinced that an immediate solution will be extremely difficult.

"The United States, of course, has indicated clearly that it is not interested in mere promises as much as it is in putting said promises into effect. It is necessary, therefore, for us to be prepared to withdraw our troops as soon as the freezing order is rescinded and materials are made available to us."

However, when their telegrams reached Tokyo, Togo was infuriated by the unauthorized actions of the Ambassadors. "The internal situation in our country is such that it would be difficult for us to handle it if we withdraw from Southern Indo-China, merely on assurances that conditions prior to this freezing act will be restored," cabled Togo. He stated categorically that submission of private proposals was not welcome by him or by General Tojo, and instructed them to proceed immediately on Proposal B. The language of the telegram was so strong that Kurusu could not but feel that it was a "severe rebuke."[15]

Meanwhile, an emergency session of the Imperial Diet was convened on November 16. Its main function was to approve the necessary budget estimates, but it was quickly turned into a propaganda forum. On November 17 Tojo made a speech which was broadcast to the nation for the first time in Japan's parliamentary history. In his speech he termed the economic sanctions "a measure little less hostile than carrying on armed warfare," adding that the Empire could by no means acquiesce to it. Unspoken but implicit in his speech was Japan's determination for war.

On November 20, the Liaison Conference approved the details for the military government of the South Sea regions after occupation. Among other things, it decided upon the spheres of primary responsibility between the Army and the Navy. Hong Kong, the Philippines, British Malaya, Sumatra, Java, and British Borneo were to be placed under the Army's control, and the rest, including other islands of the Dutch East Indies were to be placed under the Navy's jurisdiction.

Rejection of Modus Vivendi. Against this background Japan's final offer, Proposal B was presented to Secretary Hull at noon, November 20 (Tokyo time, November 21, 2 a.m.). The proposal, reproduced in full in the early part of this chapter, was in the nature of a *modus vivendi*, in an attempt to arrive at a stopgap arrangement in order to give more time to the settlement of larger issues. No attempt was made to answer the fundamental issues. The only concrete step Japan would take was to remove its troops from the southern part of French Indo-China to the northern part. In return Japan expected resumption of commercial relations as they existed before the freezing order, and a guarantee for a fixed amount of oil import from the United States and the Netherlands East Indies.

Secretary Hull was already familiar with the content of Japan's *modus vivendi* through the "magic" intercepted messages. He was quick in grasping the import of what amounted to an "ultimatum." The commitments the United States would have to make were "virtually a surrender," remarked the Secretary:

"We on our part should have to supply Japan as much oil as she might require, suspend our freezing measures, and resume full commercial relations with Tokyo. We should have to discontinue aid to China and withdraw our moral and material support from the recognized Chinese Government of Chiang Kai-shek. We should have to help Japan obtain products of the Netherlands East Indies. We should have to cease augumenting our military forces in the western Pacific.

"Japan, on her part, would still be free to continue her military operations in China, to attack the Soviet Union, and to keep her troops in northern Indo-China until peace was effected with China. There was no limit on the troops Japan could send into Indo-China. Her willingness to withdraw from southern Indo-China to northern Indo-China was meaningless because those troops could return within a day or two. Japan thus clung to her vantage point in Indo-China which threatened countries to the south and vital trade routes."[16]

Of this meeting Nomura reported that Hull was terribly aroused by the demand that aid to China be discontinued. The Secretary intimated that unless Japan adopted a policy for peace, the aid to China would have to be continued which was of similar nature as aid to Britain. He then reiterated his objection to Japan's continued adherence to the Tripartite Pact.

Hull's latter remarks prompted Kurusu to visit Hull alone the following day, to give the Secretary his own interpretations of the Pact. He stated that Japan could independently interpret its obligations under the Tripartite Pact, and "the Japanese Government would not involve the nation in war at the command of a foreign government." The Secretary knew that the Japanese Ambassador had nothing more to offer and was unimpressed. After Kurusu left he gave warnings to Admiral Stark, Chief of Naval Operations, that Japan might attack at any time.

In Tokyo there was visible pessimism. The Liaison Conference of November 22 discussed two alternatives. First, if the United States rejected all of Japanese demands, and second, if the United States accepted its demands. In the first instance, Japan would resort to war. In the second instance, Japan would require that the United States guarantee Japan's annual oil import quota of 3,500,000 tons from the United States and 2,000,000 tons from the Dutch East Indies. This was duly cabled to Ambassador Nomura in Washington. In a separate telegram Togo also told Nomura that the deadline could be extended to November 29 from the previous deadline of November 25, provided agreements could be secured from the United States, Great Britain and the Netherlands. Beyond that no extension would be possible, and "things are automatically going to happen."[17]

While Tokyo staked its hope of success on its stopgap arrangement as contained in Proposal B, Washington was also engaged in the study of its own *modus vivendi*. Earlier in the course of conversations with Japan, the President himself had devised some kind of arrangement which would keep the conversations going for another six months, or might even lead to an eventual comprehensive settlement. In a penciled note, Mr. Roosevelt speculated under the heading "Six Months":

"1. U. S. to resume economic relations—some oil and rice now—more later.

"2. Japan to send no more troops to Indo-China or Manchurian border or any place south (Dutch, Brit. or Siam).

"3. Japan to agree not to invoke tripartite pact if U. S. gets into European War.

"4. U. S to *introduce* Japs to Chinese to talk things over but U. S. take no part in their conversations.

"Later on Pacific agreements."[18]

The Far East Division of the State Department also studied the possibility of bringing Japan and China into a direct amicable negotiation for a peaceful settlement of their differences. On November 11 it submitted a draft of a proposal to Secretary Hull which called for immediate Japanese-Chinese negotiations during which there would be an armistice between these two countries. The United States would hold in abeyance the shipment of supplies of a military character to China, and Japan would not increase its military forces in China and French Indo-China. Upon the conclusion of a peace settlement between Japan and China the United States would negotiate with both China and Japan for the resumption of normal trade relations.

On November 18 Secretary of the Treasury Morgenthau also came up with a program of his own which would involve a comprehensive settlement between Japan and the United States. Under the Morgenthau draft, the United States was to: (1) withdraw the bulk of its naval forces from the Pacific; (2) sign a twenty-year non-aggression pact with Japan; (3) promote a final settlement of the Manchurian problem; (4) put Indo-China under a five-power joint commission, composed of the British, French, Japanese, Chinese, and American representatives, which would assure most-favored-nation treatment to these five powers until the end of the European War. In addition the Administration would recommend to Congress to repeal the Immigration Act of 1917, and negotiate a trade agreement with a most-favored nation clause and with other concessions, including (1) a two billion dollar credit to Japan at two percent for twenty-years, and (2) setting up of a stabilization fund of five hundred million dollars to which the United States and Japan were to contribute one-half each. The restrictions on Japanese funds in the United States would at once be removed.

On its part Japan was to: (1) withdraw all forces from China beyond the frontiers of 1931, and from Indo-China and Thailand; (2) discontinue support of any government other than that of Chiang Kai-shek;

(3) sell to the United States up to three quarters of Japan's current output of war materials, including naval air ordinance, and commercial ships on a cost-plus-twenty-percent basis; and (4) negotiate a ten-year non-aggression pact with the United States, China, Britain, the Netherlands East Indies, and the Philippines.

It was unlikely that Japan would have accepted this program, since it implied that Japan renounce its expansionist policies and the Axis alliance, in return for financial and economic aid from the United States. Yet the State Department took the suggestion seriously. War Plans Division also saw "no objection to its use as a basis for discussion," emphasizing "it is of grave importance to the success of our war effort in Europe that we reach a *modus vivendi* with Japan." [19]

On November 22 the Far East Division of the State Department completed the first draft of a counterproposal in reply to the Japanese note of November 20. It was in two sections. The first section contained a *modus vivendi* as an alternative to the one suggested by the Japanese. Among other things, the American *modus vivendi* called for a temporary truce of three months and would restore the status quo prior to Japanese occupation of southern Indo-China [20]

Concurrently the State Department worked on an outline of a ten-point peace settlement to accompany the *modus vivendi*. Even though the Secretary felt that there was "probably not one chance in three that the Japanese would accept our *modus vivendi*," and that he and his associates "had reached a stage of clutching at straws to save the situation," serious considerations were given to both the Japanese proposal and U. S. counterproposal. It must be noted that the two documents were similar in many respects, with the major deviation in the American insistence on limiting Japanese forces in Indo-China to 25,000 men.

The State Department became daily a scene of prolonged conferences. Mr. Hull called in the British, Chinese, Netherlands and Australian envoys and reviewed together the Japanese proposal of November 20 and the American *modus vivendi*. Except Dr. Hu Shih, the Chinese Ambassador, each of the representatives seemed well pleased with the U. S. counterproposal. On Monday, November 24, these envoys went back to Mr. Hull's office. Only the Netherlands Minister had received instructions from his government, endorsing the American *modus vivendi*. Hull was disappointed at "the lack of interest and lack of disposition to cooperate," and decided not to hand the *modus vivendi* to Nomura that day. [21]

Later on that day, at Mr. Hull's suggestion, Mr. Roosevelt cabled

Churchill in London explaining the proposed *modus vivendi*. He concluded that the modus vivendi "seems to me a fair proposition for the Japanese but its acceptance or rejection is really a matter of internal Japanese politics. I am not very hopeful and we must all be prepared for real trouble, possibly soon."[22]

On November 25 the draft proposal was again revised in the State Department, and was shown to Secretaries Stimson and Knox. The so-called "War Council" composed of President Roosevelt, Secretaries Hull, Stimson and Knox, General Marshall, and Admiral Stark met at the White House. In the words of Secretary Stimson, "The situation was how we should maneuver them into firing the first shot without allowing too much danger to ourselves." The content of the revised draft proposal was more restricted. As he read through it, Secretary Stimson thought it was too drastic, and there was no chance of the Japanese accepting it. "In return for the propositions which they were to do: namely, to at once evacuate and at once to stop all preparations or threats of action, and to take no aggressive action against any of her neighbors, etc., we were to give them open trade in sufficient quantities only for their civilian population. This restriction was particularly applicable to oil."

London also urged a similar course of action. Evidently thinking that the Japanese would not fight, Foreign Secretary Eden suggested that any American counterproposal "should stipulate for the total withdrawal from Indo-China not merely of the Japanese 'troops' as in the Japanese proposal but of Japanese naval, military and air forces with their equipment and for the *suspension of further military* advances in China in addition to satisfactory assurance regarding other areas in South East Asia, the Southern Pacific and Russia . . . . " All in all, Mr. Eden sought a counterproposal that would set "our demands pitched high and our price low."

Violent opposition to the U. S. *modus vivendi* came from Chungking. Chiang Kai-shek had shown a "very strong reaction." His American political adviser, Owen Lattimore had "never seen him so agitated." Through his ambassador, Chiang protested that the United States Government "has put aside the Chinese question in its conversations with Japan instead of seeking a solution, and is still inclined to appease Japan at the expense of China."

Not satisfied with the protest through his ambassador in Washington, Chiang sent a message of protest to Prime Minister Churchill, and also instructed his brother-in-law, T. V. Soong, who was in Washington, to appeal directly to Secretaries Stimson and Knox. T. V.

Soong enlisted the aid of "a former official who had recently taken up the practice of law in Washington," to stir up accusations of American appeasement of Japan in the press and among Congressmen and Senators. The Chinese opposition was successful. There was a rush of appeals not to "sell China down the river." Dr. Hu Shih came to see Mr. Hull on the evening of November 25 to deliver Chiang's vehement protest. Mr. Hull was disappointed that the Chinese Government could not see the point of view he held. Yet at that time he still favored presenting the *modus vivendi*. He felt that it could keep the record clear, even though there was but a very slight chance of Japan's accepting it.[23]

Then came a telegram from Winston Churchill. Apparently influenced by Chiang's protest, the Prime Minister declared: "Of course it is for you to handle this business and we certainly do not want an additional war   There is only one point that disquiets us. What about Chiang Kai-shek? Is he not having a very thin diet? Our anxiety is about China. If they collapse our joint dangers would enormously increase. We are sure that the regard of the United States for the Chinese cause will govern your action. We feel that the Japanese are most unsure of themselves."

Meanwhile intelligence reports indicated movement of Japanese troops to the South.

In the afternoon of November 26 Mr. Hull conferred with the President. This had been preceded by a conference between the President and Dr. Hu Shih and T. V. Soong. Mr. Hull decided that the *modus vivendi* be dropped: "in view of the opposition of the Chinese Government and either the half-hearted support of the actual opposition of the British, the Netherlands, and the Australian Governments, and in view of the wide publicity of the opposition and of the additional opposition that will naturally follow through the lack of an understanding of the vast importance and value otherwise of the *modus vivendi* . . . . " The Secretary later recalled that he reached this decision, since "it became clear that the slight prospects of Japan's agreeing to the *modus vivendi* did not warrant assuming the risks involved in proceeding with it, especially the serious risk of collapse of Chinese morale and resistance and even of disintegration of China."[24]

Mr. Roosevelt approved Secretary Hull's recommendation that a copy of the comprehensive basic proposal be handed to the Japanese Ambassadors while withholding the *modus vivendi*.

The November 26 Note. At 4:45 in the afternoon the two Japanese Ambassadors arrived at the State Department for their fateful conference with Secretary Hull. There the Secretary presented his ten-point program, which he called an "Outline of Proposed Basis for Agreement between the United States and Japan." In accordance with Mr. Hull's refusal to enter into "negotiations," it was marked "Tentative without Commitment." The ten points, which were preceded by Mr. Hull's four principles, are reproduced in full below:

"1. The Government of the United States and the Government of Japan will endeavor to conclude a multilateral non-aggression pact among the British Empire, China, Japan, the Netherlands, the Soviet Union, Thailand and the United States.

"2. Both Governments will endeavor to conclude among the American, British, Chinese, Japanese, the Netherlands and Thai Governments an agreement whereunder each of the Governments would pledge itself to respect the territorial integrity of French Indo-China and, in the event that there should develop a threat to the territorial integrity of Indo-China, to enter into immediate consultation with a view to taking such measures as may be deemed necessary and advisable to meet the threat in question. Such agreement would not seek or accept preferential treatment in its trade or economic relations with Indo-China and would use its influence to obtain for each of the signatories equality of treatment in trade and commerce with French Indo-China.

"3. The Government of Japan will withdraw all military, naval, air and police forces from China and from Indo-China.

"4. The Government of the United States and the Government of Japan will not support—militarily, politically, economically—any government or regime in China other than the National Government of the Republic of China with capital temporarily at Chungking.

"5. Both Governments will give up all extraterritorial rights in China, including rights and interest in and with regard to international settlements and concessions, and rights under the Boxer Protocol of 1901.

"6. The Government of the United States and the Government of Japan will enter into negotiations for the conclusion between the United States and Japan of a trade agreement, based upon reciprocal most-favored-nation treatment and reduction of trade barriers by both countries, including an undertaking by the United States to bind raw silk on the free list.

"7. The Government of the United States and the Government of

Japan will, respectively, remove the freezing restrictions on Japanese funds in the United States and on American funds in Japan.

"8. Both Governments will agree upon a plan for stablization of the dollar-yen rate, with the allocation of funds adequate for this purpose half to be supplied by Japan and half by the United States.

"9. Both Governments will agree that no agreement which either has concluded with any third power or powers shall be interpreted by it in such a way as to conflict with the fundamental purpose of this agreement, the establishment and preservation of peace throughout the Pacific area.

"10. Both Governments will use their influence to cause other governments to adhere to and to give practical application to the basic political and economic principles set forth in this agreement."[25]

Ambassador Kurusu vehemently opposed several of the provisions of the American note, commenting that the multilateral treaty as suggested in point 2 would bring back the old order similar to the one under the Nine-Power Pact, and thus nullify Japan's past four years' effort in China. On Points 3 and 4, calling for the evacuation of China and Indo-China and for the support of the Chungking regime and the abandonment of the Nanking regime, Kurusu said that if this represented the idea of the American Government he did not see how any agreement was possible. If they did report this proposal back to Tokyo, declared Kurusu, the Japanese Government "would be likely to throw up its hand."

On November 27 the Liaison Conference held two sessions in the Imperial Palace. The deadline for reaching an agreement with the United States was near. While Foreign Minister Togo was explaining that it was almost impossible to receive a satisfactory answer from the United States, two telegrams arrived from Washington. They were from the Military and Naval Attachés, giving an outline of the November 26 note. The telegram from the two Ambassadors had not arrived. But on the basis of the incomplete outline given by the attachés, the Liaison Conference concluded that the Hull note was tantamount to an ultimatum and Japan could not accept it. The Conference decided to call an Imperial Conference on December 1 to get the imperial sanction for war.[26]

The Japanese reaction to the Hull note was summarized in the words of its Foreign Minister: "If we yielded to the present demands of the United States," said Mr. Togo, "Japan's international position would be inferior even to that which it occupied prior to the Manchurian Incident, and its very existence itself would be endangered."

The two Ambassadors in Washington doggedly tried their hands. There were still two and one-half days to go before the deadline. Before they met the Secretary on that fateful day, Ambassador Nomura cabled Tokyo, suggesting that the Government might consider sending a personal message from the Emperor to President Roosevelt. After the receipt of the Hull note, he sent only a brief resume to Tokyo first, which was followed by a telegram admonishing the Tokyo Government not to attack the United States while the negotiations were still going on, lest Japan be blamed "for the rupture of the negotiations." Mr. Hull had arranged for the two Ambassadors to meet with the President the following day, and they hoped that the meeting might bring out something concrete that would enable the two countries to avoid catastrophe. However, despite the President's friendliness, the two envoys were to find that the President shared the Secretary's views, and there was no indication of readiness to reconsider.

It was a point of no return. It is academic whether a more compromising note would have averted the war. It was not likely that the Japanese militarists would have been content with anything less than their Proposal B. A day before the Hull note was received, the Naval High Command ordered the task force assembled at the Hitocup Bay to proceed to its destination. Another fleet composed of twenty-seven submarines had already disembarked for Pearl Harbor on November 21. Large forces and landing equipment were assembled in Hainan Island, Southern French Indo-China, and Formosa during the month of November. While these troop movements were not in themselves conclusive proof of Japan's ultimate intentions, (since the task force could still be recalled, and the troops despatched elsewhere), there was little doubt that a war was in the offing. Only a miraculous force could have saved it."

Equally tense was the situation in Washington. The words attributed to Secretary Hull in his telepohne conversation with Secretary Stimson, "I have washed my hands of it and it is in the hands of you and Knox," hardly need repetition. The Secretary also held an unusually long press conference outlining the status of discussions with the Japanese. He emphasized that the Japanese reinforcements were pouring into Indo-China, and that a Japanese attack might come within a few days. His action was hailed almost unanimously by the press as the rejection of another Munich. While America rejected a Far Eastern Munich, Japan was determined to do away with another possible "Triple intervention of 1895." The crisis was at hand.

On November 28 Togo sought Lord Privy Seal Marquis Kido's

advice on the matter of the Emperor sending a personal message to President Roosevelt as suggested by the two Ambassadors. Kido rejected it as impractical and refused to communicate the idea to the Throne. He was also shown the text of the Hull note, upon which he registered sharp disappointment, saying that the acceptance of the note might lead to civil war. The two Ambassadors were informed that the Japanese Government could not use the Hull note as the basis for further negotiations. Togo promised a report of the views of the Japanese Government to be sent within two or three days. He declared that the negotiations had to be suspended for all practical purposes, though the Ambassadors should avoid giving the impression that this was the case.

Decision for War. No dissenting voice was raised in the Liaison Conference of November 27 which decided for war. This included Foreign Minister Togo, the most moderate of the Cabinet ministers. At the Emperor's suggestion, the Tojo Cabinet also called a meeting of all Senior Statesmen, or Jushin, who had previously held the post of premiership.

There Tojo's insistence that Japan's "gradual privation" caused by the American embargo could only be saved by going to war evoked Yonai's terse comment: "It sounds like you are trying to avoid 'gradual privation' by going bankrupt first." Otherwise with the notable exception of Prince Konoye, most former Prime Ministers expressed their confidence in the Government.

After communicating to Tojo his doubt about the wisdom of entering into war and conferring with the Chief of Naval Operations and the Navy Minister, the Emperor reluctantly consented to the holding of an Imperial Conference. Whatever chance Japan might have had for peace was thus sealed. The Imperial Conference of December 1 formally ratified the decision for war.

Meanwhile, on November 30, the Japanese public was informed that their soldier Premier had made a speech declaring that the British and American influence in the Far East ought to be purged: "The fact that Chiang Kai-shek is dancing to the tune of Britain, America, and communism at the expense of able-bodied and promising young men in his futile resistance against Japan is only due to the desire of Britain and the United States to fish in troubled waters of East Asia by pitting the East Asiatic peoples against each other and to grasp the hegemony of East Asia. This is a stock in trade of Britain and the United States."[28]

The message was actually never delivered. November 30 was Sunday, and advance copies were given to newspapers the night before. It was drafted for Tojo by the staff of the East Asian League, which was responsible for the celebration of the first anniversary of the Japanese-Manchukuo-Wang treaty. Tojo himself had not seen the draft, nor was he present at the celebration. Yet, the message was soon cabled to the United States by Ambassador Grew and by the United Press. It was headline news in major papers, and caused President Roosevelt who was resting at Warm Springs, Virginia to return to Washington.

The two Ambassadors were dismayed by the violent statement from Tokyo. "Incredible," exclaimed Kurusu when he learned the whole story. Yet they had the unpleasant task of explaining away the speech and the troop movements in Indo-China. Neither Nomura nor Kurusu were informed of Tokyo's irrevocable decision for war. Thus both of them again suggested to Tokyo a possible top level conference between Prince Konoye and Viscount Ishii, a veteran diplomat, on Japan's side, and Vice President Wallace and Harry Hopkins, representing the United States to meet at Honolulu. Their suggestion was promptly vetoed by Tokyo.

On December 2, the Liaison Conference met to consider the method of declaring war. The Navy wanted negotiations to prolong until the day of actual attack, and demanded that the notice of the rupture of negotiations be given in Tokyo rather than in Washington to insure the success of the surprise attack.

On the same day the Liaison Conference was held, the Combined Fleet received the order to "climb Mt. Nitaka," meaning "attack Pearl Harbor." The X day or the zero hour was definitely set to be December 8, Tokyo time. After the Conference Togo also directed the Embassy in Washington, and the Legation in Ottawa and all consular offices in North America to burn the diplomatic code.

A few days earlier, on November 28, the Foreign Office formally instructed its Ambassador in Berlin, General Oshima, to inform the Reich Government that the United States and Great Britain had adopted a challenging attitude and had been reinforcing their forces in the Far East, and that if a war broke out, Japan expected Germany and Italy to join immediately. The Ambassador was to initiate negotiations for a No-Separate-Peace treaty. Japan had not been truly faithful to its Axis partner in the past, but in this instance it declared that the main obstacle to the success of the negotiations in Washington had been its insistence upon maintaining its treaty obligations and its faithfulness to the Tripartite Pact.[29]

Berlin was unaware of the imminence of war. Ambassador Oshima was away in Vienna atending the Mozart festival, and it was not until December 2 that Oshima actually presented the Japanese request to Ribbentrop. The latter was unable to give definite answer since the Führer was at the Russian front. On December 5, a formal German acceptance of the Japanese requests was handed to Oshima.

In Rome, similar requests were presented to Ciano and Mussolini. The former was cautious, but the Duce was "not at all surprised" at the prospect of war with the United States, "in view of the utter bull-headedness of the United States and the meddlesome nature of President Roosevelt." Mussolini readily granted the Japanese requests when presented. However, he did reserve the right to consult with Hitler.

Japan got the German-Italian promise with little or no price to pay on its part. Togo refused to intercept any American shipment of munitions going to Russia through Vladivostock. Japan had made it clear that its participation in the war against Russia was definitely out of question. To the repeated inquiries from the Germans and from its own Embassy in Berlin whether Japan would later join Germany in war against Soviet Russia, the Army High Command avoided definite commitment.

Meanwhile, the Liaison Conference formulated a basic policy toward Thailand. Subsequently on November 23, Ambassador Tsubogami was instructed to ask from the Thai Government facilities for passage of Japanese troops through the Thai territory, and for taking preventive measures to insure that there would be no clashes between the Japanese and Thai troops. The negotiations were not to start before 6 p.m. on X minus one day, nor after midnight. Thai's public statement that it would regard any power that first invaded its territory as aggressor complicated the issue, but the Japanese Government was certain that Premier Phibun Songkhram would accept Japanese demands provided Japan gave enough bait, such as territories in Burma and Malaya in return for Thai's cooperation.

In Washington, Nomura and Kurusu were making a desperate last minute attempt to revive the defunct *modus vivendi*. They conferred with Bernard Baruch, Rev. E. Stanley Jones, Bishop Walsh, and Postmaster General Walker. These people were interested in the idea of the United States acting as an "introducer." But their activities, coming at this late stage, left no visible change in the attitude of the Roosevelt Administration. However, Kurusu credited Rev. Jones with taking an active part in persuading the President to send a personal message to the Japanese Emperor.[30]

The idea of sending a personal message to the Japanese Emperor had been under discussion since October. Hr. Hull was not favorably inclined to it. As he later recalled: "I felt that the Emperor, in any event, was a figurehead under the control of the military Cabinet. A message direct to him would cause Tojo's Cabinet to feel that they were being short-circuited and would anger them."[31] However, on December 6 the message was sent as a last-minute resort, and strictly "for the record." There was no hope of a favorable response. It was sent in gray code, the least secret one, which could easily be deciphered.

In Tokyo, Ambassador Grew first learned from the radio that the President had sent a message to the Emperor. The telegram which was marked "Triple Priority" did not reach him until 10:30 p.m., December 7, Tokyo time, being held up by the Tokyo Central Telegraph Office for more than ten hours at the request of an officer of the General Staff.

Mr. Grew immediately arranged an appointment with the Foreign Minister and saw him at about 12:30 a.m. on the 8th. Togo promised the Ambassador his sympathetic consideration but indirectly hinted that an audience with the Emperor would be futile. Togo consulted with Tojo and Kido, and saw the Emperor at three in the morning. Tojo, when approached by Togo, remarked: "It's a good thing the telegram arrived late. If it had come a day or two earlier we would have had a lot to do." He was greatly relieved that no one could use the telegram as a pretext for reopening the negotiations, and thus bring about unnecessary complications. When Togo reached his official residence at 3:30 a.m., he received a call from the Navy Minister that the Japanese planes had succesfully attacked Pearl Harbor.[32]

Due to the slowness of the embassy staff in deciphering, translating and typing, Nomura and Kurusu were unable to deliver the Japanese note informing the American Government of the complete rupture of negotiations at 1:00 p.m., Washington time, as ordered by the Foreign Office. They had to ask for a postponement of their appointment with Secretary Hull until 1:45, and were not in fact received until 2:20 p.m. At that time, Mr. Hull had already received a call from the President informing him that he had an unconfirmed report that Pearl Harbor had been attacked. After glancing through the

Japanese document—the content of which he was already famiLar with through the "magic"—and without asking his visitors to take seats, Mr. Hull could not help but impart his personal feelings. "In all my fifty years of public service I have never seen a document that was more crowded with infamous falsehoods and distortions—infamous falsehoods and distortions on a scale so huge that I never imagined until today that any Government on this planet was capable of uttering them."

When Ambassador Nomura, under great emotional strain, was about to say something, the Secretary nodded toward the door, and the two envoys turned without a word and walked out, their heads down.[33]

Lord Keeper of the Privy Seal Marquis Kido rose early in the morning of December 8, even though he was at the Imperial Palace until 3:30 the same morning, and went to his office at 7:15 a.m. Knowing that his country was already at war, he worshipped the rising sun and prayed for victory. Ambassador Grew was summoned at 7:30 a.m. to the Foreign Office, and was handed a copy of the Japanese note which Nomura and Kurusu had delivered to Secretary Hull. At 8:00 a.m., Ambassador Craigie also received a similar note. At 11:40 a.m. the Imperial Rescript declaring war was issued.

It was a crisp fair winter morning. Since dawn the Japanese radio network had been informing the public that Japan had entered into an armed conflict with the U. S. and Britain. The announcement was followed by the Battleship March, and then by Beethoven's Fifth Symphony. Thus fate knocked at the door.

CHAPTER XV

CONCLUSION

With the sinking of the *U. S. S. Arizona,* the capsizing of the *U. S. S. Oklahoma,* and the blazing of three other capital ships at Pearl Harbor, Commander Kanji Kato could well have said: "This is my revenge." Yet revenge played only a minor part in Japan's attack on Pearl Harbor. Two factors clearly emerge as the immediate causes of war. They were: Japan's unwillingness to withdraw its troops from China, and America's uncompromising stand on the freezing order and oil embargo. As to the Tripartite Pact, it played an insignificant role in Japan's decision for war, since the Pact had the Soviet Union rather than the United States as its primary target.

Stationing of Troops in China. By 1941 there was no end in sight for Japan's stalemate in China. However, to accept a negotiated peace sponsored by the United States would have meant a return to the *status quo* of 1937, and would result in one or more of the following three situations: (1) China would be united under Chiang Kai-shek who would receive strong backing from the popular Chinese nationalism which would be characterized by hatred and contempt for Japan. (2) Soviet Russia would, either alone or in conjunction with the Chinese Communists, thwart Japan's penetration into North China and threaten the security of Manchukuo, (3) The western powers would return to China to put a concerted effort to eliminate Japan's influence.

China was a thorn in the flesh for Japan. Nominally Wang Ching-wei's jurisdiction extended to more than half a million square miles of territory encompassing the richest and most densely populated regions of China, having a population of about 200 million. Although Japan exacted favorable terms from Wang in the basic treaty, it was unable to convert China into a base of its East Asian Co-prosperity Area. Wang Ching-wei could not transpose the hostility of the Chinese populace into one of active cooperation with Japan. Nor was he capable of serving as a liaison man between the Japanese Government and the Chungking regime to bring about total peace. The alternative policy was to negotiate directly with Chiang Kai-shek. However,

238

each attempt Japan made was coldly answered by Chiang's continued resistance and his refusal to submit.

The folly of tying down a force of one million men in China and exhausting the already limited resources was long recognized by the Army High Command. It wanted to free the manpower and resources for war against Soviet Russia and for expansion southward. It thus enthusiastically supported the Wikawa-Drought Proposal for Understanding, which seemed to contain a formula to permit Japan to withdraw most of its troops from China with honor, without sacrificing much of the gains it had obtained in the past. As negotiations dragged on, the Army realized that an understanding with the United States would require complete withdrawal from China—i.e., Japan would not have the right to station its troops in China indefinitely. However, the Army decided to persist. Its reason was twofold: (1) The right to station the troops would have pre-empted the whole of China for Japan to the exclusion of others and would enable Japan to maintain its supremacy. (2) Without this right, the semblance of unity maintained by the Army would be shattered, and would be disastrous for the Army politically.

The thirties can be characterized by the Army's attempt to make the entire nation in its own image. The Army had been a separate organism within the nation's social structure. Most of its leading officers had at one time or another served tours of duty in Manchuria, and had learned the effectiveness of an expansionist policy, totalitarian control, and planned economy. Back in Japan their watchword had been reform internally and expansion externally. The several revolts staged by young officers had only a limited degree of success. But they discovered that in the undeclared war against China the nation became more receptive to their demands. The court and financial circles pledged their cooperation in the execution of the "holy war" and granted the Army more expenditures and a greater degree of planned economy.

The internal reform the Army desired was accomplished step by step during the process of war, and the prestige of an army uniform was restored. China had become the base of power for the Army, and from there it could dictate the fate of the nation. If the Incident were ended without granting the Army the right to station troops the Army's power base would be lost forever. Furthermore, the existence of war permitted the Army to close its ranks. Even though there was no complete unity, the factional strife had generally been replaced by the excitement of fighting the war. To permit peace without the right to station troops would revive the old factional strife, and either the remnant of the Kodoha, or some other new group could successfully challenge the authority of the ruling faction, charging it with treasonable appeasement. General Tojo was aware that Japan might not win the war against the United States, but he was willing to gamble the future of the Empire in order to maintain the semblance of unity for the Army.

U.S. Economic Sanctions. The Army alone could not have fought the war without the active support of the Navy. It was the Navy which had to shoulder the main burden of war against the United States. As a whole, the Navy was opposed to a war against the United States since it knew it could not win. However, its moderating influence was replaced by agitation for war when the United States froze Japanese assets and decreed an oil embargo on Japan. The Navy's oil reserves were expected to last for only one and one-half years of active naval operation. The proud Imperial Navy would be reduced to impotency once its oil supply route was cut. It was true that the issues of stationing troops in China and the U.S. economic sanctions were interrelated. If Japan were willing to yield on the former, the United States would rescind the latter. But the Navy was no longer capable of waiting for the prolonged diplomatic negotiations, the outcome of which was by no means certain. As Admiral Nagano put it, for each hour Japan waited, the Navy wasted 400 tons of oil reserves. Thus the Navy chose action instead of perseverance.

The Navy's objective was to fight a limited war. Together with the Army, it hoped to capture Burma, Singapore, Sumatra, Java, Northern New Guinea, the Bismarck Archipelago, the Gilbert Islands, and Wake. This would permit the Navy to establish an impregnable defense perimeter which would include the Marshall Islands and would be extended northward to the Kuriles. Since the United States was not expected to go on the offensive for eighteen months or so, during this period Japan planned to fortify its defense perimeter and extract crude oil, bauxite, rubber, tin, nickel, and copper from the South Sea regions. Once freed from the position of economic dependence on the hostile western powers, Japan would be militarily in a much stronger position. The United States, having its hands tied in the European theater, might compromise and allow Japan to retain a substantial portion of its initial gains. In this way, the Navy could translate the cold war of attrition into a hot war of abundance.

Lack of Machinery for Coordination. Neither the issue of stationing troops in China nor the issue of the economic embargo was insurmountable. If cool calculation had entered into the picture, Japan might not have chosen war on the basis of these two reasons alone. However, no effective dissenting voices were raised against the decision for war. The public was ignorant of what was taking place, and was unaware of the wide gap between official hopes and stark realities, between propaganda myth and actual fact. As to the chosen few who governed the country, there was no central organ that could coordinate their policy decisions. Theoretically the Emperor ruled and reigned and he alone could arbitrate between the civilian and military branches of the Government. Yet he wielded no political power. The attempt to coordinate policies at various stages had failed—either on the Cabinet level in the form of the Four Ministers' Conference or Five Ministers' Conference, or at the sub-Cabinet level between the chiefs of the Military Affairs Bureaus and a representative of the Foreign Office. The Liaison Conference which was designed to coordinate military and foreign policies possessed no executive power. Once a decision was adopted, responsibility for its execution was passed to the Army, Navy, or the individual ministries. The process of reaching decisions had been arduous. Since decisions were often reached without efforts being made for reconciling the contradictory viewpoints, they contained seeds of future discord.

The Imperial Conference was similar in function to that of the Liaison Conference except the former was attended by the Emperor. It was employed to confirm the more important decisions reached by the Liaison Conference and garb them with the aura of imperial sanctity. The decisions would thus become irrevocable. Instead of coordinating military and foreign policies, the Imperial Conference made them inflexible. Even if the majority decided against the Imperial Conference's prior decisions, they could not change them an iota when someone in the minority would claim that to go counter to the decision was to go against the wishes of the Emperor. Examples of this were the July 2, 1941 Imperial Conference which decided the occupation of Southern Indo-China, and the September 6, 1941 Imperial Conference which set a deadline for terminating negotiations with the United States. Time and again the Foreign Office asked for reconsideration and moderation. Each time its plea was completely ignored. The Foreign Office lacked the power to decide independently on major policy questions, and it was quickly reduced to the status of a maidservant of the military. However, in the actual carrying out of diplomatic negotiations, the Foreign Office was generally free to decide on its own procedures. Only in the negotiations with China did the Army take over both the procedural and substantive matters relating to policy questions. It was true that the talks for the Tripartite Pact were initiated by the Army High Command. Yet it was a civilian Foreign Minister, Yosuke Matsuoka who brought the negotiations to a successful conclusion.

Responsibility of the Civilians. Thus it would be erroneous to assume that it was the military alone which had decided for war and the civilians were to be exonerated from the responsibility. Without the firm union of the conservative big-business (*Zaibatsu*) wing and the aggressive elements of the Army and Navy, the war planning and the war itself would have been impossible. Others in the ruling circles—the imperial court, the top bureaucrats, and the leaders of political parties—were either imbued with the bandwagon psychology to join the ascending might of the military or filled with the fear of assassination and registered no protest to the actions of the military. Their active cooperation or indifference, whichever it might have been, made it possible for the military to gain the commanding position with regard to foreign policy decisions. The establishment of the pseudo one-party system, the Taiseiyokusankai, was typical of the bandwagon psychology in action.

It would be impossible to brand one cabinet as liberal or pro-western, and another as rightist and pro-Axis during the years 1937-1941. There had been some differences in degree but not in substance in their policy approach. This holds for the Yonai-Arita Cobinet which was considered moderately pro-western. It was the Yonai Cabinet that had established Wang Ching-wei's government and started the occupation of Northern French Indo-China. It also had begun negotiations with Germany for an alliance. Many of the major policies adopted by the Second Konoye Cabinet found their direct counterparts in the policies of the Yonai Cabinet. All of these serve to illustrate that with regard to foreign policy aims, Japan maintained certain continuity irrespective of who headed the Cabinet. The continuity and affinity were especially pronounced in the China policy, in the southward advance, and in the economic policy. The third category consisted largely of how to free it from economic dependence on western powers. The irritation Japan experienced from the United States actions on economic matters—non-extension of the Commercial Treaty, embar-

goes, and the freezing order—was equally noticeable under the Yonai
Cabinet as under the Tojo Cabinet.

The Matsuoka Diplomacy. Of the civilian ministers, none could
compare with Foreign Minister Matsuoka in strong leadership. In
essence, he viewed alliance and entanglement as passing phenomena.
Each of the treaties or alliances he concluded could either be supplemented or superseded by another, or completely eradicated as
occasion demanded. It was not necessarily inconsistent for him to
conclude a Neutrality Pact with Soviet Russia and advocate war
against it shortly thereafter. Nor was it contradictory for him to align
with Germany while seeking a rapprochement with the United States.
His approach was similar to that of Germany's Iron Chancellor,
Prince von Bismarck. While Bismarck's foreign policy was backed
by his unchallenged supremacy in domestic politics, Matsuoka lacked
that power. While the Iron Chancellor could insure both continuity
and flexibility in his foreign policies, the Japanese Foreign Minister's
hands were tied, hence his failure. Despite his bellicose utterances,
Matsuoka was in many respects more moderate than his Cabinet
colleagues, including Prince Konoye. Post-war evidence discloses
that he opposed Japan's occupation of Southern French Indo-China,
and he was at heart against a conflict with the United States. His
dismissal from the Konoye Cabinet did not result from foreign policy
disputes but from his own personal trait, and from his inordinate
passion to become a Prime Minister.

The Riddle of the Tripartite Pact. The Tripartite Pact represented
Matsuoka's Herculean effort to reshape Japan's foreign policy and
assure Japan's place in the sun. Geographically Japan's foreign relations were conditioned by three key states that directly or indirectly
shared common frontiers with Japan. They were: the United States,
Soviet Russia, and China. Japan's attainment of political primacy
in the rimlands of Eurasia or in the South Sea regions would be possible
only if at least one of these three powers were effectively neutralized.
In 1940 Japan was faced with the hostility of the three nations, and
with the prospect of their joining hands to circumvent Japan's activities.
Thus any effort to neutralize one or more of these three key nations
would have to come from an alignment with a third power. Germany
was Japan's choice. Japan had an unshakable belief in the ultimate
victory of Germany. It hoped that an alliance would enhance
Japan's international standing; permit Japan to advance southward

pre-empting the field before Germany also claimed these regions for itself; and facilitate its rapprochement with either the Soviet Union or the United States. Then there was also a remote possibility that the improved situation might help Japan solve its stalemate in China. Although the Pact was commonly regarded as one primarily aimed at the United States, neither Matsuoka nor his Cabinet colleagues entertained the thought of using the Pact as an offensive weapon to declare war on the United States.

Even if Germanay had entered into a state of war against the United States, Matsuoka would have insisted on Japan's right to decide independently whether it would come to Germany's aid. In Matsuoka's mind, Japan could reach a rapprochement with the United States only from a "position of strength." The Pact was designed to provide Japan with such strength. In effect, the Pact remained as a defensive one as far as the United States was concerned. During the course of negotiations with the United States, it was hinted that the Pact might be neutralized and superseded by an agreement with the United States. On the other hand, despite the fact Soviet Russia was expressly excluded from the Pact's application, that country remained the primary target. This is further evidenced by the way in which Matsuoka concluded the Neutrality Pact with Russia.

Three overriding considerations were apparent in the Neutrality Pact. The first was to prevent a possible rapprochement between the United States and Soviet Russia. The second was to strengthen Japan's position in order to aid its negotiations with the United States. The third was to safeguard Japan's northern frontiers while it was engaged in southward advance. Once these objectives were accomplished, Japan was ready to nullify the Neutrality Pact and strike at the Soviet Union.

The Tripartite Pact permitted the Roosevelt Administration to identify Japan publicly as America's enemy even before Pearl Harbor since Japan was aligned with Hitler. This was important for propaganda purposes only.

Reflections on American Policy. If the Tripartite Pact played an insignificant part in Japan's decision to enter into the war, and the immediate causes of the war were Japan's unwillingness to withdraw its troops from China and America's uncompromising stand on the economic issues, then was there any way by which the United States could have avoided the coming of war?

The use of embargoes or pacific blockades has long been recognized by international law as a means of preventing international lawlessness. The Roosevelt Administration's measures against Japan were consistent with this viewpoint. Yet in applying economic sanctions, the timing is most important. To have been effective, the embargoes should have been imposed immediately after the outbreak of hostilities in China. Otherwise they should have been delayed indefinitely. The freezing order of July 1941 was unfortunate in that it came at a time when both sides were aware that such a measure would eventually involve the two parties in war. Had the embargoes been imposed on Japan in July 1937, the result might have been entirely different. It was not until the spring of 1939 that Japan began seriously contemplating a shift of its national economy to a full war-time basis. In July 1937, Japan's war potential was still low, and it did not have the eighteen months supply of oil to think of starting a war. If the Neutrality Act had been invoked and other economic measures had been taken at that time, Japan might have become more amenable to the suggestiton of stopping its aggression. The effect would have been beneficial to China even if it had been necessary to apply them against China as well as Japan. The absence of the U. S. aid, limited as it was in amount, could not have materially affected China's will to resist Japan's aggression. On the other hand while the United States delayed economic sanctions, Japan stockpiled war materials with the added expenditures provided for the execution of the China Incident, the United States being the largest supplier of goods to Japan.

Another critical moment in the U.S.-Japanese relations was the summer of 1941 when Prince Konoye sought a summit conference with President Roosevelt. Without discounting the likelihood of a complete breakdown of the meeting, this writer still believes that the surprise attack on Pearl Harbor could not have taken place on December 7, 1941, had there been a meeting of the two leaders.

It is true that Prince Konoye had pledged that he would "be fully prepared to break off the talks and return home. It is therefore an undertaking which must be carried out while being fully prepared for war against America. (If the talks should fail) the people will know that a Japanese-American war could not be avoided. This would aid in consolidating their determination."[1] This pledge would seem to suggest that Konoye had intended to use the proposed meeting as a cover-up for Japan's expansionist policies and for its propaganda value. Yet even if one should ascribe such a motivation to Prince Konoye's proposal, the fact remains that Japan could not have struck at the

time the meeting was to take place. October 15 was the last day
the militarists would allow such a meeting to commence. Assuming
that it had taken place and Prince Konoye had broken off the talks,
Japan could not have staged a surprise attack. Post-war evidence
indicates that by October 30 Japan was not ready for a major war.

On the other hand, if a meeting had taken place, the two leaders
could have conceivably achieved a *modus vivendi,* and some major
issues might have been solved at least temporarily. It would likely
have included a provision recognizing the United States' aid to Great
Britain as an act of self-defense, thus effectively neutralizing the Tripartite Pact. Another provision might have been Japan's withdrawal
from Southern French Indo-China, in return for which the United
States would resume a limited shipment of oil to Japan. Konoye was
also prepared to concede on the issue of Japan's right to station troops
in China. A temporary agreement would have given the United
States a longer period to prepare for the coming of war and the risk
would have been worth taking.

Sir Robert Craigie, the British Ambassador in Tokyo, was unusually critical of Mr. Hull's handling of the proposed leaders'
meeting. He thought the proposed meeting presented the best opportunity in years for bringing about a just solution of Far Eastern
issues, and that the policy of procrastination on the part of the United
States was the obstacle blocking the Japanese-American negotiations.[2]
To this contention, one should counter the obstinacy of the Japanese
Army in insisting on stationing troops in China. Yet one would
wonder if the Chinese question should loom so large in Washington's
mind that it would have to stand in the way of reconciliation with Japan.

A similar consideration should apply in the case of Mr. Hull's
November 26 note to the Japanese Government. It was at the insistence of the Chinese Government that the proposed *modus vivendi*
was discarded in favor of a stringent note. And upon the receipt of
this note, an Imperial Conference was called to decide for war. By
then a task force was sailing for Pearl Harbor.

Ironically Pearl Harbor became a blessing to Japan. It was a
beginning to the end of military domination. All they that took the
sword perished with the sword. The military who sought to retain
their supremacy through the war were utterly destroyed in the process.
The war had achieved what the combined effort of the Emperor and the
oligarchy could not accomplish. And from the ruins of the war came
the rebirth of a nation that is now shouldering its share of the burden
in building a free world.

REFERENCES

CHAPTER I

1. *The Japanese Chronicle*, June 19, 1930, p. 110, quoted in Robert A. Scalapino, *Democracy and the Party Movement in Prewar Japan*, (Berkeley and Los Angles: University of California Press, 1954), p. 246.

2. Itaro Ishii, *Gaikokan no Issho* (*A Diplomat's Life*), (Tokyo: Yomiuri Shinbunsha, 1950) p. 237. Ishii might have borrowed this phrase from Hugh Byas whose book is entitled *Government by Assassination* (New York: Knopf, 1942).

3. *Kido Diary*, entry of February 26, 1936, quoted in Yale Candee Maxon, *Control of Japanese Foreign Policy, A Study of Civil-Military Rivalry, 1930-1945*, (Berkeley and Los Angeles: University of California Press, 1957), p. 109.

4. Toshikazu Kase, *Journey to the Missouri* (New Haven: Yale University Press, 1950), p. 35.

5. G. E. Uyehara, *The Political Development of Japan*, (London: 1910), p. 19; quoted in Harold S. Quigley, *Japanses Government and Politics, An Introductory Study*, (New York: Century, 1932), p. 67.

6. *The Meiji Constitution*, Art. LV.

7. Hirobumi Ito, *Kempo Gikai* (*Commentaries on the Constitution*), 16th ed., (Tokyo: Kokkagakkai, 1935), p. 87: The *Meiji Constitution*, Art. LVI.

8. It must be noted, however, that the Privy Council played a far more important role than either house of the Diet in formulating foreign policies. The minutes of the Council provide important clues to the conduct of the pre-war Japanese foreign policy.

9. Japanese Foreign Office (hereinafter cited as JFO) *Important Decisions Relating to Japanese Policies toward China* (*Nihon no tai-Shi Seisaku ni kansuru Juyo Kettei*), Dec. 1934-Oct. 1937, SP 305, pp. 4-66, pp. 147-150; See also IMTFE Judgment, pp. 668-669.

10. Several colorful, although somewhat superficial and subjective, Japanese accounts are consulted in the writing of this chapter. They include, *Sempu Nijunen* (*Twenty Years' Whirlwind*) by Shozo Mori (Tokyo: Masu Shobo, 1945); *Diaries of General Kazushige Ugaki* (Tokyo: Asahi Shinbunsha, 1954); Tatsuo Iwabuchi's *Gumbatsu no Keifu* (*The Genealogy of the Military Caste*), (Tokyo: Chuokoronsha, 1948); and Sogoro Tanaka's *Nihon Fascism no Genryu* (*The Origin of Japanese Fascism*), (Tokyo: Hakuyosha, 1949).

The best eyewitness accounts are provided by the *Kido Diary* and the *Saionji-Harada Memoirs*. The former appears as Exhibits and other documents in the International Military Tribunal for the Far East (cited as IMTFE), and is generally available both in Japanese and English. The latter is available in English in 40 volumes, compiled by the General Headquarters Far East Command, Military Intelligence Section. The author, however, relied on its Japanese version, published by Iwanami Shoten in eight volumes between 1950 and 52 under the title of *Saionji-Ko to Seikyoku*. Citations from these documents are all in

249

the author's own translation in order to recapture the meaning of original Japanese.

Kita's and Okawa's various writings are now available in microfilm in *Archives in the Japanese Ministry of Foreign Affairs, Tokyo, Japan*, 1868-1945. See for example, IMT 71 and IMT 281.

CHAPTER II

1. JFO, *The China Incident (Shina Jihen)*, S 1. 1. 1. O-27, pp. 2634-2636; JFO, *Important Decisions Relating to Japanese Policies toward China (Nihon no tai-Shi Seisaku ni kansuru Juyo Kettei)*, Dec. 1934-Oct. 1937, SP 305, pp. 208-214; SP306, pp. 10-11, 17.

2. Harada records in his memoirs, *op. cit.*, vol. 6., pp. 50-51, the following strange story related to Foreign Minister Hirota by Vice Minister of Navy Admiral Yamamoto: "A certain staff officer of the Tientsin Garrison, Wachi by name, had been recalled to Tokyo immediately after the fighting had started.... The reason why Wachi was recalled was because if he were left over there he would cause trouble for us. We figured it would take him several days to return to Japan and that in the meantime we would be able to settle the Incident there. ...But he flew back to Japan and our objective could not be accomplished. Moreover it would have been unfavorable if he should start causing trouble while he was in Japan, so we decided to send him back. Hirota commented that it was unforgivable for the Army to mislead Japan on account of one staff officer. 'It is pitiful indeed, that the Army lacks discipline within'."

3. U. S. Department of State, *Press Release*, XVII, No. 407, July 17, 1937.

4. Text in William L. Langer and S. Everett Gleason, *The Challenge to Isolation, 1937-1940*, (New York: Council of Foreign Relations, 1952), p. 19. However, Dorothy Borg believes the President was not embarking upon some strong policies toward Japan, but was simply pursuing a variety of nebulous schemes for warding off catastrophe. See her "Notes on Roosevelt's 'Quarantine' Speech" in *Political Science Quarterly*, vol. LXXII, Sept. 1957, pp. 405-433.

5. Harada, *op. cit.*, pp. 89, 111-112.

6. S 1. 1. 1. O-27, pp. 9010-9537; IMT 349, pp. 1-6; IMTFE, *Exhibit* No. 63, *Record*, pp. 20985-20989.

CHAPTER III

1. Harada noted that even President Roosevelt was not averse to having Germany mediate in the current Sino-Japanese conflict. He attributed this information to Ambassador Saito in Washington. See Harada, *op. cit.*, vol. 6, 192 and 229.

2. IMTFE, *Exhibit*, No. 486-F.

3. IMTFE, *Judgment*, pp. 206-207, *Record*, pp. 25095 ff.

4. IMTFE, *Judgment*, p. 248.

5. Itagaki's testimony in IMTFE, *Record*, pp. 30297-30298.

6. Irving S. Friedman, *British Relations with China*, (New York: Institute of Pacific Relations, 1940), pp. 148-149.

7. JFO, *Documents Relating to Policy Decisions Concerning the China Incident,* IMT 357, pp. 263-264; S. 1. 1. 1. O-27, p. 2283.

8. JFO, *Memorandum on the Nakamura-Chiao Meeting* (*Nakamura-Kyo Nisshi Kosho ni kansuru Kaidan*), IMT 609 pp. 1-17; S 1. 1. 1. O-27, pp. 2218-2225.

9. S. 1. 1. 1. O-27, pp. 2328-2334; IMTFE, *Exhibit* 758; Mamoru Shigemitsu, *Showa no Doran* (*The Showa Armageddon*), (Tokyo: Chuokoronsha, 1952), vol. 1, pp. 199-205. Shigemitsu's book is translated in English as *Japan and Her Destiny: My Struggle for Peace,* (New York: Dutton, 1958). It is edited by F. S. G. Piggott, and translated by Oswald White.

10. Akira Kazami, *Konoye Naikaku* (*The Konoye Cabinet*), (Tokoyo: Nippon Shuppan Kyodo Kabushiki Kaisha, 1951), p. 132.

CHAPTER IV

1. JFO, *Concerning the Strengthening of the Anti-Comintern Pact* (*Bokyo Kyotei no Kyoka Kosaku Yoryoshu*) in S 1.1.1.0-27, pp. 2075-2079, 2080, 2084, 2106-2108, 2125-2128, 2381-2383, under the dates of June 21 and 23, 1938.

2. The London *Economist* originally regarded the association of Germany with Japan in the Anti-Comintern Pact as primarily one of blackmail which in time of peace could effectively harass England and France both in Europe and Asia, but in war would be rather ineffective. See Ernest L. Presseisen, *Germanay and Japan, a Study in Totalitalian Diplomacy, 1933-1941,* (Hague: Martinus Nijhoff, 1958), p. 121. Even if Japan had been successful in concluding an alliance against Russia alone, its impact on the western powers might have been still the same.

3. Shigenori Togo, *Jidai no Ichimen* (*Another Façade of Our Times*). (Tokyo: Kaizosha, 1952), p. 116. Translated and edited by Togo's son-in-law, Fumihiko Togo, and Ben Bruce Blakeney as *The Cause of Japan* (New York: Simon and Schuster, 1956). On the Army's attitude toward Togo, see also Kasahara's testimony in IMTFE, *Record,* pp. 33716-33727, *Exhibit* No. 3493.

4. Thus the Navy was not necessarily moderate in its foreign policy approach as generally assumed. Its attitude as described above was probably responsible for many of Japan's key decisions, including the conclusion of the Tripartite Pact and the occupation of Southern Indo-China. In modified form, the same attitude was evident in the decision for war. In this connection, Captain Takagi's secret communication to Harada for transmittal to Prince Saionji is most relevant. It is contained in Harada *op. cit.,* vol. 6, pp. 268-269.

5. It must be noted that the fault should have been equally shared by Tokyo as well. The following testimony rendered by Usami on Oshima's behalf at the Tokyo Trial is of interest: "Tokyo's instructions . . . never denied the duty of war participation. Only they gave a very broad interpretation to the term by including measures which could not be interpreted normally as war participation and instructed Oshima to secure Germany's consent to that interpretation. The instructions were ambiguous and difficult to understand and Oshima was sometimes hard put as to how to make them clear. He found out later that the ambiguity was due to the fact that the instructions were drafted as a result of oral compromise while the difference of opinions remained unreconciled." IMTFE, *Record,* p. 34008.

6. See Harada, *op. cit.*, pp. 334-339; IMTFE, *Record*, pp. 30492 ff.   (Itagaki's cross examination).

7. IMTFE, *Exhibit* No. 504, *Record*, pp. 6108-6110.

8. Joseph C. Grew, *Ten Years in Japan* (Simon and Schuster, 1944), p. 282.

9. Harada, *op. cit.*, pp. 361-362.

10. Cordell Hull, *The Memoirs of Cordell Hull*, (New York: Macmillan, 1948), vol. 1, pp. 631 ff.

11. R. Sontag and S. Beddie (ed.), *Nazi-Soviet Relations, 1939-1941*, (Washington: Government Printing Office, 1948), pp. 72-73.

12. On Hiranuma's resignation, see IMTFE, *Exhibit* No. 2735-A.   On Japanese-German negotiations during this period, Frank W. Iklé points out the pro-German sentiment existing in the Japanese Army which provided the fovarable climate for negotiations, even aside from political reasons.   See Iklé *German-Japanese Relations, 1936-1940* (New York: Bookman Associates, 1956).   Francis C. Jones' *Japan's New Order in East Asia, 1937-1945* (London: Oxford University Press, 1954) gives a general account of this period based on Tokyo War Trials documents.   It does not give the reason for the Navy's decision to support the alliance.   This is treated in pages 47-48 of this work.

CHAPTER V

1. Tokuzo Aoki, *Taiheiyo Senso Zenshi* (*A History of Events Leading to the Pacific War*), (Tokyo: Gakujitsu Bunken Fukyukai, 1953), vol 2, pp. 224-225; Harada, *op. cit.*, pp. 65 ff.

2. The best example was that of Kurihara, chief of the East Asian Bureau. Kurihara was sympathetic to the Army's course, and advocated their policies. In return, he received young officers' support.   In the absence of a full-time foreign minister, Kurihara was able to control important policy decisions.   The Abe proclamation immediately following the outbreak of the European War was written by him.   He repeatedly told the Counselor of the French Embassy that the proclamation was solely aimed at the elimination of French and British influence in China.   Abe was much embarrassed when he learned of this.   See Harada, *op. cit.*, p. 90.

3. JFO, *Efforts for the Improvement of U.S.-Japanese Relations* (*Nichi-Bei Kankei Dakai Kosaku*), S 1. 1. 1. O-43, pp. 178 ff.

4. U.S. Dept. of State, *Foreign Relations of United States: Japan: 1931-1941*, (Washington: Government Printing Office, 1943) vol. 2, pp. 19-29; Grew, *op. cit.*, pp. 288-297.

5. JFO, *Policies to be Taken Toward Great Britain and the United States With Regard to Chinese Questions* (*Shina Mondai ni kansuru Tomen no Tai Ei-Bei Shisaku Yoryo*), S 1.1.1.0-43, pp. 217-226.

6. *Foreign Relations of the United States: Japan*, vol. 2, pp. 193-196.

7. JFO, *Basic Foreign Policy Aims* (*Taigai Shisaku Hoshin Yoko*), S 1. 1. 1. O-43, pp. 520-540.

8. Shigemitsu, *op. cit.*, p. 252.

9. Quoted in Aoki, *op. cit.*, p. 239; see also Harada, *op. cit.*, pp. 173 ff.

10. *Tokyo Asahi*, February 3, 1940.

11. IMTFE, *Exhibit* No. 520; *Record*, pp. 6162-6165.

12. The War Minister, however, favored fighting against Great Britain, if

necessary. On the other hand he felt Italy's participation in the alliance useless. This sentiment was widely shared. See, IMTFE, *Record*, p. 6229 and *Exhibit No.* 528.

13. Harada, *op. cit.*, p. 278; see also Ott's and Kido's views on this incident in IMTFE, *Exhibit* No. 531, *Record*, p. 6239, and *Exhibit* No. 532, *Record*, pp. 30893-30901; The establishment of the Wang regime gave false hope of an early termination of the China Incident. See Chapter VI.

14. Teiji Yabe, "Taiseiyokusankai (The Association to Aid the Imperial Rule)," in Toshio Uyeda, *Taiheiyo Senso Geninron (The Origin of the Pacific War)*, (Tokyo: Tokyo Shinbun Gekkansha, 1953), p. 127. Yabe participated in Konoye's new order movement, and his account is highly useful, even though somewhat biased.

15. Yonai seemed to think that Hata had no part in the plot, See IMTFE, *Record*, pp. 28926, 28933-34. But see Harada *op. cit.*, 285. Yale Candee Maxon has a full account of Hata's dilemma in his *Control of Japanese Foreign Policy, A Study of Civil-Military Rivalry, 1930-1945.* (Berkeley and Los Angeles: University of California Press, 1957) pp. 146-148.

16. Most western works on this period treat Yonai's Cabinet as a pro-western one. See for example, Langer and Gleason, *op. cit.*, and Francis C. Jones, *Japan's New Order in East Asia, 1937-1945*, (London: Oxford University Press, 1954).

CHAPTER VI

1. Speech of Wang Ching-wei as recorded in Tokuzo Aoki, *Taiheiyo Senso Zenshi (A History of Events Leading to the Pacific War)*, (Tokyo: Gakujitsu Bunken Fukyukai, 1953), vol. 2, p. 305.

2. JFO, *Events Leading to the Establishment of the New Nanking Government (Shin Nanking Kokumin Seifu Seiritsu keii)* S 1.1.1.0-27, pp. 5019-5134; JFO, *Movements of Wang Ching-wei before the Establishment of the New Chinese Central Government (Shina Shin Chuo Seifu Juritsu zen ni o keru O Sei-ei no Dosei)*, UD 59, pp. 1-83. These documents are used extensively in this chapter. The documents include intelligence reports, day-to-day correspondence of Tokyo and its officials in China, and Wang's position papers both in Chinese and Japanese. Most of these documents have not been published anywhere or used in the Tokyo War Trials.

3. Yamazaki Keizai Kenkyusho, *Report to the Foreign Office on Wang Ching-wei*, in UD 59, pp. 84-97.

4. UD 59, pp. 174-175.

5. Wang's demands were recorded in JFO, *Drafts of Conditions Negotiated Between the Ume Agency and Wang Ching-wei (Ume Kikan to O Sei-ei to no Sesshochu no kaku Dankai ni okeru Ambun Kankei)* which compare Wang's demands with Japan's in a double column setup, and the minutes of six meetings evaluate Wang's stand. S 1.6.1.1.-9, pp. 1-606; an account of his visit to Tokyo is given by an interpreter in IMTFE, *Record*, pp. 22262 ff.

6. After Wang's demands were known, the predominant opinion of the Five Ministers' Conference of June 6 was to establish a coalition government with Wang's forces joining hands with the existing puppet governments. The Five Ministers decided that Wang should not be given the exclusive rein. See JFO, *Documents Relating to the Establishment of the New Chinese Central Government*

by Wang Ching-wei (*O Sei-ei no Shina Chuo Seifu Juritsu Kankei Ikken*), SP 302, pp. 772-798, 1303-1307. Wang's demands were submitted to Tokyo for discussion on May 28, just before his visit took place.

7. JFO, *Documents Relating to the Details of the Principles to Guide the Central Political Consultative Conference* (*Chuo Seijikaigi Shido Yoryoan no Saimoku ni kansuru Ambun Kankei*), S 1.6.1.1-8, contains drafts by the Army, pp. 4-18; by the Ministry of Finance, pp. 19-22; by the China Board, pp. 23-29; and by the North China Governing Council, pp. 31 ff. The diverse opinions were ironed out in the Liaison Conference of October 30, 1939, which is recorded in SP 302, pp. 1254-1258; the *Minutes of the Wang-Kagesa Conferences* are contained in S 1.1.1.0-27, pp. 5260-5285 for the first meeting, and pp. 5285-5469 for the subsequent meetings.

8. Toyu Yoshida, trans., *Shu Fukkai Nikki* (*Diaries of Chou Fu-hai*) (Tokyo: Kenmin Sha, 1953), p. 35.

9. Japan's guidance paper drafted by Kagesa and his associates, dated January 5-7, is contained in S 1.1.1.0-27, pp. 5580-5606. Compare the decisions reached by the conference as contained in *ibid.*, pp. 5617-5645. They are almost identical.

10. The money actually belonged to the Chinese Customs Administration. Its proceeds were then deposited in the Yokohama Specie Bank. Wang wanted to have full rights to the deposit, but a compromise was worked out in the form of a loan.

11. For example, Chou Fu-hai wrote in his diary, *op. cit.*, p. 256 under the date of November 30, 1940, the day the basic treaty was signed: "The best course we can adopt for the future is that there must be a secret understanding between Chiang and Wang. Whether the new era opened today as the result of the signing of the basic treaty is good or bad for us we cannot predict. But one of us can side with the Axis powers and another one of us can side with Great Britain and the United States. Then regardless of whichever side wins, China can be saved. We are thus spared from making a fatal decision of only siding with one camp. Both Wang and Chiang agree on this, but alas they cannot tolerate one another."

CHAPTER VII

1. Robert Craigie, *Behind the Japanese Mask* (London: Hutchinson & Co., 1946), p. 60.

2. This author does not subscribe to the view expressed by Toshikazu Kase, *Journey to the Missouri* (New Haven: Yale University Press, 1950), p. 87, that "The liaison conference in fact served the Supreme Command as a convenient tool for imposing its will upon the government." See also Yale Maxon *op. cit.*, p. 156, which quotes Kase's statement with approval.

3. Teiji Yabe, *Konoye Fumimaro* (Tokyo, 1952), vol. 2, pp. 118-119. Yabe's book contains Yoshida's reminiscence of the Ogikubo conference on pp. 120-121. Yoshida, the only survivor of the Ogikubo Conference after the war, insists that the meeting was informal. With the exception of Prince Konoye who read his memorandum, no written record of the meeting was kept. And the meeting ended in confirming some of the policy decisions reached by the Yonai Cabinet, notably the recommendations by the War, Navy, and Foreign Ministries for strengthening the Axis ties.

4. Akira Kazami's Memoirs, *Konoye Naikaku* (*The Konoye Cabinet*), (Tokyo: Nippon Shuppan Kyodo Kabushikikaisha, 1950) describes in full the dilemma that both Konoye and political parties had to face. See pp. 210 ff.

5. Yabe, *op. cit.*, p. 140.

6. Konoye's talk to Tomida, as recorded in Yabe, *op. cit.*, p. 106, Translation slightly abridged.

Chapter VIII

1. IMTFE, *Record*, pp. 6307-6321, *Exhibit*, No. 541; background materials concerning the prior decisions are found in JFO, *Minutes of Joint Conferences of the Army, Navy and Ministry of Foreign Affairs Officials on the Intensification of Cooperation Between Japan, Germany and Italy, July 12 and 16, 1940*, IMT 253 pp. 6-37 and IMT 267 pp. 1-20.

2. JFO, *Collection of Documents Relating to the Conclusion of the Tripartite Alliance* (*Nich-Doku I Domei Jyoyaku Teiketsu Yoroku*), IMT 630 (IPS Doc. no. 3376), contains the complete minutes of conversations between Matsuoka and Stahmer. These remarkable documents, once believed lost, contain Matsuoka's marginal notations as well. In this author's view, these are the most important source of information of the Tripartite Pact. See especially pp. 55 ff. An equally important document is IMT 162, *The Tripartite Alliance and Cooperation Between Japan, Germany, and Italy: From the Papers of Matsuoka*. (IPS Doc. no. 1037).

3. IMT 162, p. 71, upper and lower columns.

4. *Ibid.*, pp. 23, 63; Matsuoka later told the Privy Council that the alliance was "radically different from the one contemplated by the Hiranuma Cabinet. Germany had already told us that she did not need Japan's participation in the European War. She strives to avoid American participation, and Japan on her part intends to avoid a conflict with the United States. Our policy of non-intervention in the European conflict is not affected by the alliance." IMT 228, p. 17, IMT 293, p. 14.

5. Yoshie Saito, *Azamukareta Rekishi* (*The Distorted History*), (Tokyo: Yomiuri Shinbunsha, 1955), p. 88. While somewhat biased, most of Saito's statements in his memiors are supported by documentary evidence in the Foreign Office Archives.

6. Grew, *op. cit.*, p. 333.

7. IMT 162, pp. 21 ff; Saito, *op. cit.*, p. 102 ff.

8. Fumimaro Konoye, *Circumstances Surrounding the Tripartite Alliance*, IMT 52 (IPS Doc. no. 573), p. 8.

9. Saito, *op. cit.*, p. 5. The present study differs from others in that it points out the anti-Russian nature of the Tripartite Pact. It thus indirectly supports Paul W. Schroeder's contention that the Tripartite Pact played no part in the United States decision to oppose Japan's moves. The Pact was employed by both the United States and Japan as a propaganda weapon. See Schroeder, *The Axis Alliance and Japanese-American Relations, 1941*, (Ithaca: Cornell University Press, 1958). Other works generally accept the view that the alliance was primarily directed against the United States. See the works by Iklé, Jones, Langer and Gleason, and Presseisen, as cited in the bibliography.

CHAPTER IX

1. U. S. Department of State, *Foreign Relations of the United States: Japan*, (Washington: Government Printing Office, 1943), vol. 2, p. 169; Cordell Hull, *The Memoirs of Cordell Hull*, (New York: Macmillan, 1948), vol. 1, p. 909.

2. R. Sontag and S. Beddie, ed., *Nazi-Soviet Relations, 1939-1941* (Washington Government Printing Office, 1948) gives a highly useful account of this critical period. See pp. 197 ff.

3. JFO, *Documents Relating to the Neutrality Pact between Japan and the USSR (Nisso Churitsu Joyaku kankei ikken)*, S 2.1.0.0.-23, pp. 26-31.

4. *Nazi-Soviet Relations, op. cit.*, p. 260.

5. William L. Langer and S. Everett Gleason, *The Undeclared War*, (New York: Council on Foreign Relations, 1953), pp. 293 ff.

6. Chuji Ohashi, *Taiheiyo Senso Yuraiki: Matsuoka Gaiko no Shinso* (The *Origin of the Pacific War: The Truth about Matsuoka's Diplomacy*), (Tokyo: Kaname Shobo, 1952) pp. 46 ff.

7. JFO, *Treaties Concerning the Basic Relationships between Japan and China (Nihonkoku Chuka-Minkoku kan Kihon ni kansuru Joyaku)*, SP 303 pp. 144-148 contains proceedings of the Privy Council; see also Eigo Fukai, *Sumitsuin Juyo Giji Oboegaki (Memoranda of Important Privy Council Proceedings)*, (Tokyo: Iwanami Shoten, 1952), p. 120 ff., and Saito, *op. cit.*, pp. 83 ff.

8. JFO, *Documents Relating to the Establishment of the New Chinese Central Government by Wang Ching-wei (O Sei-ei no Shina Chuo Seifu Jurittsu kankei ikken)*, SP 302, p. 1382 ff.

9. Kotaro Sakuda, *Tenno to Kido (The Emperor and Kido)*, (Tokyo: Heibonsha, 1948), p. 135. Sakuda was Kido's defense counsel at the Tokyo trials, and his book contains some documents which are not available elsewhere.

10. JFO, *Draft Outline of the Points to be Negotiated with Germany, Italy, and the U.S.S.R. (Tai-Doku-I-So Koshoan Yoko.)*, IMT 597, pp. 1-6.

11. *Nazi-Soviet Relations*, pp. 284-285, 291; see also IMTFE, *Exhibit* Nos. 573, 577, *Record*, pp. 6485-6498.

12. See Matsuoka's testimony before the Privy Council, Fukai, *op. cit.*, pp. 145-159.

13. *Nazi-Soviet Relations*, pp. 323-324; see also Tatekawa's report in S 2.1.0.0.-23 pp. 77-78.

14. Saito, *op. cit.*, pp. 184 ff.

CHAPTER X

1. For details of negotiations, see JFO, *Development of Negotiations for the Conclusion of a Franco-Japanese Agreement Concerning the Advance of Japanese Troops into French Indo-China (Nihongun Futsu-In Shinchu ni kansuru Nichi-Futsu Kyotei Teiketsu Kosho Keii)*, IMT 603, pp. 6-27.

2. Maxine Weygand, *Mémoires: Rappelé au Service* (Paris: 1950), 336-339, cited in Langer and Gleason, *op. cit.*, p. 12.

3. JFO, *Privy Council Proceedings, Minutes of the Plenary Session on the Ratification of the Treaty between Japan and Thailand (Nihonkoku-Taikoku kan Joyaku Gohijun no Ken)*, IMT 160, p. 12.

4. *Nazi-Soviet Relations*, p. 302.

5. IMTFE, *Exhibit* No. 1312, *Record*, p. 11814.

6. Fukai, op. cit., p. 164; see also IMFE, *Exhibit* No. 1045, *Record*, pp. 11862-11882.

CHAPTER XI

1. Tokuzo Aoki, *Taiheiyo Senso Zenshi* (*A History of Events Leading to the Pacific War*), (Tokyo: Gakujitsu Bunken Fukyukai, 1953), vol. 3, p. 138.

2. JFO, *Documents Relating to Negotiations between Japan and the United States*, IMT 265 p. 5.

3. U.S. Department of State, *Foreign Relations of the United States: Japan* (Washington: Government Printing Office, 1943) vol. 2, pp. 123-129.

4. Kichisaburo Nomura, *America ni Shishite* (*My Mission to America*) (Tokyo: Iwanami Shoten, 1950), pp. 36 ff.; Compare the U.S. official record in *Foreign Relations of the United States: Japan*, vol. 2, pp. 387 ff.

5. Nomura, *op. cit.*, pp. 39 ff; telegram of Nomura to Matsuoka, Nos. 136 (a) and (b), dated 3-8-41, in Aoki, *op. cit.*, pp. 38-43; compare Hull's version in IMTFE, *Exhibit* Nos. 1056, 1057, *Record*, pp. 9847 ff. Nomura's version, as usual, was incomplete. However, this was the one on which the Japanese Foreign Office had to base its decisions, and this writer chose to base his discussion on Nomura's version. It would explain more clearly some of the actions taken by the Japanese later.

6. JFO, *Documents Relating to Diplomatic Negotiations between the U.S. and Japan Immediately before the Outbreak of the War* (*Nichi-Bei Kaisen Chokuzen ni okeru Ryogoku kan Gaiko Kosho Kankei*), UD 63 p. 9. UD 63 is the basic source material on U.S.-Japanese relations.

7. The full text of Wikawa's letter is contained in Yabe, *op. cit.*, pp. 237 ff. Wikawa's name is pronounced Ikawa with no value being given to "W".

8. Yabe, *op. cit.*, contains the full text at pp. 239 ff.

9. *U.S. Congress Joint Committee on the Investigation of the Pearl Harbor Attack*, XX, pp. 4284, 4291-4293. This was conducted during the 79th Congress, Second Session. It is hereinafter cited as *Pearl Harbor Attack* with appropriate volume numbers.

10. *Foreign Relations of the United States: Japan*, vol. 2, pp. 406 ff.; IMTFE, *Exhibit* No. 1061, *Record*, pp. 9867-9868; Hull *op. cit.*, p. 995; but compare Nomura's version in UD 63, pp. 23-40.

11. IMTFE, *Exhibit* No. 1059; *Foreign Relations of the United States: Japan*, vol. 2, pp. 398 ff.; Nomura, *op. cit.*, English part, pp. 5-6.

12. UD 63, pp. 52-59; for Nomura's reply see *ibid*, pp. 69-79, 80-85.

13. Japanese Ministry of War, *Opinions Concerning the Proposals Made by Ambassador Nomura*, received by JFO, 4-23-41, UD 63, pp. 91-98; IMTFE, *Record*, p. 36221.

14. Kase, *op. cit.*, p. 45. For Matsuoka's conversations with Steinhardt, see UD 63, pp. 12-17; and *Foreign Relations of the United States: Japan*, vol. 2, pp. 143 ff.

15. See for example, Langer and Gleason, *op. cit.*, pp. 467-468. There the authors cite Memos of Father Drought to Postmaster General Walker, and Iwakuro's affidavit in IMTFE, *Defense Document* No. 2589. Both Father Drought and Colonel Iwakuro overestimated their own influence.

16. See especially the marginal notes on a copy of Nomura's April 17 telegram. Note also Konoye's signature over these pages. UD 63, pp. 23-40.

17. IMT 265, pp. 18-28; IMTFE, *Exhibit* No. 1070, *Record*, pp. 9893-9903; IMT 265, p. 318 marginal note; and UD 63, pp. 121 ff. Hereafter no specific references are made to telegrams contained in UD 63, and/or IMT 265.

18. The two Ki's were Tojo Hide*ki*, War Minister, and Hoshino Hide*ki*, President of the Government Planning Board and Minister without Portfolio. The three Suke's were Matsuoka Yo*suke*, Foreign Minister, Kishi Nobu*suke*, Vice Minister of Commerce and Industry, and Ayukawa Gi*suke*, President of the Board of the Nissan Concern. Ayukawa was the only one not a member of Konoye's official family. Note: In this footnote, family names are given first.

19. IMTFE, *Exhibit* 1077, *Record*, pp. 9935-38 contain the record of conversations between Hull and Nomura on May 28, *Exhibit* 1078 is an American draft proposal to adjust relations (also at *Record*, pp. 9939-9940). See also Nomura's telegram to Matsuoka, No. 380, of the same date, in IMT 265, pp. 102-130. The Foreign Office made an analysis which is in IMT 265, pp. 131-150. One of the documents extensively used but not specifically cited is JFO, *Negotiations Concerning the Proposal for Understanding, to May 20, 1941*, in IMT 265 pp. 95-98.

CHAPTER XII

1. The telegram is contained in UD 63, p. 169.

2. *Kido Diary*, entries of 6-6-41 and 6-20-41 in IMTFE, *Exhibit* No. 1084 and IMT 2, pp. 281-282; Fukai, *op. cit.*, pp. 168 ff.

3. Prince Konoye, "Circumstances Surrounding the Tripartite Alliance," in IMT 52, pp. 7-8.

4. IMTFE, *Exhibit* No. 588, *Record*, pp. 6558, 6567-6569, 7904.

5. IMTFE, *Exhibit* Nos. 1091 and 1092, *Record*, pp. 10001-10019; *Foreign Relations of the United States: Japan*, vol. 2, pp. 483 ff.

6. Cordell Hull, *The Memoirs of Cordell Hull* (New York: Macmillan, 1948), vol. 2, pp. 1010-1011.

7. U.S. Congress, *Joint Committee on the Investigation of the Pearl Harbor Attack, Report* (79th Cong., 2nd Session, 1946), pp. 295-296.

8. UD 63, pp. 256, 278; Nomura, *op. cit.*, English part, pp. 82 ff.

9. Nomura, *op. cit.*, p. 73; IMTFE, *Documents*, No. 4052F, cited in Langer and Gleason, *op. cit.*, p. 640.

10. Yabe, *op. cit.*, p. 321.

11. Text of High Command's plan reproduced in Yabe *op. cit.*, pp. 323-324.

12. *Foreign Relations of the United States: Japan*, vol. 2, pp. 527 ff.

13. Fukai, *op. cit.*, p. 176; The freezing order actually took Tokyo by surprise. The earliest date Japan became seriously concerned about the prospect was July 21, only a few days before the order was actually issued. On July 21, the China Board studied various steps to be taken in anticipation of the freezing order, See JFO, *The China Incident (Shina Jihen)*, S 1.1.1.0-27, pp. 1577 ff.

14. Konoye was deeply concerned with the Navy's strong stand, *Kido Diary*, entry of 8-2-41, IMTFE, *Exhibit* No. 1129, *Record*, p. 10197.

15. *Kido Diary*, entry of 8-7-41, IMTFE, *Exhibit* No. 1130, *Record*, pp. 10199-10201.

CHAPTER XIII

1. *Foreign Relations of the United States: Japan*, vol. 2, pp. 546-550; *Konoye Memoirs* in *Pearl Harbor Attack* XX, p. 3998; IMTFE, *Record*, p. 36268.

2. See especially the document prepared for Konoye's audience with the Emperor on this matter, UD 63, pp. 546-552. The text of his proposal is in Yabe, *op. cit.*, pp. 337-39.

3. *Konoye Memoirs* in *Pearl Harbor Attack* XX, pp. 3999-4000, IMTFE, *Exhibit* No. 2866; *Tojo Memorandum*, IMTFE, *Record* pp. 25767, 36269.

4. *Pearl Harbor Attack* IV, pp. 1785 ff. containing memo of conversation between Roosevelt, Churchill, Welles, Hopkins and Codogan, August 11, 1941.

5. Winston Churchill, *The Grand Alliance* (Boston: Houghton Mifflin Co., 1951), pp. 439-440, containing Churchill's telegram to Anthony Eden, dated 8-11-41.

6. U.D. 63 pp. 478-486, 572-579; IMTFE, *Exhibit* No. 2880, *Record*, pp. 25776-25780.

7. Otto D. Tolischus, *Tokyo Record*, (New York: Reynal & Hitchcock, 1943), pp. 234-236.

8. UD 63, pp. 585-587, 630-633.

9. The text reproduced herein is the official translation by the Japanese Foreign Office, in UD 63, pp. 692-698, Nomura, *op. cit.*, English part, p. 103 ff.; compare *Foreign Relations of the United States: Japan*, vol. 2, pp. 572 ff.

10. Nomura, *op. cit.*, p. 107; Aoki, *op. cit.*, p. 332.

11. UD 63, pp. 852-890; *Foreign Relations of the United States: Japan*, vol. 2, pp. 593, 608; JFO, *Documents Relating to Negotiations Between Japan and the U.S., 1941*, IMT, 263, pp. 105-111.

12. Memoranda of Staff Conference attended by Oka, Muto and Imamoto, 9-6-41, including an *Outline for Explanations of Policy Objectives at the Imperial Conference*, UD 63, pp. 896-922.

13. *Tojo Memorandum*, IMTFE, *Record*, p. 36281; see also IMTFE, *Exhibit* No. 588.

14. Proceeding of the Liaison Conference of September 13, 1941, UD 63, pp. 988 ff.; *Pearl Harbor Attack* XVIII, p. 2952.

15. *Konoye Memoirs* in *Pearl Harbor Attack* XX, p. 4006.

16. JFO, *The U.S.-Japanese Understanding and International and Domestic Law Considerations*, UD 63, pp. 1010-1013, 1106-1135.

17. *Foreign Relations of the United States: Japan*, vol. 2, pp. 64 ff.; Grew, *op. cit.*, pp. 436 ff. *Pearl Harbor Attack* XX, pp. 4425 ff, *Committee Report*, pp. 315, 321; Hull, *op. cit.*, p. 1025.

18. Takushiro Hattori, *Daitoa Senso Zenshi* (*A History of the Great East Asian War*), (Tokyo: Masu Shobō, 1953), vol. 1, p. 196.

19. Before the four ministers met, Admiral Oka, Chief of Naval Affairs Bureau of the Ministry of Navy, called on Cabinet Secretary Tomida, informing him that while the Navy wanted to avoid war, it could not openly say so for political reasons. Therefore, the Navy Minister would defer the matter to the Prime Minister if the question should be brought up at the conference.

CHAPTER XIV

1. IMTFE, *Record*, pp. 10292, 36311-36315, 35671; Shigenori Togo, *The Cause of Japan* (New York: Simon and Schuster, 1956), pp. 54-55.

2. Otto D. Tolischus, *Tokyo Record*, (New York: Reynal & Hitchcock, 1943), p. 272.

3. Hull, *op. cit.*, p. 1054.

4. Grew, *op. cit.*, pp. 467, 470; *Pearl Harbor Attack* XIV, 1045-57; *Foreign Relations of the United States: Japan*, vol. 2, pp. 701-704.

5. Togo, *op. cit.*, pp. 115 ff.

6. *Kido Diary*, entry of 10-23-41, IMTFE, *Exhibit*, Nos. 1161, 1162, *Record*, pp. 10312-10314.

7. IMTFE, *Exhibit* Nos. 1328, 1329, *Record*, pp. 11923-11935, contain the minutes of this meeting. See also Tojo's testimony in IMTFE, *Record*, pp. 35690-35699.

8. Texts in UD 63, pp. 1786-1805, Togo, *op. cit.*, pp. 129-130, 134.

9. Saburo Kurusu, *Nichi-Bei Kosho Hishi* (*Untold Stories of U.S.-Japanese Relations*), (Tokyo: Sogensha, 1952), pp. 89 ff.

10. IMTFE, *Exhibit* Nos. 809 and 1265.

11. *Pearl Harbor Attack*, XI, p. 5420, *Committee Report*, pp. 336-339.

12. UD 63, pp. 1923-1927; *Pearl Harbor Attack* XII, pp. 113-116; *Foreign Relations of the United States: Japan*, vol. 2, pp. 715-719.

13. UD 63, pp. 2056-2067, 2124-2126; *Pearl Harbor Attack* XII, pp. 127-129, 149-152.

14. Hull, *op. cit.*, p. 1063.

15. UD 63, 2214-2220; *Pearl Harbor Attack* XII, p. 155, *Committee Report*, p. 358; Kurusu, *op. cit.*, p. 134.

16. *Foreign Relations of the United States: Japan*, vol., 2, pp. 753-757; Hull, *op. cit.*, pp. 1069-1071; Nomura, *op. cit.*, p. 154.

17. UD 63, pp. 2302-2304; IMTFE, *Exhibit* 1183, *Record*, pp. 10400-10401; *Pearl Harbor Attack* XII, p. 165; in 1940 Japan imported 3,300,000 tons of oil from the United States. The demand to the Dutch East Indies for 1940 was 1,800,000 tons. Thus the new demands represented higher amounts.

18. *Pearl Harbor Attack* XIV, p. 1109. The Joint Committee believed that the memo was probably written around November 20, 1941.

19. *Pearl Harbor Attack* XIX, pp. 3688 ff., *Committee Report*, pp. 366-367.

20. Text in *Pearl Harbor Attack* XIV, pp. 1110-1115.

21. Hull, *op. cit.*, pp. 1073-1074, 1077.

22. *Pearl Harbor Attack, Committe Report*, pp. 373 ff.

23. *Ibid.*, p. 376-381; *Pearl Harbor Attack* XIV, pp. 1160-1161, 1167-1174; Hull, *op. cit.*, p. 1080.

24. *Pearl Harbor Attack, Committee Report*, p. 381; Hull was nevertheless furious with the propaganda laid by the Chinese. See Hull, *op. cit.*, p. 1089.

25. *Foreign Relations of the United States: Japan*, vol. 2, pp. 766-770.

26. Anticipating Hull's rejection of his Proposal 'B' Togo called on the Emperor on November 26 and explained Japan's basic positions, see UD 63, pp. 2039-2043; The Liaison Conference meetings of November 27 were covered in Togo's testimony at the Tokyo Trial, IMTFE, *Record*, p. 35706, and *Kido Diary*, entry of 11-27-41, IMTFE, *Exhibit*, No. 1190. By then the Navy had definitely

set the X day, the day of attacking Pearl Harbor, for December 8, Japanese time, see Shimada's testimony in IMTFE, *Exhibit* No. 1128-A, *Record*, p. 10428.

27. On Japan's naval preparations, see Hattori, *op. cit.*, pp. 177 ff.

28. *Foreign Relations of the United States: Japan*, vol. 2, pp. 148-149; Japanese envoys' explanations in *Ibid.*, p. 778.

29. UD 63, pp. 2441-2447; IMTFE, *Exhibit* No. 1199, *Record*, pp. 10467-10470; *Pearl Harbor Attack* XII, p. 205.

30. UD 63, pp. 2528-2529, 2540-2549, 2552-2559; Kurusu, *op. cit.*, pp. 164 ff.

31. Hull, *op. cit.*, p. 1092.

32. Togo, *op. cit.*, pp. 221-222; Grew, *op. cit.*, pp. 486 ff; UD 63, pp. 2590-2595 contains Foreign Office discussions of the President's personal message.

33. *Foreign Relations of the United States: Japan*, vol. 2, pp. 786-787; Hull, *op. cit.*, pp. 1096-1097; Kurusu, *op. cit.*, pp. 179 ff. Tokyo was unaware of the delay, and Togo's word should be accepted. See cross examination of Togo, IMTFE *Record*, p. 36101.

Chapter XV

1. Joseph C. Grew, *Turbulent Era: A Diplomatic Record of Forty Years, 1904-1945*, (Boston: Houghton Mifflin Co., 1952) vol. 2, p. 1303n quotes this statement.

2. IMTFE, *Exhibit* No. 2908, *Record*, p. 25847.

SELECTED BIBLIOGRAPHY

OFFICIAL DOCUMENTS

Archives in the Japanese Ministry of Foreign Affairs, Tokyo, Japan, 1868-1945, microfilmed for the Library of Congress, 1949-1951. Documents cited in this work are represented by suffixes S for Showa Documents; UD for Unindexed Documents; SP for Special Studies; and IMT for War Trials Documents. For further information, consult the *Checklist* compiled by Cecil H. Uyehara (Washington: Library of Congress, 1954).

Documents on German Foreign Policy, 1918-1945: From the Archives of the German Foreign Ministry. Ser. D, 9 vols. Washington: U. S. Government Printing Office, 1949-1956.

Foreign Relations of the United States. Washington: U. S. Government Printing Office, 1937- .

Foreign Relations of the United States: Japan, 1931-1941. 2 vols. Washington: U. S. Government Printing Office, 1943.

Führer Conference on Matters Dealing with the German Navy, 1939-1945. 7 vols. Washington: Office of Naval Intelligence, 1947.

International Military Tribunal for the Far East (Record of the Proceedings, Narrative Summary of the Record, Exhibits, Prosecution Documents Not Used in Evidence, Rejected Defense Documents, and Judgments and Opinions). Tokyo: Unpublished material on microfilm and in mimeographed form, 1946-1948. A *Functional Index* to the proceedings is compiled by Paul S. Dull and Michael T. Umemura and published by the University of Michigan Press in 1957.

Nazi Conspiracy and Aggression. 12 vols. Washington: U. S. Government Printing Office, 1946.

Nazi-Soviet Relations, 1939-1941, edited by R. Sontag and S. Beddie. Washington: U. S. Government Printing Office, 1948.

Peace and War: United States Foreign Policy, 1931-1941. Washington: U. S. Government Printing Office, 1943.

Trial of the Major War Criminals at the International Military Tribunal (Official Documents, Proceedings, and Documents in Evidence). 42 vols. Nuremberg: Secretariat of the Tribunal, 1947-1949.

U. S. Congress Joint Committee on the Investigation of the Pearl Harbor Attack, *Pearl Harbor Attack: Hearings Before the Joint Committee.* (79th Cong., 1st Sess.) 39 parts in 15 vols. Washington: U. S. Government Printing Office, 1946.

————. *Investigation of the Pearl Harbor Attack: Report of the Joint Committee.* (79th Cong., 2nd Sess.) Washington: U. S. Government Printing Office, 1946.

U. S. Strategic Bombing Survey, Naval Analysis Division. *The Campaign of the Pacific War.* Washington: U. S. Government Printing Office, 1946.

UNOFFICIAL COMPILATIONS OF DOCUMENTS

Aoki, Tokuzo. *Taiheiyo Senso Zenshi* (*A History of Events Leading to the Pacific War*). 3 vols. Tokyo: Gakujitsu Bunken Fukyukai, 1953.

Hattori, Takushiro. *Daitoa Senso Zenshi* (*A Complete History of the Great East Asian War*). 8 vols. Tokyo: Masu Shobo, 1953-1956.

Jones, S. S., et al. *Documents on American Foreign Relations, 1939-* . Boston: World Peace Foundation, 1940- .

Toynbee, Arnold J., ed. *Documents on International Affairs, 1939-1946.* 3 vols. London: Oxford University Press, 1951.

MEMOIRS IN ENGLISH

Churchill, Winston S. *The Second World War.* Vol. I, *The Gathering Storm,* Vol. II, *Their Finest Hour,* Vol. III, *The Grand Alliance.* Boston: Houghton Mifflin Co., 1948-1951.

Ciano, Count Galeazzo. *The Ciano Diaries, 1939-1943.* Edited by Hugh Gibson. New York: Doubleday & Co., Inc., 1946.

Craigie, Sir Robert. *Behind the Japanese Mask.* London: Huchinson & Co., 1946.

Dirksen, Herbert von. *Moscow, Tokyo, London.* Norman: University of Oklahoma Press, 1952.

Grew, Joseph C. *Ten Years in Japan.* New York: Simon and Schuster, 1944.

————. *Turbulent Era. A Diplomatic Record of Forty Years, 1904-1945.* Edited by Walter Johnson. 2 vols. Boston: Houghton Mifflin Co., 1952.

Hull, Cordell. *The Memoirs of Cordell Hull.* 2 vols. New York: Macmillan Co., 1948.

Kase, Toshikazu. *Journey to the Missouri.* New Haven: Yale University Press, 1950.

Saionji, Kimmochi, and Harada, Kumao. *Saionji-Harada Memoirs.* 24 parts in 40 vols. Tokyo: General Headquarters Far East Command, Military Intelligence Section, General Staff, Civil Intelligence Section, 1946-1947.

Shigemitsu, Mamoru, *Japan and Her Destiny: My Struggle for Peace.* Edited by F. S. G. Piggott. Translated by Oswald White. New York: Dutton, 1958.

Stimson, Henry L., and Bundy, McGeorge. *On Active Service in Peace and War.* New York: Harper and Brothers, 1948.

Togo, Shigenori. *The Cause of Japan.* Translated and edited by Togo Fumihiko and Ben Bruce Blakeney. New York: Simon and Schuster, 1956.

Tolischus, Otto D. *Tokyo Record.* New York: Reynal and Hitchcock, 1943.

Van Mook, Hubertus J. *The Netherlands Indies and Japan: Battle on Paper.* New York: W. W. Norton and Co., 1944.

Weizsäcker, Ernst von. *Memoirs.* London: Victor Gollancz Ltd., 1951.

Welles, Sumner. *The Time for Decision.* New York: Harper and Brothers, 1944.

MEMOIRS IN JAPANESE

Arima, Yoriyasu. *Seikai Dochuki* (*Journey Through the Political World*). Tokyo: Nippon Shuppan Kyodo Kabushiki Kaisha, 1951.

————. *Shichiju-nen no Kaiso* (*Reminiscence of My Seventy Years*). Tokyo: Sogensha, 1953.

Fukai, Eigo. *Sumitsuin Juyo Giji Oboegaki* (*Memoranda of Important Privy Council Proceedings*). Tokyo: Iwanami Shoten, 1953.

Harada, Kumao. *Saionji-ko to Seikyoku* (*Saionji-Harada Memoirs*). 8 vols. and Appendix. Tokyo: Iwanami Shoten, 1950-1952, 1956.

Hashimoto, Tetsuma. *Nichi-Bei Kosho Hiwa* (*Untold Story of the U. S.-Japanese Negotiations*). Tokyo: Shiwunso, 1946.

Hosokawa, Moritada. *Joho Tenno ni Tassezu* (*News Never Reached the Emperor*). 2 vols. Tokyo: Isobe Shobo, 1953.

Ikeda, Seihin. *Zaikai Kaiko* (*Reminiscence of the Financial World*). Tokyo: Sekai no Nihon Sha, 1949.

Ishii, Itaro. *Gaikokan no Issho* (*A Diplomat's Life*). Tokyo: Yomiuri Shinbunsha, 1950.

Kase, Toshikazu. *Dai-niji Sekai Taisen Hishi* (*Untold History of the Second World War*). Tokyo: Kadokawa Shoten, 1957.

Kazami, Akira. *Konoye Naikaku* (*The Konoye Cabinet*). Tokyo: Nippon Shuppan Kyodo Kabushiki Kaisha, 1951.

Konoye, Fumimaro. *Heiwa e no Doryoku* (*My Effort for Peace*). Tokyo: Nippon Dempo Tsushinsha, 1946.

Kurusu, Saburo. *Homatsu no Sanjugonen* (*Thirty-five Years in Vain*). Tokyo: Bunka Shoin, 1948.

————. *Nichi-Bei Gaiko Hiwa: Waga Gaikoshi* (*Untold Story of the U. S.-Japanese Diplomatic Relations: Our Diplomatic History*). Tokyo: Sogensha, 1952.

Morishima, Morito. *Imbo, Ansatsu, Gunto* (*Conspiracy, Assassination and Sword*). Tokyo: Iwanami Shoten, 1950.

Muto Akira. *Hito kara Sugamo e* (*From the Philippines to Sugamo*). Tokyo: Jitsugyo no Nihon Sha, 1952.

Nomura, Kichisaburo. *Beikoku ni Shishite* (*My Mission to America*). Tokyo: Iwanami Shoten, 1951.

Ohashi, Chuichi. *Taiheiyo Senso Yuraiki: Matsuoka Gaiko no Shinso* (*The Origin of the Pacific War: The Truth About Matsuoka's Diplomacy*). Tokyo: Kaname Shobo, 1952.

Okada, Keisuke. *Okada Keisuke Kaikoroku* (*Memoirs of Admiral Okada*). Tokyo: Mainichi Shinbunsha, 1950.

Saito, Yoshie. *Azamukareta Rekishi* (*The Distorted History*). Tokyo: Yomiuri Shinbunsha, 1955.

Shigemitsu, Mamoru. *Gaiko Kaisoroku* (*Diplomatic Memoirs*). Tokyo: Mainichi Shinbunsha, 1953.

————. *Showa no Doran* (*The Showa Armageddon*). 2 vols. Tokyo: Chuokoronsha, 1952.

Togo, Shigenori. *Jidai no Ichimen* (*Another Façade of Our Times*). Tokyo: Kaizosha, 1952.

Ugaki, Kazushige. *Ugaki Nikki* (*Ugaki Dairies*). Tokyo: Asahi Shinbunsha, 1954.

Yoshida, Toyu, ed. and trans. *Shu Fukkai Nikki* (*Diaries of Chou Fu-hai*). Tokyo: Kenminsha, 1953.

GENERAL WORKS IN ENGLISH

Allen, George C. *Japanese Industry: Its Recent Development and Present Condition.* New York: Institute of Pacific Relations, 1940.

Beard, Charles A. *President Roosevelt and the Coming of the War, 1941: A Study in Appearances and Realities.* New Haven: Yale University Press, 1948.

Beloff, Max. *The Foreign Policy of Soviet Russia, 1929-1941.* 2 vols. London: Oxford University Press, 1947-1949.

Bisson, Thomas A. *American Policy in the Far East, 1931-1940,* with a supplementary chapter by Miriam S. Farley, rev. ed. New York: Institute of Pacific Relations, 1941.

————. *Japan in China.* New York: Macmillan Co., 1938.

Bloch, Kurt. *German Interests and Policies in the Far East.* New York: Institute of Pacific Relations, 1940.

Borton, Hugh. *Japan since 1931: Its Political and Social Development.* New York: Institute of Pacific Relations, 1940.

————. *Japan's Modern Century.* New York: Ronald Press, 1955.

Brown, Delmer M. *Nationalism in Japan.* Berkeley: University of California Press, 1955.

Butow, Robert J. C. *Japan's Decision to Surrender.* Stanford: Stanford University Press, 1954.

Byas, Hugh. *Government by Assassination.* New York: Alfred A. Knopf, 1942.

Chamberlain, William H. *Japan over Asia.* 2nd rev. ed. Boston: Little, Brown, 1939.

Cohen, Jerome B. *The Japanese Economy in War and Reconstruction.* Minneapolis: University of Minnesota Press, 1949.

Colegrove, Kenneth W. *Militarism in Japan.* Boston: World Peace Foundation, 1936.

Craig, Gordon. *The Diplomats, 1919-1939.* Princeton: Princeton University Press, 1953.

Dallin, David J. *Soviet Russia and the Far East.* New Haven: Yale University Press, 1948.

Feis, Herbert. *The Road to Pearl Harbor: The Coming of the War between the United States and Japan.* Princeton: Princeton University Press, 1950.

Friedman, Irving S. *British Relations with China: 1931-1939.* New York: Institute of Pacific Relations, 1940.

Griswold, A. Whitney. *The Far Eastern Policy of the United States.* New York: Harcourt Brace, 1938.

Hishida, Seiji. *Japan among the Great Powers: A Survey of Her International Relations.* London: Longmans, Green & Co., 1940.

Iklé, Frank W. *German-Japanese Relations, 1936-1940.* New York: Bookman Associates, 1956.

Jones, Francis C. *Japan's New Order in East Asia, 1937-1945.* London: Oxford University Press, 1954.

Johnstone, William C. *The United States and Japan's New Order.* New York: Oxford University Press, 1941.

Kato Masuo. *The Lost War.* New York: Alfred A. Knopf, 1946.

Kennan, George F. *American Diplomacy, 1900-1950.* Chicago: University of Chicago Press, 1951.

Langer, William L. and Gleason, S. Everett. *The Challenge to Isolation, 1937-1940.* New York: Harper and Brothers, 1952.

————. *The Undeclared War, 1940-1941.* New York: Harper and Brothers, 1953.

Levi, Werner. *Modern China's Foreign Policy.* Minneapolis: University of Minnesota Press, 1953.

Lockwood, William W. *The Economic Development of Japan: Growth and Structural Changes, 1868-1938.* Princeton: Princeton University Press, 1954.

Lory, Hillis. *Japan's Military Masters.* New York: Viking Press, 1943.

Maki, John M. *Japanese Militarism: Its Cause and Cure.* New York: Alfred A. Knopf, 1945.

Maxon, Yale C. *Control of Japanese Foreign Policy: A Study of Civil-Military Rivalry, 1930-1945.* Berkeley: University of California Press, 1957.

Millis, Walter. *This Is Pearl! The United States and Japan, 1941.* New York: William Morrow and Co., 1947.

Moore, Frederick. *With Japan's Leaders: An Intimate Record of Fourteen Years as Counsellor to the Japanese Government, Ending December 7, 1941.* New York: Charles Scribner's and Sons, 1942.

Moore, Harriet L. *Soviet Far Eastern Policy, 1931-1945.* Princeton: Princeton University Press, 1945.

Morrison, Samuel E. *The Rising Sun in the Pacific, 1931-April, 1942.* Boston: Little, Brown, 1948.

Pal, Radhabinod. *International Tribunal for the Far East: Dissenting Judgment.* Calcutta: Sanyal and Co., 1953.

Presseisen, Ernst L. *Germany and Japan: A Study in Totalitarian Diplomacy, 1933-1941.* Hague: Martinus Nijhoff, 1958.

Quigley, Harold S. *Far Eastern War, 1937-1941.* Boston: World Peace Foundation, 1942.

————. *Japanese Government and Politics: An Introductory Study.* New York: Century, 1932.

Royama, Masamichi. *Foreign Policy of Japan, 1914-1939.* Tokyo: Institute of Pacific Relations, 1941.

Scalapino, Robert A. *Democracy and the Party Movement in Prewar Japan.* Berkeley: University of California Press, 1953.

Schroeder, Paul W. *The Axis Alliance and Japanese-American Relations, 1941.* Ithaca: Cornell University Press, 1958.

Sherwood, Robert E. *Roosevelt and Hopkins: An Intimate History.* New York: Harper and Brothers, 1948.

Spykman, Nicholas J. *America's Strategy in World Politics: The United States and the Balance of Power.* New York: Harcourt, Brace and Co., 1942.

Storry, Richard. *The Double Patriots.* Boston: Houghton Mifflin Co., 1957.

Supreme Commander for the Allied Powers, Government Section. *Political Reorientation of Japan, September 1945 to September 1948,* 2 vols. Washington: U. S. Government Printing Office, 1949.

Takeuchi, Tatsuji. *War and Diplomacy in the Japanese Empire.* New York: Doubleday, Doran, 1935.

Tamagna, Frank M. *Italy's Interests and Policies in the Far East.* New York: Institute of Pacific Relations, 1941.

Tolischus, Otto D. *Through Japanese Eyes*. New York: Reynal and Hitchcock, 1945.
Willoughby, Charles A. *Shanghai Conspiracy: The Sorge Spy Ring*. New York: Dutton, 1952.
Yanaga, Chitoshi. *Japan since Perry*. New York: McGraw-Hill Book Co., 1949.

GENERAL WORKS IN JAPANESE

Fuchida, Mitsuo. *Kido Butai (The Task Forces)*. Tokyo: Nippon Shuppan Kyodo Kabushiki Kaisha, 1951.
Fukudome, Shigeru. *Kaigun no Hansei (Self-Examination of Our Navy)*. Tokyo: Nippon Shuppan Kyodo Kabushiki Kaisha, 1951.
Ishida, Bunshiro. *Shinbun Kiroku Shusei: Showa Daijiken Shi (Big Events during the Showa Era: Compilation of Newspaper Articles)*. Tokyo: Kinseisha, 1955.
Ito, Hirobumi. *Kempo Gikai (Commentaries on the Constitution)*. 16th ed. Tokyo: Kokka Gakkai, 1935.
Iwabuchi, Tatsuo. *Gunbatsu no Keihu (The Genealogy of the Military Caste)*. Tokyo: Chuokoronsha, 1948.
Kazanishi, Mitsuhara et al. *Nihon ni okeru Shihonshugi no Hattatsu (Development of Capitalism in Japan)*. 2 vols. and a chronological table. Tokyo: Tokyo University Press, 1950-1953.
Kinoshita, Hanji. *Nippon Fascism Shi (A History of Japanese Fascism)*. 2 vols. Tokyo: Iwazaki Shoten, 1950.
Mori, Shozo. *Sempu Nijunen (The Twenty Years' Whirlwind)*. 2 vols. Tokyo: Masu Shobo, 1946.
Nippon Kindaishi Kenkyukai. *Kindai Jimbutsu Seijishi (Biographical History of Modern Politics)*. 2 vols. Tokyo: Toyo Keizai Shinposha, 1955-1956.
Rekishigaku Kenkyukai. *Taiheiyo Senso Shi (A History of the Pacific War)*. 6 vols. Tokyo: Toyo Keizai Shinposha, 1953-1954.
Sakuda, Kotaro. *Tenno to Kido (The Emperor and Kido)*. Tokyo: Heibonsha, 1948.
Shiobara, Tokishiro. *Tojo Memo (Tojo Memoranda)*. Tokyo: Handbook Co., 1952.
Tanaka, Sogoro. *Nihon Fascism no Genryu: Kita Ikki no Shiso to Shogai (The Orgin of Japanese Fascism: The Life and Thought of Ikki Kita)*. Tokyo: Hakuyosha, 1949.
Takagi, Sokichi. *Taiheiyo Kaisenshi (A History of Naval Operations in the Pacific War)*. Tokyo: Iwanami Shoten, 1949.
Uyeda, Toshio, ed. *Taiheiyo Senso Geninron (The Origin of the Pacific War)*. Tokyo: Shinbun Gekkansha, 1953.
Watanabe, Eizo. *Jimetsu no Tatakai (The War of Self-Extinction)*. Tokyo Shubunkan, 1947.
Yabe, Teiji. *Konoye Fumimaro*. 2 vols. Tokyo: Kobundo, 1952.

INDEX

ABCD encirclement, 151, 185, 195, 201.
Abe, Nobuyuki: Premier, 59, 60, 62, 67-70; Ambassador to Nanking, 96, 124, 128.
Anami, Korechika, 75, 76.
Anglo-Japanese Alliance, 1.
Arima, Count Yoriyasu, 29, 101.
Anti-Comintern Pact, 23, 41, 45, 49, 50, 80, 82, 90.
Aoki, Kazuo, 60.
Araki, Sadao, 5-7, 35, 47, 176.
Arita, Hachiro, 39, 45, 47, 51-53, 70, 72, 74, 75.
Atlantic Charter, 193-195.
Axis Pact between Germany and Italy, 54-55, *see also* Tripartite Pact.

Baba, Eiichi, 12, 29.
Ballantine, Joseph W., 186.
Brussels Conference, 21.
Burma Road, 126, 127, 201.

Cabinet (*Naikaku*): 6-10, 28; Advisers' Council, 28, 29.
Catroux, Georges, 142, 143.
Central China, 78, 85, 89, 91.
Chang Chun, 37.
Chang Fa-kwei, 84, 89.
Changkufeng Incident, 37-39.
Chen Kung-po, 80.
Chiang Kai-shek, 14, 24, 25, 27, 74, 78-83, 88, 90, 92, 93, 124-130, 137, 148, 164, 169, 218, 221, 224, 226, 228, 229, 233, 238; Madame, 84.
Chin-Doihara Agreement, 13.
China: civil war, 14, 126; communism in, 14, 84, 126; Japanese designs on, 12, 13, 23-25, 81, 82, 85, 90-93, 100, 125, 155, 238-240; relations with France, 141, 142, with Great Britain, 14, 37, 63, 126, 127, with U. S. A., 27, 63, 127, 155, with

U. S. S. R., 19-20, 137; stationing of Japanese troops in, 81, 191, 197, 200, 201, 204, 205, 207-209, 212, 214, 216, 219, 226, 230, 238, 239, 246; Tripartite Pact and, 126, 127; in U. S.-Japanese negotiations, 157, 160, 161, 164, 169, 178, 179, 181, 197, 230, 239, 245, 246.
China Board, 39, 87, 92, 158.
Chou Fu-hai, 80, 93, 96.
Churchill, Winston S., 71, 72, 97, 193-195, 220, 228, 229.
Ciano, Galeazzo, 48-51, 95, 138, 166, 235.
Commercial Treaty between U. S. and Japan, 62-64, 66, 70, 149, 154, 242. 242.
Control faction, *see* Toseiha.
Craigie, Robert, 19, 36, 133, 220, 237, 246.

Darlan, Jean François, 186, 188.
Decoux, Jean, 143, 145.
Diet, Japanese, *see* Gikai, also *Shugi-in* and *Kizoku-in.*
Dirksen, Herbert von, 24-27.
Doihara, Kenji, 13, 85-87.
Drought, James M., 160-163, 167, 239.
Dutch East Indies: Japanese designs on, 67, 72, 74, 108, 124, 141, 148-153, 154; in U. S.-Japanese negotiations, 160, 185, 187, 189, 201, 224.

East Asia Co-Prosperity Area, 152, 165, 177, 186, 192, 212, 238.
Economic sanctions, 62-67, 70, 116, 120, 144, 154, 179, 187, 188, 198, 201, 216, 220, 223-226, 231, 238, 240, 242, 244, 245.
Eden, Anthony, 36, 228.
Emperor, 8-12, 241; *see also* Hirohito, Emperor.
European war, 60-61, 169, 182.

269

DATE DUE

MAY 21 '65		
MAY 13 '66		
MAY 21 1968		
NOV 1 5 1978		
DEC 3 1 1978		
GAYLORD		PRINTED IN U.S.A.